DILEMMAS OF
SOCIAL REFORM

D1392641

DILEMMAS OF SOCIAL REFORM

Poverty and Community Action
in the United States

Peter Marris and Martin Rein
Second Edition
With a new Preface

THE UNIVERSITY OF CHICAGO PRESS

The University of Chicago Press, Chicago 60637

© 1967, 1973, 1982 by Peter Marris and Martin Rein
All rights reserved. Published 1967
Second edition 1973. University of Chicago Press edition 1982
Printed in the United States of America

89 88 87 86 85 84 83 82   1 2 3 4 5

Library of Congress Cataloging in Publication Data

Marris, Peter.
  Dilemmas of social reform.

  Bibliography: p. 297.
  Includes index.
  1. United States—Social policy. 2. Community
organization—United States. 3. Poor—United
States. I. Rein, Martin. II. Title.
HN65.M3   1982   361'.973   81-16361
ISBN 0-226-50657-6 (pbk.)   AACR2

CONTENTS

ACKNOWLEDGEMENTS

We would like to thank the Ford Foundation and the President's Committee on Juvenile Delinquency and Youth Crime for their financial support, and in particular, Paul N. Ylvisaker and the staff of the Foundation's Public Affairs Programme for their friendship, for the stimulus of their ideas, and for their tactful encouragement of ruthless impartiality. Few of our ideas can pretend to be original. As we went round talking to project directors, research directors and programme staff; interviewed mayors and civic leaders; discussed with members of Federal departments, we absorbed their insight and knowledge, and tried to make a coherent synthesis of all these points of view. If we have abused their ideas, we can only plead the inherent complexity of the events and issues to be understood, and thank them all the more for their time and patience. Besides members of the Projects' staff, we have learned a great deal from discussion with other sociologists—especially Herbert J. Gans, S. Michael Miller, Frances Piven, and Frank Riessman. Many of these read the book in draft, and helped us with their comments and corrections. We would like to thank all those associated with the President's Committee, the Office of Economic Opportunity, and members of the staff and advisory committee of the Institute of Community Studies who also gave us their comments. Diana Rodricks typed the manuscript. Tom Knutt helped prepare much of the additional material for the epilogue. Besides those we have already mentioned, we would like to thank Daniel P. Moynihan and Robert A. Levine for their comments on a draft of these additional sections.

PREFACE TO THE UNIVERSITY OF
CHICAGO PRESS EDITION

When we published the second edition of this book, the principles of reform it describes were still broadly accepted, even by a Republican administration. Poverty was acknowledged to be a grave national problem that could be solved only with government intervention and the active participation of poor people themselves. At the same time, we needed to learn by experiment what would work. Difficult as they were to reconcile in practice, these principles of a scientifically rational, locally controlled program of action against poverty, supported by the commitment of every level of government, seemed established as an internationally viable model of democratic social policy.

We reintroduce our study in a radically different political climate. The Reagan administration—encouraged by a compliant public opinion and only half-hearted opposition from the party which once endorsed community action—has repudiated the assumptions and many of the ideals which inspired that model of reform. Are the reformers of our study—with the ideals they articulated, the issues they confronted, the frustrations and contradictions they tried to surmount—now, therefore, part of an era which has ended, their preoccupations no longer relevant?

We believe that conservative government can neither relieve poverty nor successfully ignore its social consequences. Its ideology does not represent an alternative solution to the problems with which this book is concerned, but a reaction against their continued aggravation. Community action was conceived in response to an impoverishment of central cities already apparent thirty years ago. Neighborhoods were declining into slums, unemployment was rising—especially among young people—businesses were leaving, and the tax base falling.

Since then, the fiscal problems of the older industrial cities have deepened into crisis: schools close because teachers cannot be paid, public transportation systems are at the point of breakdown, whole neighborhoods disintegrate into rubble, unemployment is worse. The conservative reaction is a self-protective impulse by those who are not poor or trapped in urban ghettos, seeking to insulate their own precarious prosperity from the worse off. This retreat has been rationalized by calculations attempting to show that there is little poverty left; by depicting the beneficiaries of welfare as hustlers, cheats, loafers, and middle-class dropouts; and by blaming the fiscal problems of cities on irresponsible mismanagement. As a basis of policy, conservatives assume above all that the market economy, stimulated by tax cuts and freed from governmental interference, will regenerate economic growth, and that growth will provide employment and an adequate income for the poor, drawing business back into the city.

But the approach to reform this book describes was itself provoked by the failure of economic growth to end poverty in the 1950's. Growth is now harder to sustain, and far less likely to help the poor. As the National Advisory Council on Economic Opportunity noted in its 1980 report:

> As we have seen, the basic premise of those who proclaim the myth of the "abolition of poverty" is the idea that "the growth of jobs and income in the private economy" has been a main force in reducing poverty to "minor" proportions. The general implication is that our recent macroeconomic policy has worked well in alleviating the plight of the disadvantaged. The myth vindicates the hopes of those who have argued that poverty will be almost automatically reduced through the "trickling down" of jobs and earnings from a dynamic private economy. But a careful look at both the Census data and the results of recent special studies suggests that just the opposite is true. On the contrary, the private economy has done little by way of jobs and earnings for the poor since the mid-60's. Though economic growth did improve the situation of some groups of the poor before that time, it has since had a dwindling impact. *Virtually all of the reduction in poverty since the mid-1960's has come through the expansion of social insurance and income transfer programs.* (pp. 11–12)

Economic growth by itself will only reduce poverty substantially if both the chances of being poor and the effects of growth are evenly distributed. Then, indeed, any increase would be likely to benefit some poor people at least proportionately: their chances of employment, for instance, would improve, along with everyone else's chances. But poverty is not evenly distributed. It threatens black and Hispanic people more than white, women more than men; it is rising among the young while it falls among the old, and its incidence is much greater in some parts of the country than others.

For example, as the National Advisory Council reported, in terms of income level a woman heading a family was six times more likely to be poor than a young man in 1977. In that year, a third of employed single mothers of young children and nine out of ten, if they had no paid employment, were living in poverty. A black or Spanish-speaking woman who headed a family was more than ten times as likely to be poor as a white man. Regional disparities were as striking. For instance, between 1969 and 1975 the rate of poverty among young children rose five or six times more rapidly in Massachusetts and Ohio than in most of the nation. Other measures of poverty, taking relative rather than absolute standards, show similar patterns.

In itself, economic growth would be more likely to aggravate than remedy these selective disadvantages, as it accelerates world-wide shifts in production and investment. For twenty years, gray-area programs, community action agencies, model-city plans, community development corporations, and job training schemes have tried to attract private enterprises into impoverished inner-city neighborhoods with very little success. The reformers who initiated these experiments were neither radical nor socialist. They were as inclined to romanticize the boisterous, inventive energy of capitalist enterprise as any conservative, and as mistrustful of bureaucracy. Their conception of capitalism, too, was nostalgic—a nineteenth-century vision of sturdy, self-reliant firms bound to their community. But the poverty of cities is not a lack of small business: it arises from world-wide shifts of capital and production led by a few hundred enormous corporations that scarcely acknowledge any national or regional loyalties. There seems no reason to suppose that the new administration can achieve, without any planning or initiative, what previous administrations could not do in two decades of patient experiment.

Meanwhile, since the present administration is ruthlessly cutting the services and transfer payments which in practice have done most to reduce poverty in the past twenty years, poverty and inequality in American society seem bound to become harsher and more widespread. Even the most rigid of governments will not be able to ignore indefinitely the frustration, hopelessness and decay, the injustice and social degradation its conservative doctrines try to wish away. At some point, however reluctantly, government will have to confront, once again, the issues which the principal actors of our story struggled to place at the center of American concerns: how the resources of government, of knowledge and self-help, can be mobilized against persistent social inequality.

These swings of policy, as we discuss towards the end of our study, seem characterisic of intractable problems. Politics thrives on large promises and simplistic prescriptions. Unless, behind the rhetoric, people are prepared to learn patiently from experience, the same misunderstandings, contradictions, and disappointments merely repeat themselves in alternating cycles of brave beginnings and lame conclusions. What have we learned from two decades of experiment in social reform that could make their revival less frustrating?

The experiments began when the American economy was prosperous, stable, and expanding. Poverty seemed, then, above all, a problem of social and cultural alienation, by which people were excluded from the opportunities the economy provided. Programs concentrated on education, teaching, and social reintegration. But by the mid 1970's, it became increasingly clear that the impoverishment of older industrial city communities reflected fundamental structural changes in the American economy which no amount of local intervention or community self-help could reverse. In the preceding fifteen years, the organization of corporate capital had been undergoing a drastic concentration—to the point where most of the productive assets of the noncommunist world were owned by a few hundred international corporations. Major American corporations were at once more dominant in the national economy and less bound to it: they manufactured less and less in the United States and were often making more than half their profit overseas. A profound restructuring of employment accompanied these changes. Americans made fewer and fewer of the clothes they wore, the cars they drove, the appliances they used. But while the number of jobs in production leveled off, the national impact of this swift and profound reorganization of the world economy was softened by the expansion of employment in the public sector—in education, government, and defense. This new international division of labor and the compensatory generation of employment out of public revenues led by the mid 1970's to recurrent fiscal crises, especially in the older centers of manufacture. For while older urban economies were declining, the relative costs of public employment were rising, and inflationary pressures were making the public less and less willing to accept the taxes needed to sustain even the existing level of services. At the same time, every nation, region, and city competed for internationally mobile capital with tax breaks and financial inducements, impoverishing their revenues in an often desparate scramble to attract and hold a corporate plant or a headquarters.

The situation of poor people in American cities is the direct outcome of these changes. Tax cuts not only deprive them of benefits and services, but undercut their best chances of employment in the public sector. The traditional kinds of manufacturing jobs are disappearing. Instead, new plants offering low-paid, unskilled work, especially to women, are beginning to appear where the cost of labor and conditions of work begin to compare with alternative sites in Mexico, the Philippines, and Hong Kong. In effect, the poor are not offered the chances to compete with other Americans for economic opportunities, but only with people of nations where the standard of living is much lower. For the rest, there is generally only a chance of low-paid service work.

In these circumstances, no community-based program against poverty can hope to achieve much unless there is also a national strategy to create and distribute jobs, not only through public services and public investments, but through a much greater willingness to constrain the freedom of private corporations to invest where and when they choose without regard for the social consequences. Local protests against the closure of a plant, for instance, need the backing of national legislation that can require a company to negotiate and national resources to help communities explore alternatives.

The approach to reform this book describes was concerned with more than social deprivation. Most fundamentally, it sought to develop an ideal of social policy as a collective, democratic process of learning, responsive to knowledge and experience. We do not know well enough what people need, what prevents them from getting it, or how to overcome these obstacles, so the reformers argued, and we will not find out until we submit our actions and beliefs to systematic experiment and evaluation. This sounds such obvious good sense. Yet, it gave rise to more conflict and frustration than any other aspect of the programs. Before we once again try to use theory and systematic empirical inquiry to help solve social problems, we need to understand better how to relate knowledge and action within the framework of democratic politics.

The reformers characteristically accepted the axiom that questions of fact and of value were logically separate and that the objective pursuit of knowledge needed to be insulated from the contamination of ideological prejudice. By the mid 1960's, sociologists were questioning the ideal of a value-free social science, but experimental reform still adhered to a systematic institutionalization of scientific impartiality. In principle, politicians articulated values and purposes, scientists established the theories on which action to achieve those purposes might rationally be based, while administrators translated theory and purpose into action. Such a division of labor is not only impracticable, as the history of community action demonstrates again and again, in both America and Britain, but even in principle, it cannot be a successful way of institutionalizing social learning. The purposes, the emotions, and assumptions which provide the interpretive framework of inquiry are an integral part of what we experience.

The conventional objective evaluation of social programs merely compares the outcome to the stated purpose, confirming or verifying the hypothesis of action. This characteristically leads only to recrimination, because to the promoters of the program, the measured outcome is not a meaningful interpretation of the program's experience while their own interpretation is discredited. Correspondingly, community groups become frustrated with the pretensions of social research, because the interpretation of their own experience is taken out of their hands.

The conflicts between research and action in the programs we describe arose not only, as our study shows, because the pursuit of knowledge and political success is often incompatible, but because the attempt to institutionalize a separation between questions of fact and questions of value was itself misconceived. As the ideal of community action evolved as a popular social movement, it began to articulate more clearly the need for a community to control, not only access to knowledge, but the assumptions and procedures by which knowledge is generated and interpreted.

At the end of the book, the democracy of information emerges as a central theme of the whole movement of reform. That theme still seems to us profoundly relevant—as relevant as the deepening urban poverty which provided the context for the movement. We believe there is still much worth learning from the history of these earlier experiments about the relationship between knowledge, ideology, and political action.

INTRODUCTION

IN this book we set out to examine, in the light of one experiment, some of the principles, dilemmas and frustrations with which social reform in America must grapple. The particular projects with which we shall be concerned were few, and their scope limited, but they represent the most imaginative and ambitious attempt to manipulate deliberate social change in the years 1960–1964. These projects were promoted, and largely financed, by the Ford Foundation and the Juvenile Delinquency and Youth Offences Control Act of 1961: absorbed into the poverty programme, and diffused as a national strategy, they are now known as community action projects—local agencies, drawing on federal funds, which concert the resources of a community in a democratic, coherent attack upon the handicaps of the poor. But though, from the first, this movement of reform was concerned with poverty, it arose less from protest or moral indignation at injustice, than from a sense of breakdown in the institutions which should be diffusing opportunities to all. The reformers in the Ford Foundation, in the President's Committee on Juvenile Delinquency, and the executives of the projects they funded were intellectuals, for whom poverty was more a problem in social engineering, than a cause. They attacked it by expert knowledge and political manoeuvre, as technicians to whom the guidance of social change was a career. This study is concerned, then, with strategies of reform, as they appeared to a group of dedicated professionals working within the limits of community action.

Programmes against poverty could be analysed as relevantly from several other points of view. We could ask whether they will, in fact, show how poverty can be eradicated; or what, irrespective of their avowed purposes, they are likely to achieve. To explain why we have raised these questions only in passing—and very tentatively—it may help to discuss briefly the origins of the study, and the inherent difficulties of presenting a sociological enquiry so that it may be of some practical use.

The Ford Foundation invited Peter Marris to spend the year of 1964 as an independent observer of their 'grey area' projects. Meanwhile, Martin Rein had received a similar commission to study the projects of the President's Committee on Juvenile Delinquency. Early in the year, we met and decided to concert our enquiries. We visited projects; read through files, reports and proposals; and gathered impressions of meetings we were invited to attend, and many informal conversations. Since we could watch the projects evolve from month to month, and were sometimes present at moments of crisis, we were better placed to record the process of their development than the outcome of the endeavour. Most of the programmes were only a year or two old, and little systematic data was to be had on the numbers, characteristics and response of those they were serving. At the same time, we observed the projects primarily from the point of view of their national sponsors, looking at the movement as a whole rather than the detailed circumstances of every one. We were only able in the year to visit, between us, twelve of the seventeen projects, concentrating especially on those in cities with the longest experience. For the rest, we had to rely on information from reports and files.

By the end of the year, we had, then, a mass of notes on the projects' histories, the aims they put forward in their proposals, the range of their programmes, and a sense of the criteria by which their national sponsors were trying to guide their progress. We had also walked some of the more public corridors of power. But we could only guess at what the projects were achieving, and we could only sometimes glimpse the private political manoeuvres which lie behind every public decision. People will talk more freely of past struggles than those in which they are at the moment engaged, and an outside observer risks degenerating into a gossip-monger if he tries too insistently to unravel the personal conflicts of those about him.

The limitations of this insight are obvious enough. It provides neither a political history nor an evaluation. It tends to emphasize articulate ideas and aims at the expense both of achievements and particular political motives. And it assimilates very complex events to a more general framework of discussion. We have, for instance, written of 'The Ford Foundation', 'The President's Committee', and even of 'The reformers' (a style which some of them would repudiate as too pretentious or too tainted with earnest well-meaning, though it describes literally enough their concern with constructive changes in institutions and relationships). Each is an abstraction, treating as a unity the outcome of the inter action between men and women of diverse aims and ideas. No one, perhaps, will recognize himself in our generalized account. And just as a photographer, capturing a particular expression, seldom satisfies his subject, even where we write of individuals, they may not accept that they are truly represented by the posture in which we describe them.

Most of these limitations could be overcome with time. But here is the dilemma of research which hopes to be useful. The longer it takes, the more thorough the knowledge. But by then the events it describes are long since past, the context of decisions may have changed, and its insight is of only historical interest. And conversely, the more immediately relevant the comment, the sketchier is the understanding on which it is based. An exact, thorough analysis of a particular event can usually only be made long afterwards, when the knowledge is no longer directly useful. Paradoxically, assessment becomes more specific as events recede, and the truth refined. Thus the search for accurate judgment conflicts with the urgency of decisions. Every essay in sociological interpretation is a compromise between the need to say something to the point, before it is too late, and the need to make sure that what you say is true.

Unless he aims only at scholarship, the time at which a sociologist makes his comment must affect what he tries to say. At a meeting to formulate a project or a policy, he may have nothing to go on but the imagination he has been able to train. It may be useful then to raise the broadest questions of social purpose, in a way that would only obscure an analysis of what the policy achieved. As his knowledge grows, his interpretation tends to narrow to the aspect of events he best understands, and becomes more selective. Writing eighteen months after the events we observed, we have tried to abstract themes from a very complex history which seem to have a wide relevance, but which can be illustrated in some detail from our findings. But in a sense, the ideas about which we have organized our material are arbitrary. The interpretation is only just, so long as it is recognized to be one of many points of view from which the events might equally be examined, and which could only together provide a rounded judgment.

We decided, then, to concentrate our analysis on the process of reform, because this seemed more accessible than its achievements —either intended or accidental. We have tried, especially, to distinguish the different strategies of reform which community action took up, the relationship between them, the theories of social action and legitimate intervention which seemed to inform them. These themes are general enough to remain meaningful as community action evolves, and yet, we hope, by illustrating them from the experience of the projects, still specifically relevant to the decisions which the directors and promoters of programmes against poverty will have to take. By looking at events in this way, one can see a pattern in them which helps to clarify the characteristic dilemmas of reform: and one of the objects of the projects we studied was to explore just these problems. But from any other point of view—as an enquiry into the nature of poverty, as an analysis of the political history of community action, or an evaluation of anti-poverty programmes—this account would be both inadequately informed and over-simplified. In chapter one, we have outlined the historical background, and later we discuss the initial success of educational and vocational programmes in a few projects: the analysis of the strategies of reform would have seemed too abstracted apart from these accounts. But neither is more than a sketch, and the evaluation implied in the discussion of the experience of action cannot yet be confirmed. Since it would be tiresome to repeat these cautions on every page, we hope the reader will bear in mind the perspective from which we have assembled this account.

In the first chapter, then, we discuss the origins of community action in the social problems which, towards 1960, had begun to preoccupy the Ford Foundation, the Federal Government and its advisers; and we have summarized the community action projects which, by 1964, had already been established. These problems were all aspects of poverty in the United States, and in the second chapter, we have tried to analyse how community action, as a movement of reform, interpreted the causes of poverty in devising its policy. The third chapter examines the initial success of some of the programmes, to show what light the experience of action seems to throw on the assumptions about poverty from which these programmes derived. These first three chapters will, we hope, describe enough of the social and political context of community action to frame the discussion of the strategies of reform which occupy the rest of the book. Chapters four to eight examine the strategies themselves—the dilemmas of each, their relationship to each other, and the constraints under which the reformers acted. The last two chapters are concerned with the evolution of community action under the Economic Opportunity Act, and its meaning as an illustration of the possibilities and inhibitions of reform in American society.

PREFACE TO THE SECOND EDITION

The original material for this study was gathered in 1964, and the book was written in the following year. For this new edition, we have brought the history of community action up to date by adding an outline of events between 1965 and 1970—model cities legislation, the decline of the anti-poverty program, the use of legal intervention as a strategy of reform. We have not altered the original text, because it still seems the best attempt we can make to understand the ideals, dilemmas, and politics of community action in the earlier years. More recent history has again and again repeated the same endeavors and encountered the same conflicts. But in the new material we have gone back over the origins of the anti-poverty program, to bring out more clearly why President Kennedy's concern to make poverty an issue of policy should have led to an emphasis on community action, and how this influenced the controversies that followed. We have reviewed other interpretations of these controversies—especially Daniel P. Moynihan's *Maximum Feasible Misunderstanding*—which differ from our own.

We have also added a further section on community action interpreted as an attempt to revitalise the processes of government, for it is in this sense—rather than as a means of relieving poverty—that we think it has the most lasting importance. We have tried to articulate the criticisms of established democratic process which the principles of community action implied, and to show where its own conception of reform faltered.

So this new chapter, as well as discussing the subsequent five years, also tries to set the study in a broader context: first, by interpreting the political motives and constraints that led to the adoption of community action as a principal strategy of a nationwide war on poverty; second, by discussing the underlying weaknesses of democracy that community action implied and sought to tackle. Both these issues are as relevant now as when the first tentative proposals for experimental demonstrations of reform were put forward over a dozen years ago.

Since the book was initially written for both British and American readers and the British edition happened to be the first to appear, English spellings have been retained in the American edition for convenience of publication. We have also taken American institutions and the traditions of American democracy less for granted than if we had been writing for American readers alone. We are very concerned with the relevance and productiveness of community action, and at the same time, we have tried to present it as a characteristic aspect of American political processes—that blending of radical imagination with conservatism, at once shrewd, hypocritical, idealistic and dispairing. But if detachment makes one see the uniqueness of America more sharply, it also suggests comparisons. The history we have recorded here is important, not only because it reveals something of the inherent dilemmas of social reform in America, or because it helped to articulate a new conception of the democratic rights implied in the constitution of the United States. It raises issues which any highly industrialised urban democracy must struggle to resolve.

I

THE ORIGINS OF
COMMUNITY ACTION

A REFORMER in American society faces three crucial tasks.
He must recruit a coalition of power sufficient for his
purpose; he must respect the democratic tradition which
expects every citizen, not merely to be represented, but to play
an autonomous part in the determination of his own affairs; and
his policies must be demonstrably rational. These criteria are not
peculiar to the United States—nor irrelevant even to totalitarian
societies—but each gains in America a particular emphasis. In the
first place, the distribution of authority is uniquely complicated.

No other nation organizes its government as incoherently as
the United States. In the management of its home affairs, its
potential resources are greater, and its use of them more inhibited
than anywhere else in the world. Its policies are set to run a
legislative obstacle race that leaves most reforms sprawling help-
lessly in a scrum of competing interests. Those which limp into
law may then collapse exhausted, too enfeebled to struggle
through the administrative tangle which now confronts them,
and too damaged to attack the problems for which they were
designed. This humiliation of the will of government is popularly
reckoned no bad thing. Both the abundance of resources, and the
hamstringing of their exploitation, express alike the triumph of
democracy.

The political obstacles are rooted in the deadlock of entrenched
interests which—despite the diversity of their doctrines, ideolo-
gies, and the constituencies whose needs they represent—must
be manipulated into a coalition by any effective political leadership. Presidential power confronts independent centres of
congressional power, based on the safe seats of one-party districts,
whose venerable intransigence frustrates social legislation not

7

only by its votes, but by control of the machinery—'the committees, the caucus and conference, the promotion system, the movement of legislation, procedure on the floor . . .'[1] Leadership is therefore at the mercy of a coalition of congressional support which can rarely be contrived except in an overriding national emergency. The faith in divided powers inhibits government at every level, setting executive against legislature, state against nation, city against county—elaborating overlapping, partial jurisdictions in an almost obsessive distaste for effective government.

The same pattern of fragmented authority confuses the administrative structure. 'There are altogether over eighty different government departments and agencies which report direct to the President of the United States. They are not grouped in any hierarchy which would permit the President to restrict his dealings to a smaller number of intermediaries who would make reports and carry back the Government's decisions to the agency chiefs. Each of them has the right of access to the man at the top and is determined to use it. It is almost inconceivable that a coherent policy could emerge out of an administrative welter of this kind. Its effect under any but the strongest President is to turn the offices of the Government into a loose confederation of more or less hostile bodies competing with one another for more money and more power.'[2] In local administration, the rivalries are as fierce, and autonomy even less domitable, since agencies answer to different governments, or to none at all.

Yet this political and administrative muddle has fostered the most prosperous economy in the world's history, and protects the liberties of the greater part of its citizens more ably than most societies. The impulse to reform is repelled between the frustrations of impotence, and fear of upsetting a delicate balance which has already achieved so much. Effective government has to be reconciled with the peculiarly American tradition of democracy, which believes profoundly in the vitality of local autonomy as an expression of personal freedom. Even problems common to the whole society tend to be seen as a complex of local difficulties, to which national policy should offer support rather than

[1] James MacGregor Burns, *The Deadlock of Democracy: Four-Party Politics in America* (New Jersey: Prentice-Hall, Inc., 1963), p. 196.
[2] Andrew Shonfield, *Modern Capitalism* (Oxford University Press, 1965), p. 319.

direction. Every major reform has therefore to deal with a question of its structure, as difficult as the social problems it seeks to solve. It has to manipulate many levels of government, many semi-autonomous administrative agencies into coherent action, respecting even in the act of planning the anarchic bias of society.

This devolution of power extends beyond any formal jurisdiction to the citizen himself. He is expected, ideally, to be an active promoter of the well-being of his community—his children's school, the amenities of his block, neighbourhood affairs. Any conception of social welfare which appears to patronize its clients, or to leave them merely dependent on its services, is therefore suspect. Nothing should be done for people, that is not also done with them. Any help offered that would not ultimately enable people better to help themselves is held to be degrading. A reformer must, then collaborate with those he seeks to help as conscientiously as with the jurisdictions which claim an interest. A mandate from established power does not excuse him from securing the endorsement and participation of the people themselves.

But, thirdly, reform needs an argument, as well as political and democratic support. In a secular society, where religion is treated as a matter of private conscience, morality is an uneasy ground from which to argue any specific proposal. The sense of shared beliefs begins to dissolve in the light of intellectual analysis. Even though some moral commitment must lie at the foundation of any social policy, it is wiser to pursue, as long as possible, a more dispassionate line of argument. A technologically sophisticated culture promotes, besides, the prestige of scientific problem-solving. Analysis, expert planning, experiment begin to be as much a convention of social policy, as of industrial development or defence strategy.

Thus the movement of reform whose experience we shall discuss was largely preoccupied with these three aspects of legitimate change, and tried to evolve strategies of action at once politically viable, radically democratic, and scientifically rational. As we pursue our analysis, we shall examine each in turn, exploring the beliefs which underlay them, the inherent difficulties of implementing them, and their mutual compatibility. But before we turn to the main themes of the enquiry, it may help to discuss briefly the anxieties and preoccupations which led the Foundation and the President's Committee to originate their movement of community reform.

The Growth of Inequality

The early years of President Eisenhower's conservative administration had been sustained by the doctrine that economic growth would itself, by diffusing prosperity, reduce inequalities and resolve social problems. The standard of living for all seemed to be rising, and the position of the unskilled improved more rapidly than others. The progressive tax structure, expanded welfare services, mass public education and the G.I. Bill all served the twin aims of economic growth and income redistribution. Marginal economic groups would in time 'gracefully succumb' to the diffusion of good living, and in the end, only a small residual group of incorrigibles and incompetents would remain. And for these the public dole was available.

The first chairman of the Council of Economic Advisers under the Eisenhower administration optimistically reflected this mood, when in 1951, before he was appointed to the Council, he stated 'the transformation in the distribution of our national income . . . may already be counted as one of the great social revolutions in history.'³ The share of the nation's income going to the wealthiest 5% was declining, and the traditional income pyramid seemed to be changing into a barrel-shaped distribution—bulging in the centre, and trim at either end. But by the middle of the decade, this complacency that economic growth alone would promote a more equitable distribution of income began to lose its conviction. Prosperity was not distributing its benefits as expected.

Between 1950 and 1955 real Gross National Product increased at an average annual rate of about 4·7%, but in the period of 1955–9, the rate had declined to a sluggish 2·3%.⁴ Meanwhile unemployment and prices rose persistently. Throughout the decade, as the economy moved through successive periods of recovery and recession, a disturbing pattern emerged. Each

³ Quoted in Herman T. Miller, 'Is the Income Gap Closed? "No"', *New York Times Magazine Section,* (November 11, 1962).
⁴ Harold G. Vatter, *The United States' Economy in the 1950's: An Economic History* (New York: W. W. Norton and Company, Inc., 1963), pp. 7–8.

recovery after 1953 brought a higher proportion of the labour force into the ranks of the unemployed. In 1953 the rates stood at 3·5%, in 1956 at 3·8% and in 1959 at 5·5%. An even grimmer picture emerged from unemployment rates among special groups. Blue collar workers, those in goods producing industries, teenagers, those with less than eight years of education, and non-whites suffered more sharply than the average.[5]

Negroes were especially victimized by declining economic growth and expanding unemployment, and their plight established the political context from which many of the social reforms at the end of the decade emerged. In 1940, Negro unemployment was 20% higher than among whites. By 1953 the relative rate had risen to 71% and between 1953 and 1963 the average differentials continued to rise to 112%.[6] Commenting on the long-range trends from the perspective of the 1960's, Daniel P. Moynihan has recently observed that the two-to-one unemployment ratio between Negroes and whites is now 'frozen into the economy'.

The situation of Negro teenage workers was even more serious. In 1948 they had slightly lower unemployment rates than white youth—7·6% to 8·3%. But in the years that followed, the white rate doubled while the non-white rate quadrupled. The trend was exacerbated by changes in the age distribution of the population—youngsters under eighteen years of age increased by 37% during the decade. In the early 1950's less than two million people reached eighteen annually: by 1961, two and three-quarter million. An increase to three and three-quarter million could be projected for 1965.

Unemployment rates show only part of the increased disparity between Negro and white. In 1949 the median income of Negro men (broadly defined to include wages, salary, pension, un-employment compensation, interest, etc.) was 53% of the income of white men, while Negro women earned 51% as much as white women. The relative position of Negro women continued to improve and in 1959 their incomes were three-fifths of white. But the relative position of the Negro men grew progressively worse, falling 3 to 4% in the South, the North, and the West. The

---

[5] Margaret S. Gordon, 'United States Manpower and Employment Policy: A Review Essay', *Monthly Labor Review*, Vol. 87, No. 11, (November 1967).

[6] Herman T. Miller, 'Poverty and the Negro', (Paper presented at the University of West Virginia Conference on Poverty, May 3, 1965, mimeographed).

national Negro–white ratio had declined only slightly to 52%.[7] While the relative income of Negro men had declined, their absolute income dramatically improved. Between 1940 and 1960, according to Herman Miller, Negro men's wages have 'shown a remarkable rise . . . there was a threefold increase in Negro purchasing power', as the wages and salaries, in 1960 dollars, rose from $1,000 to approximately $3,000.[8] Thus, they were caught in a bind of rising expectations and declining relative achievement. Absolute standards of living had increased but, compared to the rest of society, income and employment had become steadily worse.

During the 1950's, migration to the North and West, and from rural to urban areas, served to reinforce this sense of deprivation. Between 1950 and 1960, one million four hundred thousand Negroes left the South. Racial inequality acquired a physical definition, as the newcomers crowded into the dilapidated ghettoes of the centre city, while the middle-class white population settled into the suburbs. In ten years, the central cities of the twelve largest metropolitan areas lost over two million white residents, and gained just under two million non-whites, who by 1960 accounted for more than a quarter of their citizens. Meanwhile, the suburbs had added only marginally to their meagre coloured residents. The disparity of living standards was clear for all to see. In the slums, Negro parents—half of whom had been educated in the backward schools of the South—struggled to find and hold the jobs which no one else wanted, while their children's chances depended on an impoverished inner city school system, whose teachers scarcely disguised their contempt for their new pupils. Meanwhile, across the city boundary, white society consolidated its advantage. Migration and a rising living standard only served to show Negro Americans the bitterness of their frustration.

Were these problems symptoms of a basic disorder in society, which would not yield to rising productivity? Negro income and employment apart, whole regions were in persistent economic decline. Senator Douglas, a distinguished economist as well as

---

[7] Allan Batchelder, 'Decline in the Relation of Income of Negro Men', *Quarterly Journal of Economics*, Vol. LXVIII, (August 1964).

[8] Herman T. Miller, 'Poverty and the Negro', (Paper presented at the University of West Virginia Conference on Poverty, May 3, 1965, mimeographed), p. 2.

political leader, discovered the depressed areas of Southern Illinois in his 1954 election campaign. The Council of Economic Advisers noted the chronic unemployment of these regions in its annual report of the following year, though it believed at first that the difficulties could be resolved locally. Douglas proposed new legislation, and the debates on its passage turned on the implications of technological change for structural unemployment. Would the hardship of coal miners in eastern Pennsylvania or Kentucky be relieved by an increased aggregate consumer demand alone? It seemed, rather, that changes in technology were creating a surplus of workers whose skills were either redundant or inadequate. By 1959, average income per head in depressed areas was more than a fourth lower than in the nation at large.

The issues raised in the late 1950's—the sluggish economic growth, the unrelenting rise in unemployment, racial disparity, the implications of automation, the neglect of education, the assimilation of more and more young people into the labour force, migration and depressed areas—were all related, and converged especially in the plight of Negro boys growing up in the city slums. A third of them were soon to be out of school and out of work—a whole generation of misfits, driven from the poverty of the South to the more humiliating frustrations of an urban ghetto.

The economic doctrine which had justified government in-action seemed less and less plausible. But reform still faced a congressional stalemate, and in the last years of Eisenhower's presidency it seemed unlikely that government would, or could, attempt any radical initiative. The Civil Rights Law of 1957 was little more than a gesture; the President had vetoed legislation directed at impoverished districts in depressed areas which included both Negro and white; and though the Social Security Act was amended in 1956 so that social services might be used to reduce economic dependence, Congress failed to appropriate funds. The most promising legislation dated back to Truman's administration.

The Housing Act of 1949, amended in 1954, provided through urban renewal a means to tackle at least one aspect of social and racial inequality. Slum clearance, with Federal subsidy, was to revitalize the declining finances of the central city. New houses would retrieve the well-to-do from the suburbs, offering the harassed suburban commuter once again the convenience and diversity of city life. His spending would revive the shops, the theatres, and department stores; his taxes would pay for education and social services; his needs would provide employment. Meanwhile, as the slum dwellers were relocated, their welfare could be tackled afresh in new surroundings, released from the demoralizing culture of the ghetto. Urban renewal dealt at once with the fiscal, social and racial problems of the city, restoring a mutually supportive diversity of race and income.

But it was crucially flawed. Where were the slum dwellers to be relocated? Unable to afford decent housing in the real estate market, excluded from the suburbs, reluctant to submit to the humiliating conditions of a public housing project, they crowded into the marginal neighbourhoods near their old homes—no better housed, and at higher rents. Urban renewal became, for the city's poor, a cynical expropriation in the interests of business, real estate, and the tax base.

The movement of reform, whose history we follow in this book, arose out of disappointment with urban renewal, seeking a form of social planning that would complement physical redevelopment. But it reflected all the concerns which had become explicit in the previous decade—the assimilation of migrants, of young people, the relief of depressed areas, education, unemployment—and it faced the same political and administrative tangle which frustrated government action. These issues converged in the 'grey area' projects of the Ford Foundation.

The Grey Area Projects

The grey area projects take their name from that zone of deteriorating real estate which, in so many American cities, lies between downtown and the suburbs. In these grey areas, the newcomers to the city have always settled, and presented their claim upon the American promise of dignity, prosperity and freedom for all. But here, too, the disappointed have remained or returned; and here racial discrimination has mostly contained the Negro migrants from the South. As technology raises its demands on human skill, and turns indifferently from those who cannot readily meet its standards, the grey areas become a symbol of hope abandoned, alienation and retreat. The Ford Foundation projects set out to show how the city might redeem its broken promise. They sought to challenge the conservatism of an impoverished school system; open worthwhile careers to young people disillusioned by neglect; return public and private agencies to a relevant and coherent purpose; and encourage a respect for the rights and dignity of the poor. The projects could not claim, in themselves, to realize so ambitious a programme of reform. But they proposed to demonstrate—in neighbourhoods of five cities, and one state—how the problems might be solved.

In the 1950's, the Public Affairs Programme of the Ford Foundation had interested itself in two approaches to the city's difficulties: metropolitan government and urban renewal. Both sought to reintegrate the central city and its suburbs, the first by merging fiscal and administrative jurisdictions, the second by attracting back to the centre the prosperous residents and businesses whom the poorer, more problem-ridden newcomers were displacing. Either way, resources would, it was hoped, accrue to renovate the impoverished and now desperately inadequate institutions of urban civilization. But disillusionment followed. The cause of metropolitan government seemed less and less promising, while urban renewal revealed its inherent weakness—it had little or nothing to offer those whom it displaced, and only aggravated the social distress it was supposed, ultimately, to relieve.[9] About 1957, the Public Affairs department was, then, looking for a new approach to the social problems of cities bolder

[9] In an address of philosophical resignation, Paul Ylvisaker, Director of the Public Affairs programme, illustrated the disappointment of these hopes by two imaginary profiles. In the first, the mayor of a centre city weighs the implications of metropolitan government: should he not support a reform ideally so rational, championed by influential liberal opinion, and which offered a means of retrieving revenue from the affluent citizens and taxable industries just out of reach beyond his municipal boundary? And yet, was metropolitan government at heart a more self-interested manoeuvre by these very citizens and industries to re-establish their control of the centre city, just as the less fortunate were coming into their own? Would the suburbs, with a majority of votes, underwrite expenditure in the centre, when the grossly underestimated cost of suburban development was itself beginning to cause alarm? Calculating, too, that the cause of metropolitan government would be a very doubtful ally of his own political fortunes, the mayor shrewdly forsakes it by declaring the proposed reform inadequate. In the second profile, an idealistic executive of a private development agency finds himself driven against his conscience to condone, in the interests of slum clearance, a racial quota in a housing scheme.
'Diversity and the Public Interest—Two Cases in Metropolitan Decision Making'. (Speech to the 16th Conference on Science, Philosophy and Religion in their Relation to the Democratic Way of Life, August 1960).

and more hopeful than metropolitan government, physical renewal, or support for research. But, restrained by their interpretation of the Foundation's legitimate role, they were largely dependent upon an outside initiative which they could exploit.

The first grants in direct support of the social needs of the city's decaying neighbourhoods arose in response to a request from the school superintendents of the largest cities. In January 1959, the superintendent of the Chicago school system wrote that he and the superintendents of fourteen other cities had been meeting over the past three years, and would like secretarial help to enable them to exchange views more effectively, especially as to the needs of the 'culturally handicapped'. The Foundation seized the opportunity to put forward a much more ambitious proposal. The Public Affairs department was already convinced that the central city presented social problems which could not be met by physical redevelopment alone, and that these problems arose largely through migration. Education seemed the most obvious, and perhaps the most important means of learning to adapt to society. Schools could, too, become intimately involved with the community they served—educating not only the children, but their parents, and, by a programme of evening activities, the adult population at large. So the Foundation saw in the school system of the city an opening for its policies which it eagerly exploited. In March 1960, an initial grant was proposed of one and a quarter million dollars to seven schools systems—Chicago, Cleveland, Detroit, Milwaukee, Philadelphia, Pittsburgh and St. Louis.

The ideal, which the Foundation sought to promote by these grants, is suggested by a paper prepared by Henry Saltzman of the Public Affairs department in the same year. A school would be planned in relation to an urban renewal neighbourhood, its new principal selected well in advance. Besides its regular pupils, the school would serve the community with adult classes, facilities for teenagers, and pre-school programmes to prepare the children of poorly educated parents for kindergarten. The curriculum would stress reading, the neighbourhood, preparation for a career, and ethnic cultures, besides special programmes of remedial reading, summer camps, work-study and after-school activities. The teachers would be joined by lay workers, to assist team teaching: while 'home–school co-ordinators' and social agencies would work closely with the teachers to meet pupils' family difficulties. So, from its primary concern with children, the school would reach out to their parents and their parents' world, compassionate and instructive.

In practice, the educational experiments extemporized by the grants were much more fragmentary and diffuse. Combined as Henry Saltzman suggested, they might have made the school more widely relevant to the communities' needs; adopted sporadically, they lacked any logical coherence as a means of social betterment. Team teaching in one school, a pre-kindergarten in another, visits to parents' homes elsewhere amounted only to a rather capricious and inconsequential willingness to experiment. The value of the experiments was, besides, seldom thoroughly examined.

The response to the first grant was still hopeful enough to encourage a further appropriation of four and three-quarter million dollars for education in grey areas a year later. By now Washington, San Francisco and Buffalo had been added to the original school systems. But this purely educational approach had been seen from the outset as only an interim measure, to lay the ground for a grander strategy: 'from the start, the school grants have been regarded as a stepping-stone to larger grants that would stimulate broader and more coherent community approaches to the physical and human problems of the grey areas', Paul Ylvisaker noted. These larger grants would draw together the Foundation's concerns with education, youth, and the urban condition. But to whom were they to be made? 'A major problem arises as to the question of an appropriate grantee . . .'

Here the Foundation faced a crucial difficulty which it never altogether resolved. In its school grants, it could at least maintain the appearance of playing a supportive rather than creative role, and evade the charge of overbearing. But if the school system was too limited in scope to carry the burden of the new programmes, who could? Since the programmes were to integrate the work of both public and private services, neither the voluntary agencies nor city hall held a broad enough authority. A new kind of agency would have to be created—and created at the instigation of the Foundation specifically to receive and spend its money.

Already, in developing the school grants, the Foundation had used a team of consultants to visit likely cities, promote its ideas, and oversee the programmes which the school systems were exploring. The Public Affairs staff now toured many of the same cities, and some new candidates, looking for 'a willingness to tackle the human problems of the grey areas through joint action of governmental and civic agencies'—and hinting broadly that such willingness would be rewarded. They left in their track a stir of interest, and some uncertainty as to what, exactly, the Foundation had in mind: the first tentative response was often no more than a proposal to extend conventional practice. But by the end of the following year the first grey project was launched.

The consultants for the school grants had included Evillio Grillo, then 'juvenile control co-ordinator' of Oakland, California. He returned home much excited by the whole approach, which he discussed with the city's manager. On a journey East, the city manager himself, Wayne Thompson, took the opportunity to call at the Foundation, and followed his visit by a letter offering Oakland as 'one of the localities the Foundation may assist to undertake a significant demonstration'. Six months later, the first draft of a proposal was put forward for discussion.

In many ways, Oakland was an unlikely place to begin. Its city council was conservatively Republican, as was the City's only newspaper: nor were there any very influential civic groups calling for social reform. It had not been included in the school grants. And its original proposals for a programme seemed un-imaginative. But the Public Affairs staff were impressed by Wayne Thompson, and especially by his success in bringing schools, county and city agencies together to control delinquency. This association of agencies had a limited purpose—to co-ordinate the treatment of troublesome youngsters by police, schools, courts, probation officers and welfare department—but it suggested the kind of joint action which the Foundation had in mind. Associated agencies was, besides, a precedent for inter-agency co-operation organized from City Hall, and helped to answer the question of an appropriate grantee. More generally, Oakland had attracted many workers to its shipyards during the war, and was thought still to be receiving population from the South. It was also designated as a centre for the relocation of Indians from the reservations (though this theme was never taken up). The city seemed, then, to offer neighbourhoods where experiments in meeting the difficulties of migrants would be much to the point. On December 28, 1961—after a year and a half of negotiation—a grant of two million dollars to the city of Oakland was announced.

Comparable grants to New Haven, Philadelphia and Boston followed in the next year. In 1963, the Foundation contributed seven million dollars to create a fund in North Carolina, to stimulate similar programmes of community action in cities and counties of the state. Finally, in 1964, the Foundation completed negotiations for a grant to Washington D.C. These six experiments in reform comprised the Foundation's grey area projects.

Though the projects grew out of concern with the urban condition, they also came to incorporate programmes which derived, more specifically, from the needs of young people. Beside its exploration of the inner city's problems, the Public Affairs department included a youth and delinquency programme —a field of action originally suggested to them by the Foundation's trustees. The youth programme evolved independently, with its own consultants and preoccupations. But since its grants were precipitated by the same climate of opinion as the grey area projects, they tended to fertilize much the same ground, even if the personal loyalties of the staff were unevenly committed.

The most influential consultants to the youth programme were probably Richard Cloward and Lloyd Ohlin, at the Columbia School of Social Work. In 1960, they had just completed a book on the theory of delinquency,[10] and were seeking to translate its principles into action in a project on the Lower East Side of New York. They argued, essentially, that delinquency was a response to frustration. Society held up for emulation only middle class ideals, yet denied to millions of youngsters—by the inadequacy of its schools, racial discrimination, and the squalor in which it left them to grow up—the hope of realizing these ideals by legitimate means. Delinquency could be interpreted either as an illegitimate attempt to secure the symbols of prestige, or as a retreat from the struggle. Thus the causes of delinquency were taken out of the context of individual pathology, and reinterpreted in terms of inequality in economic and educational opportunity. Whatever the difficulties of this approach as a comprehensive theory of

[10] Richard Cloward and Lloyd Ohlin, *Delinquency and Opportunity*.

delinquency, it justified delinquency programmes in seeking as broad a scope of intervention as the grey area projects, for the conclusions were the same. The process of assimilation into the main stream of society had broken down, and the remedy must lie in a reopening of opportunity.

The Cloward and Ohlin theory was influential, not only because it was the most up-to-date interpretation of delinquency, and allowed a wide scope of intervention, but because they were already trying to put their ideas into practice. Since 1957, the Henry Street settlement house on the Lower East Side of New York had been seeking funds for a comprehensive neighbourhood programme that would 'make use of everything we know to help children and families'—and more specifically, to get at the underlying causes of gang delinquency. To the settlement house 'everything we know' was more than adequate, if only money were there to put knowledge to use: but it had reluctantly concluded that no grants were to be had, without a gesture towards research. At the end of 1958, it approached the Columbia School of Social Work for help in a research design. So Richard Cloward and Lloyd Ohlin became closely involved in the development of a research and action programme, for which the National Institute of Mental Health provided a two-year planning grant. This programme, Mobilization for Youth, was conceived somewhat earlier than the grey area projects and always stood somewhat apart from them—bolder and more confident of its strategy. It exerted great influence, especially over the President's Committee.[11]

The President's Committee on Juvenile Delinquency

The grey area projects had originated at a time when a divided Congress under a conservative president was neither willing nor able to initiate major reforms. The projects had therefore been conceived primarily in terms of a power vacuum: by concerting a coherent leadership in cities, they hoped to demonstrate how reform might circumvent the stultification of national policy. The President's Committee, by contrast, was conceived within the

---

[11] For an account of the origins of Mobilization for Youth see Frances Piven, 'Conceptual Themes in the Evolution of Mobilization for Youth', (Paper prepared for the Columbia University and Mobilization for Youth Training Institute Programme, April 1964, mimeographed).

Federal Government by a new regime determined to grasp the initiative, and override the politics of sectional interests by the sheer force of rational analysis.

The Kennedy family had a long-standing interest in the problems of youth, and the President was eager to give substance to the campaign slogan of a new frontier by a series of innovative programmes. Soon after the inauguration, David Hackett—friend and schoolmate of Robert Kennedy (the newly appointed Attorney General), and a member of the campaign staff—was designated to develop a new Federal initiative against delinquency. Hackett had no previous experience of the problem or expert knowledge, but he was not a career bureaucrat, and so uncommitted to any school of official thought. The President had been shocked to discover how inflexible bureaucracies could be, and it was characteristic of his administrative style to place an independent intelligence, paralleling the establishment, in a strategic position to forge new ideas without administrative constraint.

David Hackett was assigned to the Justice Department, and collaborated closely with the Attorney General. He began to inform himself of current thinking, consulting with the National Institute, the Children's Bureau, police officials, universities and research centres. At this time, when his ideas were still unformed, the Ford Foundation got in touch with him. David Hunter and Dyke Brown, who ran the Foundation youth programme, introduced him to the philosophy of Mobilization for Youth and the grey area projects, which set delinquency in the context of social frustration and alienation, and took the conventions of institutional practice as the principal target of reform. Innovative, intellectual, anti-bureaucratic, this line of thought appealed to the spirit of the new frontier, and Hackett was readily persuaded to align his own policy accordingly. He invited Lloyd Ohlin, as joint author of the theory which rationalized this policy of wide-ranging social intervention, and co-director of research at Mobilization, to help him develop the Federal programme. In the following months, while they revised legislation which had been put forward without success since 1955, they developed the idea of a special executive committee, with power to draw together the many Federal departments, institutes and bureaux concerned with delinquency.

The President's Committee on Juvenile Delinquency and Youth

Crime was established by executive order on May 11, 1961. Its members comprised the Attorney General, the Secretary of Labour and the Secretary of Health Education and Welfare, each of whom was to appoint a special assistant as his alternate—Hackett for the Attorney General, Ohlin for HEW, and Salinger (who, however, also had other duties) for Labour. The Attorney General took the chair. The Committee was to 'review, evaluate and promote the co-ordination of the activities of the several departments and agencies of the Federal Government relating to juvenile delinquency and youth crime'; 'stimulate experimentation, innovation and improvement in Federal programmes'; 'encourage co-operation and the sharing of information between Federal agencies and state, local and private organizations . . .' and 'make recommendations to the Federal departments and agencies on measures to make more effective the prevention, treatment, and control of juvenile delinquency and youth crime'.[12] The Committee was thus to be a cabinet pressure group for coherent reform. The executive order also created an auxiliary Citizen's Advisory Council of recognized authorities on delinquency.

At the same time, new delinquency legislation was promoted. The proposed bill, like those which had been before Congress for the past six years, provided for grants to states and communities for demonstration and research projects, training of personnel, and technical assistance. But it differed from its predecessors in two important features. Firstly, its preamble was revised to emphasize the relationship of delinquency to unemployment and educational attainment. 'Delinquency and youth offences occur disproportionately among school drop-outs, unemployed youth faced with limited opportunities and with employment barriers, and youth in deprived family situations . . . prevention and control of such delinquency and youth offences require intensive and co-ordinated efforts on the part of private and governmental interests.'[13] Secondly, the bill abridged the authority to be vested in the Secretary of the Department of Health Education and Welfare. While he was authorized to make grants for demonstrations, research and training, he was directed

---

[12] Executive Order 10940, May 11, 1961, section 2.
[13] Public Law 87–274, 'The Juvenile Delinquency and Youth Offences Control Act of 1961'.

to consult and consider the recommendations of the President's Committee.

Towards the end of 1961 representatives of the Committee began to broadcast the provisions of the new legislation and invite applications. Richard Boone, who joined the Committee from the Public Affairs department of the Ford Foundation, initiated interest in forty or fifty communities. William Lawrence, who had worked with Lloyd Ohlin in Mobilization for Youth, followed up the more promising of these initial contacts. In search of innovative ideas in education, work-training, or the manipulation of street gangs, he visited many of the cities in which the Foundation was also interested, through the grey area programme or the earlier great cities school projects. Meanwhile, Lloyd Ohlin and David Hackett prepared for a six-week tour of a dozen cities, where they were to promote the range of programmes in education, employment, medical care and delinquency which marked the New Frontier.

The President's Committee and the grey area projects drew upon a common fund of ideas. But once the Foundation had introduced the Committee to its point of view, the two programmes went their own ways. They differed most in their provision for planning. The Committee tried to guard the integrity of its aims against political pressures by insisting that each community work out a conceptual framework, from which the goals and methods of action were to derive. Every proposal was to be justified by reference to this rational analysis of the nature of the problems. The Committee therefore always made a separate grant for a year or more's thorough preliminary planning, before it would consider funding any action.[14] The Foundation was less explicit about the planning procedure. It made grants only after some acceptable proposals had already been negotiated, and then left the executive director and his board free to explore other possibilities for which it held funds in reserve. It trusted less to any intellectual rationale, than to the power of veto it held over release of the development fund. Though it lacked the authority of government, the Foundation was readier to maintain a continuous, direct control over the community's affairs than the Federal bureaucracy.

[14] Mobilization for Youth excepted. It had already had a two-year planning grant from NIMH.

We shall take up the implications of these different approaches, when we come to explore the experience of planning. But despite what sometimes seemed an almost obsessive bias towards rationality, the President's Committee shared too much in common with the grey area projects to quarrel with their concrete suggestions. Both placed the emphasis upon changing the environment, rather than the individual, and both recognized education and vocational opportunities as crucial aspects of the environment. Reform, they both believed, must grow out of a much more coherent integration of relevant institutions. They both concentrated their resources in a few projects, for which they claimed wide relevance as demonstrations: and the logic of this demonstration strategy led them equally to seek objective evaluation of their success. Both, too, were concerned to create a local constituency for their approach—not only by securing a commitment from the leadership of the communities, but by drawing the people to be helped into the planning of their own welfare.

So although the Foundation and the Committee sent out independent teams to canvass their proposals, the grants tended to converge in the same cities. Four of the six grey area projects also received funds through the President's Committee, and Mobilization for Youth was supported by both sponsors. In all, by the end of 1964, there were seventeen community action agencies in being. The organization of these projects was variously contrived, but they nearly all sought to establish, as their controlling authority, a workable coalition of government and non-government, official and unofficial representation. According to the balance of local power, this coalition might be all-inclusive and amorphous, or closely knit, but only Los Angeles attempted to keep authority wholly within the hands of government.

Inspired by a common philosophy, the projects also introduced a similar range of experiments—educational innovations, both in and out of the classroom, on the lines of the earlier great cities schools programme; vocational training and employment services for young people; legal aid and community service centres. Both in their organization, and the programmes they designed, these projects became a model for the community action agencies which, under the second title of the Economic Opportunity Act, became the most adaptive strategy of President Johnson's campaign against the 'paradox of poverty in the midst of plenty'.

So though many of these seventeen projects have been absorbed into the poverty programme, and others have been displaced, their earlier experience is still relevant. For the dilemmas with which they wrestled have not been resolved. But before we take up the analysis of these issues, it may help to summarize the structure and resources of the projects at the end of 1964.

The Projects in 1964

First, there were six grey area projects, initiated chiefly by the Ford Foundation, though four also received grants from the President's Committee, and most had some other funds:

The Oakland Inter Agency Project: financed through a trust fund set up by the City Council, and run within the framework of City government. The City Manager was chairman of its Executive Committee, which included officials of City and County departments (such as Welfare, Recreation, Probation and Health), of the school system, and the Council of Social Planning. There were five other advisory committees—of citizens, departmental research directors, departmental co-ordinators, programme directors, and research consultants drawn from the University of California. The Ford Foundation made a three-year grant of two million dollars in December 1961, of which three-quarters of a million were placed in a development fund: by 1964 it was beginning to press for some commitment of matching funds from the city as a condition of a second grant.

Community Progress Incorporated, New Haven: an independent agency, but working very closely with the Mayor. Three of its Board of nine directors—'selected to reflect what might be termed a coalition of community interests'—were appointed by the Mayor; and one each by the Redevelopment Authority, the Board of Education, the Community Council, the United Fund, the Citizens Action Committee, and Yale University. With a consistent prejudice in favour of executive control, the Board remained small, and CPI did without the advice of the usual committees of public officials, academics, and local worthies, preferring to hire consultants as it needed them. New Haven is smaller and more compact than the other cities, and leadership securely in the hands

C　　　　　　　　　25

of the Mayor's 'executive centred coalition'. cpi's executive director ran a staff of about one hundred, in four divisions—programme development and training, research, neighbourhood services and manpower. Its own staff apart, about five hundred people were employed in its programmes. The Foundation made a three-year grant of two and a half million in April 1962—larger than Oakland, though the city has only about half the population. Of this, $650,000 were development funds. In addition, cpi recruited about one and a quarter million dollars in grants from the President's Committee and the Department of Labour, besides smaller local contributions. It spent in all about three million in 1963–4, and expected to spend four million in the following year—roughly eighty dollars for every man, woman and child in the neighbourhoods its programmes served.

Action for Boston Community Development: also an independent agency. Its Board of thirty-four 'was organized as a microcosm of Boston. Its members . . . reflect the economic, religious, racial and institutional interests of the community. The political leadership of the city, represented by the Mayor and several department heads, and the public and private health and welfare organizations on both the City and State levels were substantially represented on the Board'. There were two other committees. The President of the Board was the Dean of Brandeis University graduate school, reflecting abcd's bias towards research. Its staff, in 1964, was slightly smaller than in New Haven, but a much higher proportion was employed on research than in cpi or any other project—over a third. abcd had secured two planning grants in its formative stages, from a Boston Foundation and United Community Services. In September 1962, the Ford Foundation made a grant of $1·9 million, and a few weeks later the President's Committee awarded a planning grant, which led, in January 1964, to a seven hundred thousand dollar grant to implement the proposals. Meanwhile, abcd had secured nearly four hundred thousand from the Department of Labour. Altogether, its budget for 1964 amounted to just four million.

Philadelphia Council for Community Advancement: an independent agency with a Board of fifty-three, representing 'those major institutions, public and private, in the fields of education, health, recreation, government and welfare, whose interest it is to advance the physical, moral and economic well-being of the community', and 'lay and professional leadership familiar with the principal demonstration area, North Philadelphia'. PCCA was also originally encumbered with an unwieldly structure of task forces, similarly constituted. The President's Committee made a planning grant in June 1962, and the Foundation a grant of $1·7 million in December, of which one million was a development fund. Later $150,000 was also recruited from the Department of Labour. By the end of 1963, PCCA had a small, rather unstable staff, and had spent about half a million dollars.

United Planning Organization, Washington: Though the Foundation had early decided to promote a grey area project in the Capital, the complexity and amorphousness of the city made for slow progress. UPO was incorporated at the end of 1962, but did not receive a substantial grant from the Foundation until February 1964. This was still only a preliminary quarter of a million dollars, to engage a staff and develop the programmes—the balance of one and a third million had still not been finally committed at the end of the year. Meanwhile, the President's Committee had made a planning grant to its own creation, Washington Action for Youth. The two organizations were amalgamated in 1964, and UPO secured in late autumn a commitment of five millions from the Committee. The thirty trustees of UPO's Board were designated by the President of the United States, the Metropolitan Washington Council of Governments, the Health and Welfare Council, the National Capital Planning Council and Planning Commission, the Washington Board of Trade, Labour Council, and Centre for Metropolitan Studies: ten other members were elected at large. Both in its name, and the composition of its Board, UPO reflected the bias of its original conception towards regional planning.

North Carolina Fund: The Fund itself is not comparable with the other projects. Under a Board of fourteen, chaired by the now-retired Governor, it acted as an independent statewide agency, to promote, and in part finance, community action programmes in the cities and counties of North Carolina. Each such project was itself incorporated, prepared its own proposals, and applied for grants. The Fund's function was to stimulate the creation of these community agencies, advise them, and provide enough money to equip a basic organization. It also took an overall responsibility to evaluate the experiments. The fund grew out of discussions between Governor Sanford and the Foundation early in 1963. By October of the same year, Ford was ready to announce a grant of seven million for five years. Three million were held in reserve, and two more million allocated to a statewide education programme. A further million—apart from matching funds from the State—were put up by a foundation in Winston-Salem. The Fund promptly advertised its aims throughout North Carolina, and invited applications. By the spring of the following year, it was overwhelmed by 51 proposals representing two-thirds of the State's hundred counties. From these, the fund chose seven for immediate support.

Apart from these six, the Foundation also granted two million dollars to *Mobilization for Youth,* though—perhaps because the negotiations had concerned David Hunter rather than Paul Ylvisaker—the project was not included in the grey area programme. As we saw, MFY originated in the Henry Street Settlement House, but its final board was swollen to accommodate much broader interests. It included 11 representatives of the school system, 22 from local institutions, 22 city officials, 7 local residents, 5 influential laymen from the public at large and 11 professionals from the Columbia School of Social Work. From this was derived a more manageable Executive Committee of 26. In 1963–4, MFY's annual budget ran to five and a quarter million dollars, of which about one and a half million each came from the National Institute of Mental Health and the City of New York, seven to eight hundred thousand each from the Ford Foundation and the President's Committee, and two hundred thousand from the Office of Manpower Automation and Training. NIMH also provided about half a million for research. These resources were directed to the poorest 20% of the 107,000 people living below 14th Street on the East River.

In all, by 1964 the Foundation had committed about 20 million dollars to support experimental community action.[15] By compari-

---

[15] Including two related grants—to the Kansas City Association of Trusts and Foundations (see Chapter VIII) and Action Housing in Pittsburgh, a project which remained more closely within the context or urban renewal. Apart from these, the Foundation also supported specific programmes with similar aims to those of the grey area projects.

son, the President's Committee had only $10·7 millions to spend on demonstration projects in its first three years,[16] and a third of this went in planning grants. The rest was to be concentrated in the five or six cities which produced the best proposals. In practice, the ruthlessness of competitive selection was softened by political discretion, and besides the six major grants—to Boston, New Haven, Los Angeles, Syracuse, Cleveland and HARYOU-ACT in Harlem—the Committee funded specific single programmes in other communities. By the end of 1964, the scale of Federal support for these original projects was rapidly increasing, under appropriations of the Labour Department and the new Office of Economic Opportunity, while the Ford Foundation was preparing gradually to withdraw. At Congressional hearings on the extension of the Juvenile Delinquency Act, early in 1965, the Department of Health Education and Welfare gave the listing of current grants as shown on page 30.

Though the table lists only grants then current, it includes all but two of the communities which the President's Committee supported.[17] Philadelphia and Detroit received planning grants also, but no programmes of action were funded by the Committee after these grants had lapsed.

The evolution of these projects can be summarized as a continual broadening of interests, and refinement of strategy. Starting from the shortcomings of relocation, and the impoverishment of the centre city, more and more problems were drawn into the context of coherent, experimental community action—migration, the cultural handicaps of slum children, delinquency, unemployment amongst young people, adult illiteracy, the abuse of those too poor to defend their legal rights, or too discouraged to protest their needs, and last, more generally, the persistence of poverty in so prosperous a nation. As the conception broadened, so too more and more institutions became involved—in the communities, at first the school systems, then the redevelopment authorities,

[16] Apart from a special appropriation of five millions for Washington, which was released at the end of 1964. Formally all these grants were made through the Office of Juvenile Delinquency and Youth Development of the Department of Health Education and Welfare.

[17] The table includes one grant—to the San Francisco Committee on Youth—which was not intended to support a comprehensive project. HARYOU and ACT were originally separate agencies, and received separate planning grants. After a much publicized struggle between the Harlem leadership they were amalgamated under Federal pressure.

CURRENT FUNDING OF THE OFFICE OF JUVENILE DELINQUENCY AND
YOUTH DEVELOPMENT DEMONSTRATION PROJECTS, APRIL 1965*

Grantee	Current grant period	Office of Juvenile Delinquency	Funds from Department of Labour	Office of Economic Opportunity
1. Crusade for Opportunity in Syracuse and Onondaga County, Inc.	July 1, 64– Apr. 30, 65	$639,437	$758,510	$483,610
2. Houston Action for Youth Inc.	June 1, 64– May 31, 65	200,000	—	—
3. St. Louis Human Development Corp.	Apr. 22, 64– June 30, 65	364,927	—	1,092,050
4. Community Health and Welfare Council of Hennepin County Inc., Minneapolis	Aug. 1, 64– July 31, 65	250,000	—	1,114,061
5. Youth Opportunities Board of Greater Los Angeles	Aug. 1, 64– July 31, 65	782,540	1,698,716	2,729,683
6. HARYOU-ACT Inc., Harlem	Sept. 3, 64– Sept. 2, 65	1,000,000	—	—
7. San Francisco Committee on Youth	Sept. 14, 64– Sept. 13, 65	84,968	1,241,986	—
8. Joint Youth Development Committee, Chicago	Sept. 30, 64– Sept. 30, 65	250,000	—	—
9. Appalachian Action for Youth, Charleston	Feb. 1– Oct. 31, 65	325,000	1,187,907	—
10. Community Action for Youth Inc., Cleveland	Jan. 1– Dec. 31, 65	700,000	289,721	—
11. Progress for Providence, Inc.	Jan. 18, 65– Jan. 17, 66	285,000	—	61,850
12. Lane County Study Board, Eugene, Oregon	Feb. 15, 65– Feb. 14, 66	328,309	685,580	—
13. Community Progress Inc., New Haven	Nov. 1, 64– Oct. 31, 65	700,000	1,423,661	785,879
14. Action for Boston Community Development Inc.	Feb. 1, 64– Apr. 30, 65	704,071	691,737	680,050
15. Mobilization for Youth Inc., New York City	Apr. 16, 62– June 30, 65	1,969,000	1,284,725	—
16. United Planning Organization, Washington D.C.	Oct. 12, 64– Oct. 11, 65	1,500,000	491,432	1,623,756
Total Current Finding		$ 10,083,252	9,753,975	8,570,939

*Hearings . . . United States Senate . . . to Extend the Juvenile Delinquency and
Youth Offenses Control Act of 1961, April 7 and 8, 1965, p. 126. The list of Federal
grants is not exhaustive.

councils of voluntary agencies, local philanthropies, city and county governments, universities, the schools again, welfare departments, churches, and Civil Rights groups; in the states, employment services and departments of vocational training; in the Federal Government, the President's Committee (with its own complex relationships to the Attorney General's Office and the Department of Health Education and Welfare), the Department of Labour, under whose Manpower Development and Training Act the projects financed their vocational experiments, and finally the Office of Economic Opportunity. And the further the conception evolved from its origins in specifically urban problems, so too, from project to project, the field of action tended to enlarge—from one neighbourhood to the city, from city to metropolitan area, and ultimately to a whole state. The North Carolina Fund undertook to promote programmes from the tidewater to the mountains.

To have drawn so many interests together was itself a triumph of diplomacy and disinterested idealism. To have concerted a strategy with so universal a range was all the more impressive. The principles of action became on the whole only sharper and less compromising as their scope grew more ambitious. The criteria of planning included research and analysis; the participation of all relevant agencies; the endorsement of political and informal leadership; and later, the involvement of those the programmes were to benefit. The approach was to be experimental and its success methodically evaluated. Whether or not the new instrument of reform was organized within city government, the city was to assume the ultimate responsibility for the future of the demonstration, once its value had been proved. This strategy, to which so many institutions were brought to commit their support, was no mere gesture towards co-operation, but a purposeful and exacting formula.

It acknowledged the power of professional politics, even while it sought to change the principles which informed it. Unlike a popular reform movement, it did not rest on idealism and faith so much as on technique. The professional reformers addressed themselves to the professional rulers, rather than the public upon whom their power ultimately rested. At the same time, the reformers sought to influence the framework of social analysis and democratic sensitivity within which the politicians manoeuvred. Though, at the outset, their conception was preoccupied with the incoherence of political and administrative jurisdictions, it recognized each of the three fundamental criteria of reform: it was not only to mould the structure of power, but to enhance the dignity of every citizen, however poor, and to approach social problems rationally and empirically. Each principle was to counterpoise the bias of others, and the strategies which derived from them would be mutually reinforcing. Theory would educate government, while intellectual idealism would be forced to come to terms with political feasibility. Both would be tempered by the direct participation of those whom they served.

The next chapter looks at some of the assumptions about poverty and the shortcomings of community institutions, by which the projects interpreted this new approach.

II

THE UNDERLYING
ASSUMPTIONS

As experimental demonstrations of community action, the projects needed to justify their initiative, by showing how their programmes derived from their understanding of the cities' problems. In this chapter we shall try to interpret the assumptions of which they relied. But these assumptions were not always explicit, or fixed. They were obscured by diplomatic evasions and they were continually reinterpreted in the light of experience. Much of the time, the conceptual framework was shelved to make room for the problems of the day. It was only intermittently taken down, dusted off, and put into working repair. At every stage performance reacted upon the indeterminate beliefs which had inspired it, and the two evolved together.

Any practical organization will naturally develop by such a pragmatic fusion of means and ends. An initial purpose leads to a preliminary framework of action, that framework suggests other purposes which it might fulfil, the further organization of action takes these new purposes into account—and so on, until a working structure is evolved which has its own momentum. Once the organization begins to function, it tends to be as preoccupied with finding a use for its resources as with adapting resources to a pre-determined purpose. But as practice diverges from theory, and the internal demands of the organization's structure impose their own logic, the coherence of the whole enterprise is endangered. 'What are you really trying to achieve?' asks the naïve critic, and finds he has thrown down a provocative challenge. From time to time, the ultimate aims have to be re-examined—both to justify and rationalize the direction of effort.

This interplay between the exploitation of means and the realization of ends can be seen continually in the organizations created by

The Underlying Assumptions

the Ford Foundation and the President's Committee. Sensitive sounding of influential groups by Foundation staff and Federal departments preceded any precise statement of purpose: the programme proposals which followed were, characteristically, criticized for lack of clear aims; the final proposals were a compromise, in which expediency was rationalized by very generalized goals. This was largely a process of political accommodation, by which people of varying aims and resources sought a common purpose compatible with a realizable instrument of institutional coordination. But it was also a process of intellectual exploration, as ideas were redefined in the search to give them form.

Once the projects began to put their programmes into effect, their actions were more than ever shaped by the means to hand. They were under pressure to produce results, and reluctant, at the outset, to run too great a risk of failure: so they accomplished first the programmes which came easiest—a summer camp, vacation jobs for high-school students, training courses for well-qualified applicants, holiday tasks for college volunteeers—rather than those which mattered most. Sometimes they even appropriated to their sponsorship activities already in being. And in developing their plans, they went after new money, rather than new ideas. The organizations soon acquired an interest in their own survival, growth and influence which upset their original agenda.

Yet it would have been as futile to insist upon purposes they could not achieve, or were not ready to attempt, as to exploit means to no worthwhile end. No statement of intent could foresee all the consequences of action, and even the most rigorous theoretical planning remained indeterminate. After a while it seemed better to set to work, and see what came of it. If the projects were distracted by the struggle to establish their viability, the more efficient were also sophisticated by it. They came to interpret their purposes more pointedly and selectively.

This constant interaction of means and ends makes the goals and assumptions of the projects hard to define. Statements from different sources, or at different times, offer varying explanations of intent. A programme to reduce 'the volume and seriousness of criminal-type behaviour on the part of male youth 12 through 16 years of age'[1] is not, at first sight, the same as 'a concerted effort to

[1] 'The Boston Youth Opportunities Project: A Report and a Proposal', (ABCD, December 1963), p. 57.

34

strengthen and improve employment, education, health, housing, family life and recreation (to) reinforce the city's urban renewal programme'. But Action for Boston Community Development offers both definitions of its objectives—the first in its proposal to the President's Committee in 1963, the second in its annual report a year later, to both the Committee and the Ford Foundation. The second definition is given as an interpretation of the original intentions of the organizers in 1961, and the report goes on: 'After two years of operating experience, ABCD reaffirms these purposes and seeks to achieve them in the following ways:

1. By developing, in concert with other agencies, new community service programmes, with emphasis on the needs of Boston's disadvantaged people especially in areas where urban renewal is providing new opportunities.

2. By reviewing existing services and pressing for a redirection of resources . . .

3. By improving the co-ordination of services . . .

4. By testing and evaluating new methods for reducing social problems.

5. By informing and educating the public in areas related to ABCD's programmes and objectives.'[2]

This statement is not only more explicit and modest than the general purposes it reaffirms: it has a different bias. The relationship to urban renewal is presented more loosely, and the emphasis has shifted to planning, analysis, research and information at the expense of direct achievements.

A similar successive reinterpretation can be traced through the documents of other projects, and in the records of the funding agencies. As time went by the Foundation talked less of newcomers—who had pride of place in Oakland's original proposal; and Paul Ylvisaker began to wonder whether the co-ordination of many services about a problem was, after all, as essential or effective as a single imaginative experiment. The President's Com-

[2] A Report on ABCD Activities, September 1963–August 1964, Appendix C, p. iv.

mittee relaxed, one by one, its stringent principles of rational planning. Nor did experience point everyone in the same direction. As they were forced to choose between alternative conceptions of their purpose, the projects began to diverge.

But in the summer of 1964, on the eve of President Johnson's campaign against poverty, these divergencies were still latent. There was then more of a consensus of purpose than at any time before or will likely be again. The negotiations between the national and local sponsors had resolved their differences, however precariously, in a framework of action; the experience of the earlier projects had established a range of viable initial programmes; and for the most part, the various interests upon which the projects rested had not yet proved so patently irreconcilable as to force an explicit choice between them. A set of common assumptions can be disentangled from the diffuse and seemingly inconsistent statements which—rambling or crisply underscored, pedantically precise or dignified by sociological metaphysics—articulate the proposals and reports.

The preamble to New Haven's 1962 prospectus for a 'comprehensive programme for community progress' opens with a characteristic statement of the projects' line of argument:

The United States has become an urban nation, but ironically American cities have never before faced as grave problems as now. Cities are the centre of our civilization, the seat of culture, the heart of the economic system, and the leader of thought. But more and more the central cities of the metropolitan complexes are becoming places where much of the deprivation of our society is concentrated. Poverty is contrasted with wealth, and ignorance with great learning...

The city is a place where people come because there is opportunity in many area of life. Yet for many who come to or who were born in the city there are many road blocks. Some of these barriers are cultural; others relate to the social and economic structure. Certain obstacles seem to centre in the individuals themselves, while others have a group base. A fundamental task is to alter the opportunity structure in education, employment, housing and other aspects of city life.

The city is the people. New jobs can be provided but some people are unwilling or afraid to apply for them. New housing projects can be built but some tenants will turn them into slums. New community centres can be opened but only a few people may choose to use them. Exciting educational programmes can be conceived but the people can let them die for lack of participation. Therefore, attention must be paid to the underlying motivations, attitudes and values of the people of the city.

The city is the birthplace of democracy, and today it is a testing ground for the effectiveness of the democratic process . . .[3]

This passage announces the themes from which a common philosophy can be derived. A great city holds out the promise of emancipation. By its anonymity, its diversity, the tolerance of supreme indifference it offers a refuge for the misfit and the aspiring. Traditionally, the American city has absorbed the poor, the rebels and protestants of the old world, and let them scramble by fair means and foul after the rewards of citizenship. It offers, not benevolence, but a liberating anarchy. Even the corruption of city politics has probably done more for the hopeful immigrant than the patrician conscience of the public-spirited elite. But the rewards of anarchy are bought at a stiff price in callousness, exploitation and ineffectual government. The elaborately structured balance of interests stultifies coherent policy, and in frustrating every bid for supremacy, forces each source of authority back upon an anxious defence of its jurisdiction. To the family in a sordid back street, the free-for-all of decentralized democracy is an interminable struggle for power from which they have learned to expect little to their advantage. Burdened with a sense of defeat before they leave school, the young men and women from these families enter a bleakly competitive world where the opportunities have all been pre-empted. They are no longer able to respond, even to such chances as remain open to them.

The philosophy thus accepted that poverty was the crucial issue, and related it to a breakdown in the distribution of opportunities. This breakdown was then explained as both a failure of the institutional structure, and of individual will. At first sight, the explanations lead towards independent arguments—the first, that opportunities are denied; the second, that people are indifferent

[3] 'Opening Opportunities: New Haven's Comprehensive Programme for Community Progress', (CPI, April 1962), pp. 2–3.

37

to them. But each is presented as an aspect of the same faltering democratic process. The New Haven document does not carry the argument further, but the themes converge in the widely acknowledged theory of the poverty cycle.

The phrase first appears, in the literature of the projects, in the prospectus of the North Carolina Fund—and gained so wide a currency that 'help break the poverty cycle' was even stamped on North Carolina's mail. The prospectus argues:

> Poverty exists for a number of reasons, and elimination of any *one* of these reasons will not in itself eliminate poverty. Inadequate education, low or non-existent income, limited job opportunities, dilapidated and overcrowded housing, poor physical and mental health, an inclination towards delinquency and crime—these and many other characteristics of poverty both cause and are caused by each other, interacting in a manner which renders it virtually impossible for the disadvantaged child, adult or family to break out of the 'cycle of poverty'. It is essential, therefore, that any attack on the problem of poverty must be comprehensive, bringing the forces of state and community action to bear on all the characteristics of the problem . . .

> We strongly suspect, for example, that simply strengthening the public schools will not benefit many of those who drop out of school early and follow the footsteps of their parents into poverty. Too many of these young people come from homes where the level of education, as well as of income and of general living environment, has been low for generations; where increasingly this cycle of poverty and frustration has blunted the desire of parents to give their children motivation for education; where the American dream of slum to affluence in three generations no longer has a meaning. Children can make their way out of poverty, but only where there is motivation, sacrifice, and opportunity. Where these do not exist, there can be no breaking of the cycle.[4]

Poverty, then, is seen as self perpetuating. The children of the poor and ill-educated start school at a disadvantage, and soon fall behind. Their parents can give them little help or encouragement; school becomes a humiliating experience, where they cannot meet the teacher's demands, and finally lose her interest. They take

---

[4] 'The North Carolina Fund: Programmes and Policies', (November 1963), pp. 10–11.

the first opportunity to drop out. Without skills or confidence in themselves, they remain marginally employable. Some work off their frustration in crime and violence, most will always be poor. Robbed of the self-respect that comes from earning a decent livelihood, the young men cannot sustain the responsibilities of marriage, and so they bequeath to their children the same burden of ignorance, broken homes and apathy by which they were themselves crippled.

The theory allows for a very flexible strategy, since it sets no order of priority. If the causes of poverty are circular, then intervention at any point may be effective, and the more the better. At the same time, neglect of any one aspect of the problem is excused by the indirect influence upon it of action elsewhere. The argument takes care of an apparent anomaly in the grey area projects. They concentrated upon the needs of youth, yet many of the poor are neither young nor in search of employment—the retired, mothers struggling to bring up families on their own, the sick and mentally handicapped. Though they recognized poverty as their fundamental concern, the projects virtually ignored many of its most characteristic forms, especially in old age, and amongst those with badly paid jobs.[5] The conception of the poverty cycle justified them in acting upon the most malleable age groups, where intervention stood the best chance.

Conversely, it entitled the President's Committee, with a nominally much more restricted mandate, to set its task in the same comprehensive framework of interrelated causes. Delinquency was interpreted in terms of the failure of socialization. Broken homes, poor school records, unemployment deprived young people of role models and ego ideals on which they could draw to overcome their frustrations and find an acceptable place in society.

This circular etiology does not explain so clearly where the institutions of society have failed. The argument seems to leave the responsibility for their poverty with the poor themselves, and even to echo the harsh moral strictures of the nineteenth century poor law reforms. 'Some of this poverty is self-imposed and some of it is deserved', states the North Carolina Fund prospectus—

---

[5] Half of those on general assistance in New York were employed, for example, and in parts of North Carolina, a truck driver might be earning only fifty dollars a week—about $2,500 a year. The North Carolina Fund, in its statistical analysis, drew the poverty line at $3,000 a year for a family.

adding more compassionately, 'All of it withers the spirit of children who neither imposed it nor deserved it'. Washington's United Planning Organization states its objective, in general terms, as 'reduction of dependency and increase of self-reliance', and New Haven talks of 'self-improvement'. Even if incompetence was understood in terms of motivation more than morals, and the sufferings of children were no longer to be left to prod the conscience of their fathers, the theory still seems to assume that the poor must face up to the demands of their society, rather than the other way about.

Yet the projects insisted upon institutional change. In itself, belief in a poverty cycle could have led to little more than an extension of conventional social work. But as the Philadelphia Council for Community Advancement affirmed in its 1963 report, institutions, not their users, were to be the target of reform.

> The major thrust of PCCA's programme is towards strengthening the individual and the family unit so that they might participate more fully in the life of the community . . . With the above mission in mind, PCCA considered three broad alternative approaches. The first would be to serve as a resource for channelling funds to agencies and institutions to develop and implement social action programmes . . . The second alternative role would be to assume that the major correction of the urban condition is via the provision of services and rehabilitation programmes directly to the people. Such an approach, if it stops at this level and does not seek to change the character of institutional services to people, assumes people have the sole blame for their difficulties. PCCA has instead accepted as its role a third approach . . . *The major objective of PCCA is to promote change, through demonstration and research, in the character of human service rendered by governmental, private and public institutions by making such services as effective and economic as possible so that its recipients are more highly motivated to participate in community affairs.*[6]

This awkwardly-phrased juxtaposition of institutional reform and individual weakness marks the projects' claim to originality. What did they believe was wrong with the institutions of society?

Here, tactfully, the argument in proposals and reports is less explicit. The North Carolina Fund prospectus observes, very generally '. . . in all of our zeal for planning at the state and com-

[6] Annual Report to the Ford Foundation, 1963, p. 11.

munity levels, we find no evidence that any one agency, public or private, is looking at the problems of the people in their totality. We find no evidence that there is any concerted effort by cities, counties, and schools, health and welfare agencies, public or private, to find new approaches to the dilemma of the poor.'[7] The complaint is not elaborated, but it implies the characteristic criticisms of institutional practice.

Firstly, the interdependence of all aspects of poverty was not fully recognized: each agency, or government, tended to understand the problems from its own limited point of view. Nowhere, within the community, were public and private services, nor the responsibilities of government at every level, co-ordinated by an overall conception. Second, the current practice was not innovative. The arguments do not explain why innovation was so necessary, fearing perhaps to antagonize the agencies on whose goodwill the projects depend. But the reasons seem to derive from a common assumption of bureaucratic conservatism. Institutions failed for lack of imagination and adaptability, rather than for lack of resources. To provide them with more money to go on as before would only confirm them in outdated practice: the priority was innovation.

In part, conservatism was seen as the failure of institutions to adapt to changes in society. A once Jewish neighbourhood becomes predominantly Negro—yet schools still assume that pupils and staff share a common white middle-class culture, and settlement houses still cater for the aspiring Jewish youngster. Training courses survive the out-dating of the skills they teach, and charities go through the motions of dispensing a benevolence no one now cares to receive. But there are also more fundamental arguments why, irrespective of such changes, institutions may regress into irrelevance.

The theory of bureaucracy, since Max Weber's classic analysis, has emphasized its reliance on impersonal relationships articulated by formal regulations. A disciplined subordination to a hierarchy of command, in which each official fulfils a carefully-defined role, protects the organization from the corruption of personal favours and an arbitrary abuse of its authority. But this also imposes on an official great pressure to conform, to the point where he becomes preoccupied with loyalty to the organization and its routine at the

[7] *Ibid.*, p. 11.

expense of its ultimate purposes. 'The bureaucratic structure exerts a constant pressure upon the official to be "methodical, prudent, disciplined". If the bureaucracy is to operate successfully, it must attain a high degree of reliability of behaviour, an unusual degree of conformity with prescribed patterns of action . . . But this very emphasis leads to a transference of the sentiments from the *aims* of the organization onto the particular details of behaviour required by the rules. Adherence to the rules, originally conceived as a means, becomes transformed into an end in itself . . .'[8] Hence even the most necessary institutions are in danger of losing a sense of purpose, and only a continual demand for innovation can break the grip of a self-justifying routine.

But if this argument is valid, it must apply as well to any new agency established to generate reform. A morbid life-cycle of bureaucracy seems to parallel the poverty cycle. When an organization fails to adapt, and loses its sense of direction, a new one is created to fulfil the neglected functions. Since the newcomer threatens the jurisdiction of established authority, it has to struggle to survive. Survival becomes the most urgent purpose, to which ultimate ends are subordinated, and the new organization too begins to lose its sense of direction. By the time it is confidently established, pressures from within have imposed an inflexible loyalty to principles and routines already doubtfully relevant. A stir of frustration begins to concoct its successor . . .

The more radical the intentions of a new organization, the more it may be exposed to this morbid introversion, since the struggle to survive is harsher. Well-disciplined revolutionary parties are notoriously unprincipled in practice. A fiercely idealistic loyalty to the organization goes with a blatantly inconsequent programme. This theory of bureaucracy requires, then, not only that the distortions of introversion be compensated, but compensated without perpetuating a cycle of repeated retreat into irrelevance: and the more drastic the correction, the greater the risk.

The danger is discussed most explicitly in the speeches which Paul Ylvisaker, director of the Foundation's grey area programme, delivered in 1964. While he argued for rational, coherent social reform, he was pulled back from his own prescriptions by an undertow of anxiety. How was a concerted plan of action to escape the

[8] Robert K. Merton, 'Bureaucratic Structure and Personality', in Merton, Gray, Hockey & Selvin (eds.) *Reader in Bureaucracy* (Glencoe, Ill.: The Free Press, 1952), p. 365.

deadening inhibitions of centralized bureaucracy? He mistrusted the very institutions promoted to carry out his purpose: the better they established themselves, the more—encrusted by success— they might harden into a self-protective instrument of public control. Though he saw that the anarchic tendencies of city life frustrated any co-operative endeavour to solve urgent problems, and left people unsupported in their struggle to come to terms with the urban environment, he still put his deepest faith in the vitality of this emancipating anarchy.

Every man for himself—the social expression of Darwin's Law of Nature. By splitting the old social atoms of family and village and by liberating the individual particles, we have released a tremendous amount of human energy. This is the power potential of the city and its role in the human system. But we constantly are in danger of dissipating that power. For the rural–urban reaction is still not harnessed: too many of our urban citizenry are unprepared for the environment—rather, the void—into which they have been discharged . . .

It will not help to try to reverse the historic trends of this urban and individualistic society, nor to paste it together with gobs of giving. It is not dependency we want to encourage but independence and choice. These are not simple goals, and the effort to achieve them will require more from the community than the mere expenditure of money.

Among others things, it will require major changes in the way we manage our public and private affairs. Yet the third characteristic of our times is the increasing resistance to collective action and planned change. We are going private with a vengeance. Our 'won't power'— the capacity to veto proposals for public action—is growing more rapidly than our will power. Those responsible for public policy at all levels of government are finding it increasingly difficult to have legislative proposals enacted.

This is understandable, because the very diversity of the society that makes a majority difficult, also argues for programmes of action which are themselves highly specific and flexible—hardly the attributes of massive and monolithic public programmes.[9]

[9] Paul Ylvisaker, 'A Relevant Christ—but a Relevant Church?', (Speech delivered at the 'Atlanta Metabagdad' sponsored by the Episcopal Church, February 1964).

He argued therefore for a programme of reform which would at once respect the diversity and individualism of city life, and release it from its collective impotence. His speeches search after the political alchemy that would transmute the institutionalized expression of a common purpose into ungoverned personal action. 'What is needed to co-ordinate and exploit the inherent power of these complicated, egalitarian societies is the development in balance of far more sophisticated nervous, circulatory and other systems than have yet been evolved either by our nation or any other. To detect and anticipate; to correlate and differentiate; to probe and carry through; to collect energy and allocate it; to reflect and reformulate; to mobilize and individualize; to gather power and liberate it.'[10] The agencies of reform were therefore to act as facilitators, analysts and catalysers, crystallizing the good intentions of many people about a common endeavour, yet without imposing on their freedom.

Though the documents of the projects themselves did not put this theory forward explicitly, their strategy implied it. The mistrust of institutions, and the belief that yet, by encouragement, they could be stimulated to promote their own reform; the faith in independent, spontaneous action, and yet the reliance on planned programmes; the search for new approaches without displacing established leadership, for an expression of commitment which imposed no specific demands are all reflected in the projects' eventual structure. They were, it is true, new organizations struggling to assert themselves. But they tried, at least in principle, to avoid a stultifying preoccupation with their own survival, and degeneration into dogmatic routine.

Firstly, they did not set out as permanent organizations: their future beyond three or five years was left deliberately open. Boston even included a clause in its articles of incorporation, which invited a majority of its board to vote it out of existence after five years, if they thought best—by then its work might be done, and an innovative spirit would pervade the establishment; or its functions might be better distributed amongst existing public and private agencies, or restructured in a new form; or perhaps the effort would have proved abortive. Secondly, the projects worked as far as possible through established institutions, stimulating

[10] Paul Ylvisaker, 'Private Philanthropy in America', (Speech to the National Council on Community Foundations, May 1964).

them rather than replacing them. By pressing for innovation, and providing attractive funds in support of it, the projects hoped to prevail over the natural conservatism of bureaucracy. Thirdly, everything they attempted was to be ruthlessly evaluated. Their own research would correct any drift into meaningless or inefficient rituals. Their practice would compensate automatically for its mistakes and obsolescence, since the research design was part of every demonstration. Finally, by consulting with the people they served, their relevance would be continually checked against the reactions of those who, themselves outside the bureaucratic structure, could alone ultimately justify the endeavour. So, even if the projects did not argue a theory of institutional pathology in our terms, their plan of action was certainly consistent with it. Correspondingly, their strategy was less consistent with the most obvious alternative explanation of bureaucratic failure.

Bureaucracy, as the instrument of power, can be taken to reflect the interests of the dominant social classes. The apparent irrelevance of social services, judged by the needs of the poor, could have a harsher explanation than the devotion to ritual of organization men. It may suit the needs of the middle classes, whose well-being would be threatened by more generous and effective service to the poor. Those who pay for, control and staff the bureaucracies may well be reluctant to tax themselves more heavily, so that slum schools may compete with the suburbs for the best teachers, and their pupils for college places or the skilled jobs already decimated by automation. Contributors to the United Fund may not wish to see voluntary agencies deploy their services only to those who cannot afford to support them, any more than agency staff may enjoy working with clients of so little status.

Even without conscious collusion or naked self-interest, the values, tastes and distastes of middle-class America naturally conspire to render as little to the less fortunate as its own security and conscience will allow. For as long as service to the poor is not highly regarded, resources will be attracted from their needs by more prestigeful activities. Even institutions which accept a responsibility for these services may neglect them for inessentials more readily appreciated by the source of their support. Social services, whether public or private, depend upon middle-class taxpayers or donors, and in appealing for funds, these are the men and women who must be convinced that their money is being put to good use. But the instrinsic quality and need of service is often hard to demonstrate: a bad teacher looks much like a good one—especially to the voter on a school bond whose own child is educated elsewhere. Where there are few obvious criteria of performance, an institution must turn to indirect symbols of achievement, especially those which earn public acclaim. But good public relations material for middle-class backers may have little to do with the authentic ideals of the service. An institution can become so preoccupied with marginal activities which enhance its prestige, that it neglects the less visible work which makes up its true purpose. Charles Perrow, who develops this argument, cites the instance of a hospital he studied, where astute public relations at once retrieved its popularity and distorted its function. The hospital's official purpose was to promote the health of the community through the care of patients—both paying and free—teaching and research. But since neither patients nor donors could readily evaluate the quality of this service, the hospital encouraged their support with a display of peripheral amenities—wine with meals, a beauty salon, television, snacks, a glamorous surgical suite, even a public museum. The beds were filled, and national awards won, but meanwhile the essential services of the hospital suffered, and those of its poorer patients most of all.[11]

> Nurses complained that requests by private patients for coffee and other services described in the brochure took time from the care required by free and part-paying patients . . . The authorities were indifferent to the ineffectiveness and disorganization of one small, unglamorous, but potentially valuable diagnostic programme, which, in untrained hands, threatened to do more harm than good. However, a proposal to build and maintain a museum of medicine on the premises which would be open to the community and the schools was actively considered, despite the expense and effort involved. Though of less value than the diagnostic programme, it could be billed as a part of the programme of preventive medicine, while substantially contributing to prestige.
>
> More striking was the fate of one service essential to the major goal of providing patient care of high quality. This was a goal far from achieved in the case of free and part-paying patients in the

[11] Charles Perrow, 'Organizational Prestige: Some Functions and Dysfunctions', *American Journal of Sociology*, Vol. LXVI, No. 4, (January 1961).

outpatient department, largely because good care there does not at present bring prestige. The department was denied funds for remedying even the grossest physical deterioration and obsolescence, attendance and performance of the staff were undisciplined, and efforts to reform the department were, for several years, not backed by the authorities in the organization. On the other hand, while the outpatient department was in a state of physical deterioration and professional neglect, funds, much energy, and inventiveness went into constructing and publicizing an elaborate, highly specialized surgical suite, even though its contribution to official goals was relatively peripheral.

Thus, in the competition for support, social services are attracted towards a middle-class clientele, and even what they do for poorer people is designed to appeal, not to those who use the services, but those who pay for them. If so, reform cannot succeed by appealing only to institutions themselves. It must either rescue them from dependence on middle-class approval, or influence the criteria by which performance is judged and resources distributed. This analysis leads to an assertion of the interests of the poor, backed by moral and political sanctions powerful enough to force concessions, and establish a new order of priorities.

None of the projects was well placed to take so militant a stand, and preferred, even if they recognized the argument, to discount its fundamental importance. The second annual report of the New Haven project, for instance, ends with a reflection on reform in which the issue is raised, only to be put uneasily aside. 'The practices and procedures of existing public and private agencies, the reformer feels, are largely out of kilter with the era. Many of these institutions, particularly those in education, employment, and welfare, reflect primarily what he calls middle-class values. And thus far, the newcomer has not made his demands on these institutions competitive with those of other segments of the population. Whether these other demands result from the direct activity of middle class groups, such as parent-teacher associations, or from the personal norms and values of agency personnel, they have, the reformer feels, been largely unchallenged by the newcomer . . . The reformer realizes, however, that few of the newcomers currently are motivated to participate in urban society, to pursue a course of upward mobility such as immigrants in the

past have done.' The discussion thus returns to the theme of the
poverty cycle. This, rather than the class analysis, is taken as fundamental. The rest of the short essay argues for gradual change,
sustained by the reformer's faith that 'agencies are willing and
able to co-operate with him'.[12]

Even Mobilization for Youth—amongst the most militant of the
projects in its style—hesitated over the implications of class
conflict. In a paper discussing Mobilization's influence on the
school system, George Brager—one of the project's executive
directors—also raises the question of the school teacher's middle
class values.

> Another goal of Mobilization is reduction of the gap which exists
> between the educational system and its low-income minority group
> clientele. The failure of such persons to achieve in school is widely
> ascribed to their 'inadequacies'. Although it is undoubtedly true that
> lower-income socialization gives a youngster poor preparation for
> managing the classroom environment, insufficient attention has been
> given to the environment itself. Most teachers are middle class in
> orientation, and those who teach in slum schools are often alien to the
> neighbourhood in which they work. Slum schools tend to have
> high teacher turnover, hence less experienced instructors and
> reduced instructional time. The curriculum reflects middle-class
> concerns. Further, as studies have shown, teachers have a generally
> low expectation of deprived children, even when their school
> achievements are good. But the youngster who is defined by his
> society as inferior will behave in such a way as to confirm that
> definition, for we tend to achieve, in part at least, in proportion to
> what is expected of us. Education must break into this vicious cycle.
>
> Many low-income people feel, with some justification in fact, a sense
> of powerlessness. As a result, they have little motivation to learn . . .
> The implication for educators is that the schools must be prepared to
> teach minority group members and persons with low incomes the ways
> in which they can achieve power and use it responsibly to affect their
> own destinies. Obviously, since the school system itself is a major
> institution of the society, this means that low-income persons must be
> taught how to influence the schools as well as other institutions.
>
> The schools do not accept the Mobilization premise that there is a

[12] Community Progress Inc., Second Annual Programme Review for the Ford
Foundation, 1963–64, see 'Reflections on a Reform Movement'.

gap between the system and its low income clientele ... The system itself subscribes to the prevailing definition of the low income adult as inadequate and a failure. School officials find it easy to deflect criticism by low-income parents onto the criticizers themselves ... It should be no surprise to learn that Mobilization's attempts to bring the schools closer to their lower-class clients have resulted in strongly defensive, near-hysterical resistance.

A further impediment to adequate educational opportunity is the rigidity of the system, its strict hierarchial ordering and intensive bureaucratic defensiveness.[13]

Thus Brager argues, in effect, that schools should teach their pupils how to assert themselves against the shortcomings of the educational system, and concludes that teachers will of course refuse to do anything of the kind. Nor did he believe that Mobilization had the power to force them: 'the task of "unfreezing" the system, encouraging creativity and innovation ... certainly appears to be beyond the resources of an outside agency, such as Mobilization for Youth'.[14] So he was forced to advocate self-assertion primarily for its psychological value. 'We believe that the personal sense of powerlessness felt by low income people is a major cause of their isolation and apathy ... To encourage education and social learning, therefore, it is necessary to decrease the sense of powerlessness.'[15] Once again, the argument returns to the theme of apathy, partly from impotence to tackle institutions more directly. Mobilization's strategy seems to have assumed that even if little could be done to alter the middle-class prejudices of school teachers, a policy of encouraging militant self-assertion by poor people would enhance their children's self-confidence, and so make them keener to learn in spite of their teacher's lack of faith in them. For all their rigidity and defensiveness, institutions might accomodate enough to enable the poor to realize their new-found ambitions.

Though Mobilization itself was never unambiguously committed to a militant ideology, and spent only a small proportion

[13] George Brager, 'Influencing Institutional Change through a Demonstration Project: the Case of the Schools', (Paper prepared for the Columbia University and Mobilization for Youth Training Institute Programme, April 1964, mimeographed).
[14] In his annual report to the staff of MFY, 1963.
[15] 'Influencing Institutional Change through a Demonstration Project: the Case of the Schools', *op. cit.*

of its funds on the organization of community protest, it stimulated an approach which diverged increasingly from the standpoint of the original projects. On this alternative view, the poor lacked not only money or will, but power. The first task of community action was therefore to enable them to assert themselves, by placing the means to reform in their own hands. The reintegration of institutional functions, and the scientific analysis of social problems was to take second place to the organization of the poor as a political force. In 1964, Harlem Youth Opportunities Unlimited published a proposal for community action in Harlem, which presents the familiar range of programmes from this altogether more aggressive point of view. The conception of a poverty cycle still pervades the analysis, but its reinforcement is related less to the intrinsic inadaptibility of bureaucracy than to racial discrimination at large. The report is subtitled 'a study in the consequences of powerlessness and a blue-print for change', and its spirit is most vividly expressed by a fifteen-year-old Harlem girl, whom the report quotes:

'We look into the schools in Harlem and we find that our young people can't read and they can't write. They don't know who they are or where they come from and they have teachers who don't care, who will never teach them this. They don't have enough teachers. They don't have enough classroom space. And we turn to our leaders who tell us the only way we can rectify this situation is to bring in white children from the other side of town. And then the black man goes back home again and says, I can't solve my problem unless I attempt to solve it with a white person at my side; that I can't fight and make a change in this system unless I have a white person at my side; I can't be a man and not ask but take what is mine unless I have a white person at my side. So he sees that he is, in fact, less than a man. We look into the housing situation. The black man has the most deplorable housing in New York, in the United States. He has landlords who do nothing but constantly rob him deaf, dumb and blind . . . (He) looks at television and he sees those news reporters saying the city is making a move to inspect housing conditions, and the man says he thinks everything is very deplorable and he's going to make a move to do something about it, and he sets up a commission or he appoints another inspector, and then the days roll by and the rat-bites still show up on the children, and parents find that they still have to sleep in shifts to keep the rats away from the baby at night, and the children are still catching pneumonia in the winter because of the cold, and are still not being able to go to school, which are inferior anyway, but are still not able to go to the schools because there is no hot water to wash up in the morning and they find that it is easier to stay bundled up in the bed in blankets. So, where are the commissions and where are the inspectors and where are the powers that be that are supposed to effect the change?

'So, all these frustrations build up within the black man day after day. The system that we live in becomes a vicious cycle and there is never a way out. He begs for change and it seems that the conditions get worse and worse and never make a move towards the better. And we find that for every step forward, we are forced by the powers that be to take five steps backward into even more deplorable conditions. So, when this anger builds up in black people, not knowing how to let it out and how to retaliate against the power structures, the black man finds a way out; but the way out is often in a bottle of wine or in a needle containing heroin or in a reefer, or in the power of his fists when he slaps his wife down. The woman finds a way out in the power of her hand when she slaps a child down, and so the cycle goes on.

'But one unique product of this system is the young Harlemite, and this Harlem youth is the only one who is in a position to step back and look at this cycle objectively because this youth has not yet, because of age, been so viciously tainted by the cycle in this system. This youth doesn't have to risk losing a job because he attempts to fight the powers that be, so the young person is the only one who can step back and look at what exists here.

'And the young person, therefore, must be the one to channel the frustrations and the anger away from the bottle and away from the wife and away from the other children and channel them towards the power structure and towards the makers of the cycle. And, therefore, HARYOU must not attempt to teach the young person in Harlem or make the young person in Harlem what HARYOU wants. But HARYOU must be taught by the young person in Harlem. HARYOU must be moulded by the young person in Harlem. HARYOU, in essence, must be the young person in Harlem.'[16]

[16] 'Youth in the Ghetto', (HARYOU, 1964), pp. 348-9.

In spirit, HARYOU was to turn the fists of Harlem youth against the power structure instead of each other. In practice—since the power structure, after all, was to provide the money—its programmes were less revolutionary. Though it blamed the demoralization of Harlem on the exploitation and neglect of middle class white America, HARYOU turned first to rehabilitation rather than protest, recommending much the same educational and vocational innovations as the earlier projects had initiated. But the implication was different: where other projects hoped to forestall conflict, HARYOU hoped to inspire the confidence and self-respect that would arm young Negro men and women to win the battle for social justice. Thus while all the projects recognized the harm which middle class preconceptions might do—especially in education—only HARYOU, at this time, was ready to argue unequivocally for class, or racial, confrontation.[17] Most saw these middle-class prejudices more as an aspect of the inflexibility and insensitivity to which bureaucracies were inherently liable. The prejudices were misguided, not malevolent rationalisations of class interest.

As a whole, the strategy of the projects seemed to assume, as Paul Ylvisaker suggested in his speeches, that urban society is essentially a benevolent anarchy. Highly competitive, the city is yet open to all ambitious enough to pit themselves in the struggle. Its harshness is mitigated by social welfare, which should not merely comfort the failures, but encourage them back into the race. And its justice is protected by an educational system which should ensure to every child an equal start. The will to compete is primary, and social agencies are to be judged, above all, by their ability to foster and sustain it. If their middle-class prejudices make them, at times, insensitive, this is only an aspect of a more fundamental tendency towards bureaucratic introversion. Thus liberal reform, like the radical right, seems to be appealing to a tradition of individualism which bureaucracy has corrupted. But

---

[17] An emphasis on racial conflict is, of course, much more orthodox—especially in the setting of Harlem—than on class conflict. Racial discrimination can be accepted as an ugly but undeniable fact of American society, without making fundamentally more disturbing inferences about the inherent injustice of the way resources are distributed in a capitalist economy. It was therefore much easier for HARYOU to adopt a radical tone, which expressed the consensus of the Harlem community as much as did the prospectuses of other projects. And it was no freer from the pressures of political accommodation, which later modified both its structure and its proposals.

unlike the right, it recognizes the justice of institutional intervention, from generation to generation, to restore an equal chance, and seeks to make that intervention more effective.

On such assumptions as these, the projects' proposals can be interpreted as the expression of a coherent argument. Poverty and delinquency were perpetuated by an inherited failure to respond, through ignorance, apathy and discouragement to the demands of urban civilization. The institutions of education and welfare had grown too insensitive and rigid to retrieve these failures, from a characteristic, morbid preoccupation with the maintenance of their organizational structure. The processes of assimilation were breaking down, and could only be repaired by an enlargement of opportunities. But this emancipation would only come about as the enabling institutions of assimilation—the schools, the welfare agencies, the vocational services—recognized their failure, and became more imaginative, coherent, and responsive. The attack was directed at a self-protective hardening of middle class American society, which at once neglected and condemned those it excluded. Yet the attack only very ambiguously challenged the middle-class values in themselves. It remained open to either more or less radical interpretation.

To restore their relevance, institutions had to be turned outward again, to look afresh at the needs they should be serving. Only a new agency, detached from the jurisdiction of any conventional department, could reintegrate them effectively, since the causes of poverty were indivisible. Yet this new agency had itself to guard against the common disease of all bureaucracy, by continually refusing to take its own validity for granted. Hence it was to proceed experimentally, testing its programmes against methodical research and the reactions of those it served; and by its empiricism, stimulate the agencies it worked with to see the problems in the same objective, self-critical light. The comprehensive approach, the involvement of the people, innovation, research, and reliance on established agencies all fall into place within the framework of this conception of poverty and bureaucratic pathology.

This interpretation of a consensus of belief is partly speculative. The projects themselves never fully articulated their assumptions, and did not pursue ideas so logically to a conclusion, reluctant to give such naked hostages to fortune. In their prospectuses and proposals, they were immediately concerned to justify a course of action, not to elaborate a theory—though the President's Committee for a while regarded theory as an essential component of planning. Above all, the projects aimed to stimulate innovation and responsiveness in agencies and government, but since they also depended upon the co-operation of those they sought to change, they could not afford to make their criticisms of institutions too explicit. By stressing the apathy and defeatism of the poor, they tried to explain the need of more imaginative ways to help them, without alienating agencies by too direct an attack upon their protective self-interest. Their philosophy was adapted to the means and resources that lay to hand, and might change as they saw their way more clearly.

Yet it would be equally mistaken to treat these assumptions as no more than an expedient rationalization. They were supported by sociological analysis; and from our observation, project directors, planners and researchers on the whole genuinely accepted them as a frame of reference for their policy. By endorsing them, they helped to spread this interpretation of the problem of poverty as a conventional wisdom. But the truth of these assumptions is also especially important to the kind of comprehensive community action which the projects attempted. Taken together, the conceptions of a poverty cycle and of bureaucratic introversion explained the breakdown of assimilation to the opportunity structure without presupposing any fundamental conflict of interest. On both sides, the breakdown was seen in terms of irrational self-frustration. If this interpretation was right, the projects could appeal to all parties to support a non-partisan programme of reform. But if it was misleading, the viability of the whole plan of intervention was seriously compromised.

No one would dispute that poor people are sometimes apathetic, or that bureaucracies are sometimes stultified by routine. But were these the most urgent problems, and did they establish an order of priorities which everyone would accept? If the denial of opportunity demoralized people, so that they could no longer respond even to what opportunities there were, which properly came first—rehabilitation or an attack on the injustice of denial? If the poor and the community's leaders did not share the same aims, the projects were left serving two masters, and research could no longer appeal to a common set of assumptions in interpreting its findings. Militancy, political accommodation and the pursuit of knowledge would each claim a separate allegiance.

In the chapter which follows, we review the progress of some of the programmes, to see how far their experience seems to support the assumptions on which they were based. Though the findings are very tentative, they help to show more clearly the nature of the problems which underlay the struggle for reform.

III

THE EXPERIENCE OF
ACTION

DESPITE the diversity of their communities, the projects' analysis of needs led them to adopt many of the same remedies. Firstly, they promoted a range of educational innovations. Nearly all initiated pre-school classes, where children of poorly educated and not very articulate parents could be trained in the conceptual skills they needed to hold their own in school. All planned experiments in the schools—remedial reading, closer relations between parents and teachers, counselling, guidance, curriculum changes and new teaching techniques, or in-service training for teachers in the cultural background of their pupils. Los Angeles introduced reception rooms for new pupils from highly transient groups. Washington was planning a complete model school district. Few of these ideas were strictly original, or untried, but they were new, at least, to the inner city school. New Haven, Boston and Oakland, amongst others, also developed out-of-school activities such as work-study programmes, tutoring, evening study centres, and summer camps. Adult education was less noticed, but there were literacy classes in New Haven, where the community schools, as centres of neighbourhood activities, were well established, and Washington also proposed courses of Civic Education. These innovations, based on the schools, merge into those promoted through the public recreation departments— club activities, outdoor play groups, evening classes in etiquette or mechanics, team games.[1]

---

[1] Oakland, especially, had a tradition of integrating social work and recreation which went back to the playground movement at the beginning of the century. In the 1920s several private settlement houses—promoted by the same public-spirited woman who had founded and presided over the recreation department— were deeded to the city, and became the recreation department's responsibility. The department had thus acquired an approach to recreation unusually closely associated with social work, and this the Oakland project reinforced. Its programme for encouraging and guiding socially responsible teenage gangs was not, however, especially original. (See Alvin N. Taylor, 'The Oakland Recreation Department: A Study in Institutional Transition', University of California Master's Thesis, 1962.)

Education apart, the projects concentrated most generally on the vocational training and placement of young people—youth employment and counselling centres, MDTA courses (see p. 71), on-the-job training, preliminary courses of adjustment to the demands of employment, and the development of more openings to worthwhile careers. Oakland was also proposing an adult training scheme, and Boston a retraining programme for older workers.

Consistent with the President's Committee's preoccupation with prevention rather than treatment, there were only a few experiments dealing directly with disturbed or delinquent children. In Los Angeles, an office was opened across the street from a police station, where social workers were to offer intensive help to the families of young people who tangled with the law. In Cleveland court workers were trained to lead neighbourhood group counselling sessions. Mobilization for Youth made contact with young people when they were committed to a correctional institution, and followed them up when released on parole, in the hope of aiding their social reintegration. Philadelphia planned a model police district, and a half-way house for boys under correction. But the projects were generally more concerned with legal services than the rehabilitation of offenders. Encouraged by the Public Affairs department's interest in legal reform, all but one of the grey area projects, for instance, proposed new services of legal aid. Apart from defence and advice, these services were seen—especially by Mobilization for Youth—as a means of challenging the administrative interpretation of welfare rulings, and guarding the rights of youngsters arrested by the police. Oakland and Boston were also planning an experiment in pre-trial release in cases where the accused could not afford bail.

Part of the legal programme in Boston was to be housed with health, family counselling and youth employment services in new neighbourhood centres, where all kinds of help would be more accessible and closely integrated. New Haven worked for a similar integration through a staff of neighbourhood co-ordinators. In Washington, the project director conceived neighbourhood centres which would not only combine services, but subject them to the critical evaluation of their users—the fulcrum, as he put it, on which the lever of neighbourhood pressure was to pivot. And this neighbourhood work was seen, everywhere, as an opportunity to employ the people of the neighbourhood themselves as nonprofessional aides. The projects were vulnerable to the charge that they benefited most immediately, not the poor, but the many professionals they recruited on to their staff—at salaries that rose rapidly with the demand—so they were anxious to make as many jobs as possible in their own organization open to neighbourhood residents.

Finally, apart from some rather peripheral programmes concerned with housing and public health, all the projects, in one way or another, sought to encourage the participation of the people they served, either by community organization or involving local leaders.

By 1964 a few projects had already implemented a wide range of proposals: most still promised more than they had as yet achieved. That spring, New Haven, for instance, had about eighteen different kinds of programme in action, and five more planned, while Boston had eighteen planned, but only three in action. Oakland had implemented twelve programmes, Philadelphia four. The educational and vocational experiments generally came first, together with community organization, and these remained the core from which the projects evolved. The legal services were potentially more challenging as reforms but began later and, being more controversial, were also more difficult to realize.

Since the experiments are so recent, most reports of their achievements are no more than official impressions, supported by stories of individual successes, and some fragmentary, roughly classified statistics. But these impressions are still worth examining, because the experiences of the programmes raise some fundamental questions about the explanation of poverty by which they were justified. And this, in turn, has implications for the strategies of community reform we shall discuss in the succeeding chapters. As the educational and training programmes were the first, and remained the most essential components of the whole endeavour, their progress in the longest established projects provide the surest evidence for an interim assessment.

The Education Programmes

The projects argued that the children of the poor were disheartened and intimidated by a system of opportunities which disparaged their chances. Teachers despaired of the ability of most of their pupils, and insisted all the more unyieldingly on alien patterns of thought and behaviour, because their own middle-class status was insecure. The tests by which schools, training institutes and employers allocated career opportunities were biased towards the verbal skills least practiced in poor neighbourhoods. Few institutions of further education were interested to offer a second chance to those who had failed at school. The crucial task was therefore to change the preconceptions of teachers, instructors, administrators and employers, and to restore pupils' confidence in themselves.

In schools, the experiments were to demonstrate the defeatism of conservative assumptions. New reading techniques, more sensitive counselling, more imaginative curricula, reorganization of the grade structure would bring out latent ability, and prove to teachers that they need not give up hope. But the teachers' prejudices were also to be more directly confronted, by persuading them to visit their pupils' homes, by explaining the culture of the neighbourhood, by revising the middle-class connotations of classroom method. If the school would only meet its pupils half way, it might evoke a new eagerness to learn.

These reforms were to be instituted in co-operation with the school system, and carried out by the teachers themselves. Only by involving the system and its staff, and so committing them to the new approach, could the limited resources of the projects inspire widespread innovation. Such a strategy called for tact and subtlety. If the teachers already acknowledged the prejudices which frustrated their efforts, the projects were hardly necessary. But if they did not, how would they co-operate in a reform whose wisdom they failed to recognize? To challenge their prejudices openly might lead, as Mobilization for Youth discovered, to 'strongly defensive, near hysterical resistance'.

The problem was handled most sensitively, perhaps, by the 'Helping Teacher' programme in New Haven, whose implementation was a model of careful preparation and diplomacy. The programme provided for teachers of skill and experience to 'assist principals in the orientation of new teachers . . . present and demonstrate new instructional material to regular classroom teachers, guide teaching procedures, direct teacher planning, and confer with parents and teachers about individual pupil achievement and advancement'.[2] It was directed by a retired assistant

[2] Community Progress Inc., *Second Annual Programme Review for the Ford Foundation*, 1963–64, p. 4.

superintendent, who had worked all her life in the New Haven schools. Disarmingly unambitious, she was trusted alike by teachers and principals, and yet understood the weaknesses of the system. Before she launched the programme, she held several seminars with the principals, and then introduced them to the CPI educational staff, when the plans were explained. Each teacher selected for the programme was given several months to consider it, and was free to refuse. The assignment carried, deliberately, no increases in salary, but several inducements: a three hundred dollar budget for materials, which the teacher could spend without authorization; regular seminars with an eminent Yale psychiatrist, where they could put their problems before a sympathetic specialist; and weekly meetings with each other, where the experience in different schools could be compared. Thus the teachers who ran the programme enjoyed the sense that their work was important enough to be worth discussing, not only with each other, but with a distinguished academic; they had more freedom of action; and both they and their principals had time to consider the programme before they were asked to implement it. They accepted the director of the programme as one of themselves, who understood and sympathized with their difficulties. The programme was therefore popular with them, and seemed at the end of its first year to be achieving results. 'Quality of classroom instruction has been improved, more effective methods are being utilized with slow-learning students and the individual classroom teacher has been strengthened by ready assistance from helping teacher. Also, students and parents have been involved more deeply in the appraisal and evaluation of pupil achievement . . . Expansion of this programme is much to be desired. New classroom teachers have welcomed the assistance. Experienced, superior classroom teachers have gained greatly from new teaching materials and techniques which curriculum assistants (the helping teachers) have researched and developed . . .'[3]

But even with these precautions, the programme encountered resistance. 'In a few cases, teachers in need of supervision have

---

[3] Second Annual Programme Review for the Ford Foundation 1963–64 (Community Progress Inc., New Haven) pp. 4–5. The programme faced, however, the dilemma that, as helping teachers were recruited from the most experienced classroom teachers, they had to be replaced in the classroom by others less experienced, which in turn increased the demand for helping teachers—and so on, circularly.

resented even the most cautious and tactful offers of assistance.'[4] And CPI was uniquely fortunate in recruiting a director both sympathetic to reform, and wholeheartedly accepted by the New Haven teachers. Elsewhere, resentment was compounded by the failure to consult the schools themselves before the programmes were to start.

The programmes were negotiated with the central staff of the school systems, who were least threatened and had most to gain from them. The reforms implied criticism of the quality of classroom teaching, rather than the administrative structure, since the school superintendent could fairly claim that if he had not done much before to promote innovations, he had no money to do it with. A grant of a million dollars to his system was, in itself, an achievement for which he could take some credit, and the programmes helped to answer growing criticism, especially from civil rights organizations, of the system's indifference to the handicaps of its Negro pupils.

At the same time, the grant was only a marginal addition to the resources of a large city, and the experiments themselves peripheral. So the superintendent and his staff tended to co-operate rather casually in the development of the programmes, endorsing plans to which they were only nominally committed. The timing, staffing and practical implementation of the programmes was often poorly co-ordinated, and the schools themselves were unprepared. Even in New Haven, despite its sensitivity to the teachers, CPI admitted: 'with the various innovations in education it has been found that extensive orientation of both old and new staff is essential. While a start was made this year with training sessions, considerably more depth is needed'.[5]

At worst, teachers found themselves assigned without notice to an experiment they did not understand, without materials, and in makeshift accommodation. The pre-school programme in Boston, for instance, was seriously demoralized at the start. 'The scarcity of staff in the Boston Public Schools made it necessary to release teachers for the programme only when it was about ready to begin. This was done on Friday, April 17, 1964. The following week was a school vacation. The newly-released teachers, however, were asked to work . . . setting up the classroom, organizing

[4] *Ibid.*, p. 5.
[5] *Ibid.*, p. 17.

equipment and materials, and participating in orientation for the pre-kindergarten programme, which was scheduled to start on Monday, April 27th. This was an initial drain on morale since the teachers were weary, had needed and counted on their holiday, and were suddenly plucked out of their own classrooms.'[6] Their new classrooms were, besides, cramped and unsuitable, some of the space had to be shared with other activities, and much of the equipment was too large or too shoddy to be of service. More generally, Action for Boston Community Development realized, at the end of its first year, the need for a much closer understanding with the schools themselves: 'When the programmes were launched . . . the demonstration staff and the regular staff in the target area schools were inadequately informed of the background and planning that had taken place, the purposes and scope of the demonstrations, the role of ABCD's Programme and Research Departments, and the roles which they themselves were to assume.'[7] They were asked to undertake experiments thrust on them by an outside agency, when a summer of demonstrations and a press campaign against the 'lack of excellence' in many Boston schools had already put them on the defensive.

Co-operation broke down partly because the projects were preoccupied with the design of the programmes—especially, in Boston, with a sophisticated method of evaluating the outcome—and neglected the practical details of implementation. They overestimated the commitment of the school system, and its sensitivity to its own teaching staff. So when they encountered resistance in the schools, they were not prepared with a strategy to manage it.

But these misjudgements reflect too, perhaps, an underlying reluctance to confront the resistance to reform. After the years of planning, the difficult negotiations, the projects were impatient. If they now had to convince teachers and principals, they would face yet more delays and compromises. Understandably, they did not want to jeopardize their hard-won programme design. But such impatience was self-defeating, if reform in classroom teaching was their aim.

The development of the programmes themselves seems also to have backed away from any radical change in the teachers' approach.

[6] A Report on ABCD Activities, September 1963–August 1964, p. 41.
[7] *Ibid.,* p. 20.

The Experience of Action

The innovations tended to ramify about the classroom, rather than it. Education was extended into holidays, evenings, or early childhood by summer school, after school and pre-school programmes, without challenging the everyday classroom routine. In school itself, the programmes introduced more new personnel—counsellors, reading specialists, curriculum assistants—than new ideas; and more incentives to pupils to learn, than to teachers to educate. And this shift of emphasis was accentuated, because the classroom innovations which were successfully put into practice concerned technique, while those which tackled the teachers' preconceptions more directly evoked a poor response.

Mobilization for Youth found, for instance, that teachers were reluctant to take part in a home visiting programme, designed to help them understand their pupils better, while they welcomed more conventional aids. CPI considered its in-service training programme doubtfully effective. In Oakland the in-service training of teachers was indifferently supported, and seems to have influenced them little. But they accepted enthusiastically a school library service, a counselling programme and even more a Youth Study Centre which provided after school tutoring. These programmes were perhaps most popular because they interfered least with a teachers' daily work: ironically, unlike several of the classroom innovations, they did not appear from preliminary evaluation to improve the students' performance.

Since Oakland was the first project to produce a comprehensive review of the success of its programmes, its interim findings are worth noting. The pre-school programme seemed to improve linguistic skills, judging by the performance of experimental and control groups of children on a reading-readiness test. But a rather similar language enrichment programme for pre-kindergarten, kindergarten and first grade children at a child care centre did not show any demonstrable improvement. The reading programmes in first, third, and fourth grade all seemed to help the children to do better than they would otherwise have done—though, in the later grades, the results were not consistent for all the experimental classes. A seventh grade reading programme, however, appeared to be ineffective. The counselling service did not make any difference to the performance of the children counselled—though it seemed to improve relationships between the school and their parents. The School Library was well used, and teachers had the

63

impression that children read more, but no attempt was made to trace its influence on school performance. Tutoring by High School students at the study centres did not seem to affect classroom achievement, at least in the period of observation. The in-service training of teachers is not mentioned in the evaluation. The inconsistency of results for apparently similar programmes—as, for instance between the reading programmes in earlier and later grades, or between the pre-school and child care centre programmes—suggests that relatively subtle differences may be crucial. Mobilization for Youth found, for instance, that after-school tutoring twice a week improved a student's performance, but once a week was ineffective.

From these findings, it seems that pre-school training, remedial reading in the regular curriculum and frequent tutoring were most successful. None of these experiments necessarily challenged the middle-class standards of performance by which pupils were judged. They showed rather how with more time, and more help, the backward pupil might be enabled to meet them. Were they, then, really experiments at all, or simply the extension to poor neighbourhoods of techniques and amenities already common to more prosperous school districts? Robert Dentler, reviewing educational programmes of the New Haven and Boston projects with others in Syracuse and New York, argues:

> I believe we cannot call the work of these action programmes in the domain of public education innovations at all! . . . Most of the programmes involve adding better guidance services, materials adapted to the life situation of the low-income urban student, greater resources for teaching reading and for remedial reading work, more lessons for teachers in human relations and urban sociology, and the employment of additional specialists of many kinds.

> Most of the programmes also spend money to buy more time for schooling—for afternoon schools, for summer schools, for week-end study, and for pre-school, work-study school and post-school schooling. In combination, the total range of educational projects seems much like an inventory of means for *exporting* the decent American suburban public school into the poorer inner city areas.[8]

[8] Robert K. Dentler, 'Strategies for Innovation in Education: A View from the Top', (Paper presented at the second workshop of the Public Policy Institute, October 15–16, 1964).

His argument slides too glibly over the 'lessons for teachers in human relations and urban sociology', which, in the setting of the city school, meant something more specific and challenging than the suburban teacher needed to understand. But since such programmes had been poorly supported, his impression seems likely to be confirmed.

If the projects do, in fact, help to upgrade the schools of poor neighbourhoods to suburban standards, and, by their example, pioneer a fairer distribution of educational resources, they will have justified themselves as a progressive influence, if not as educational innovators. But the more poor children respond to these changes, the more it seems that the projects over-estimated pupils' unresponsiveness to middle-class teachers as a crucial handicap. Perhaps, after all, children have been more frustrated by lack of opportunity to learn, and of encouragement to overcome their difficulties, than by their cultural distance from their teachers' world. The theory of the poverty cycle becomes doubtfully relevant, if the desire to respond to the school's demands is already present. 'The evidence of the pilot projects in "deprived" schools' writes Kenneth Clark, '—odd though it may appear to many— seems to indicate that a child who is expected by the school to learn does so; the child of whom little is expected produces little. Stimulation and teaching based upon positive expectation seems to play an even more important role in a child's performance in school than does the community environment from which he comes.'[9]

The progress of the education programmes suggests then, that the children of poor neighbourhoods can be helped by more teaching, even if that teaching does not greatly change its style. Yet any reform which simply provides a fairer chance to compete in middle-class terms cannot do much to help the children with little talent for conventional classwork. The widening of opportunities may leave those who cannot grasp them only more painfully isolated. So long as education turns upon standards which the student must be trained to meet, it rebuffs children who cannot—or believe they cannot—make the grade. An inner city system of education which turned instead upon the abilities of each child, which drew out and guided his talents, vitality and

[9] Kenneth B. Clark, *Dark Ghetto: Dilemmas of Social Power* (New York: Harper and Row, 1965), p. 132.

confidence in himself, would still depend on the kind of reform in teaching which the projects originally had in mind, but were forced to put aside. In a competitive society, where education so largely determines opportunities in life, so uncompetitive a system of education can perhaps never be fully realized.[10] But in their original ideals, the projects at least recognized the dilemma. Whatever they could do to reduce the numbers of the poor by upgrading children's performance in itself must entrench the poverty of the rest. They had hoped also to broaden the teacher's sympathies towards those who could never meet her preconceived standards.

Here the projects had set themselves a task which was inevitably beyond their resources. They depended upon the school system for access to the teachers, and upon their co-operation in carrying the programmes out. Innovation was therefore limited to objectives which school and project could readily agree upon—or at best, to objectives which the school could tolerate, in return for support for its own more orthodox ideas. In Mobilization for Youth, for instance, 'because the schools have reluctantly accepted a teacher home-visiting programme, Mobilization buys a guidance counselling package—with a notable lack of enthusiasm. Settlement by negotiation often involves a continuing bargaining process, for agreement is never actually reached and terms are usually insufficiently defined. Thus, while Mobilization devotes much effort to shaping the guidance programme in directions it regards as more congenial, the schools are busy subverting the home visiting programme'.[11] Since the schools were responsible for putting the programmes into effect, they seemed likely to get the best of this doubtful bargain.

It seems, then, that the projects could help the schools to develop educational methods already widely accepted in the teaching profession—remedial reading, counselling, team teaching, cultural enrichment—provided that the changes were tactfully introduced, and everyone was prepared. If they tried to insinuate more challenging innovations, which questioned the teacher's basic

[10] The comprehensive school movement in Britain for instance tries to meet the problem by combining different streams of education in a single school. But this cannot do more than soften an essentially competitive structure.

[11] George Brager, 'Influencing Institutional Change Through a Demonstration Project: the Case of the Schools', (Paper prepared for the Columbia University and Mobilization for Youth Training Institute Programme, April 1964, mimeographed).

assumptions, the schools might not give them a fair test, and the trading of unwilling commitment to each other's aims only condemned all the programmes to half-hearted and muddled implementation. If the projects went round the system, innovating where they had more freedom, they still had to face the integration of these facilities with classroom expectations they had scarcely influenced. More radical reforms would have to turn to strategies less dependent on the co-operation of practising teachers.

Pressure on the Schools

Of all the projects, only Mobilization for Youth seems explicitly to have recognized the limitations of co-operation, and used it to justify a more aggressive approach. Since Mobilization believed that the exercise of power would help the poor to overcome their apathy, it turned to the organization of pressure upon the schools. 'The use of politics or pressure methods in a change assumes basic disagreement between contending parties. Unlike the "horse-trading" of bargaining, this strategy implies that forces must be aligned, and power brought to bear. It assumes that the other strategies are too ineffectual or "soft" to result in meaningful alteration of things-as-they-are, unless the resources available for the contest are much beyond Mobilization's present capacity . . . The schools strongly resist the Mobilization change objective of increasing their responsiveness and accountability to low-income people. This, combined with the limitation upon the project's strategic manoeuvrability, clearly suggests the necessity of employing pressure methods.'[12]

Mobilization was therefore led to support protest. Under its guidance, for instance, a group of ten Puerto Rican mothers formed an organization called 'Mobilization of Mothers' to press complaints about their children's education. They invited the principal of their school to a meeting, to put forward three requests, modest enough in themselves: appointments between teachers and parents should be arranged according to the parents' needs; adults should replace pupils as messengers and monitors, since these tasks interfered with education; and the school should provide books for the children to take home. The principal at first

[12] *Ibid.*

67

refused to meet them, claiming that they should have contacted the assistant superintendent, or raised their suggestions at a meeting of the Parent-Teachers Association. He was finally persuaded to speak to a meeting of seventy-five mothers organized by MOM. He seems, however, to have been impatient of the language difficulties of Puerto Rican parents and resentful of their criticisms. The audience found his attitude insulting, he lost his temper, and the meeting broke up in confusion. MOM then drew up a petition, adding to their three original points a demand for the principal's removal.

The petitioners were privately reproved by the assistant superintendent for provoking the principal. But, though she apparently treated them rather patronizingly, she went some way to meet their original requests. This success was achieved, however, at the cost of a public outcry. The petition provoked a telegram signed by the school principals of the area, widely published in the press, demanding an investigation of Mobilization for Youth and the removal of its director. MFY, the telegram claimed, had been 'subverted from its original plan to war against delinquency to a war against individual schools and their leaders' and its staff had become 'full time paid agitators and organizers for extremist groups'. Though, at the time, the incident went no further, these charges were to be repeated six months later in circumstances which were far more damaging.

Mobilization's militancy also influenced its social workers' interpretation of their role. It had, for instance, arranged with the schools for a social worker to take part in hearings over the suspension of students. Originally, the worker was to assist the principal, assistant superintendent, guidance counsellor and others to provide for the child's future, especially through the resources of the Mobilization programmes. But in practice, Mobilization's representative became more an advocate of the accused child and his parents—charging that suspensions violated regulations, that minority groups were being victimized, or that educators and psychologists had misinterpreted the problem. The assistant superintendent felt that Mobilization had abused the original understanding, and the experiment was abandoned after only a few months.

These incidents suggest that the school system was not prepared to tolerate criticism. If the challenge came from professional services which depended upon the schools' co-operation, it would be quashed. If it came through public protest, it provoked an equally public reaction which—even when the cause was trivial, and its supporters weak—could expose Mobilization to national attention. As we shall see, Mobilization was not prepared to withstand an attack on this scale, and lacked a political constituency powerful enough to defend it. At the same time, these conflicts made co-operation with the schools in other programmes much less easy.

Mobilization for Youth found, then, that it could not pursue a militant strategy on its own terms, limiting the conflicts to issues of its choosing. Any confrontation exposed it to the risk of an overwhelmingly virulent reaction, which it lacked the resources to withstand, while co-operation robbed it of the freedom to attempt any radical innovation. The strength and pervasiveness of resistance suggests that once teachers are established in their profession they may be unable to assimilate changes which disrupt the beliefs by which they structure their roles. Intervention is then driven back to the origins of these beliefs in recruitment and training. Education in New Haven may ultimately be more influenced by the superintendent's policy of recruiting teachers from new and less parochial sources, than by all the programmes of CPI. But this only transposes the problem from the assimilation of innovation to the assimilation of innovative recruits. When, for instance, a Washington High School introduced a group of returned Peace Corps volunteers as student teachers, the discomfort of the established staff created an intolerable strain, and the experiment was finally abandoned.

It seems clear from the first years of the education programmes' experience that the projects underestimated the resistance of the schools, and lacked power to meet it. They assumed too hopefully that the aims of the programmes had been reconciled in the negotiations which preceded action. But when the schools failed to meet their commitments, as the project understood them, no effective sanctions lay to hand. If, like Mobilization, they turned to protest, they risked a public conflict where their political nonentity was exposed. Most preferred not to jeopardize their influence as facilitators of less controversial progress, for the sake of reforms they came to recognize as beyond their resources.

This resistance to change appeared as an impregnable commitment to middle-class standards of performance, which restricted the possible benefit of the programmes to those pupils who could reach them. But no system of education can flout the requirements of the society it serves. If the school system condemned pupils as failures, this was perhaps less prejudice than realism. What if the economy has, indeed, no use for them? Teachers know that educational attainment largely determines life chances, and can only do their best to equip their pupils to compete. They are naturally attracted towards those most likely to succeed, whose achievements will reward the teacher's effort. If they devote themselves to the rest, they only neglect the promising for the sake of pupils who will never do anything that society will recognize as justifying the sacrifice. The schools cannot care equally for the education of every child, whatever his skills, unless the man he will become is equally valued, whatever he can contribute. And this no competitive economy can itself ensure. The fundamental obstacle lay in the structure of opportunities, which so constricted the employment programmes.

The Employment Programmes

The employment programmes faced a different situation, since no widely established, recognized institution already trained and guided the young people in whom they were interested. Technical high schools, few as they are, cater for abler, more purposeful students: entry to their more advanced courses depends upon high school graduation and special examination. Vocational subjects in other high schools are treated as general education, and scarcely qualify a student better than his academic studies. Unions, concerned to protect the scarcity value of their skill, restrict apprenticeship to a privileged few connected with their members. Even the new resources for training created by the Manpower Development and Training Act were originally restricted to applicants more than nineteen years old, to discourage defection for high school. The sixteen or seventeen-year-old who had dropped out of school had nowhere to turn, and the Employment Services ran no special facilities for him.

To tackle the unemployment problem, the projects had first to identify the young people in need of help, and then either place them in jobs, or training that would lead to jobs—providing directly, or through other agencies, services which had not previously existed. Essentially, the plan called for Youth Employment Centres,[13] where applicants would be registered and advised; a job development and placement service, to increase opportunities; training courses that would lead directly to a worthwhile job; and more basic preparatory training for those too unsophisticated to undertake, at once, a practical vocational preparation. In 1964, only three of the projects—Mobilization for Youth, CPI in New Haven, and Action for Boston Community Development—had enough experience to suggest how this plan may work out. But it seems that, just as the education programmes were forced to go round or retreat from institutional resistances they could not overcome, so the employment programmes backed away from the crucial obstacle. They were forced to elaborate preparatory programmes, which did not lead directly to employment, because they could not substantially increase the number of jobs open to the young people they served.

In Boston and New Haven the centres had registered over a thousand applicants within a few months of their opening. Only about ten per cent of the Boston intake could be placed immediately in jobs. Two thirds of the applicants were high school dropouts under seventeen, for whom few opportunities either in training or employment were open. New Haven, which did not restrict its service to young people, managed to place twenty per cent in jobs, but half its applicants had dropped out of high school, and were not qualified for most of the vacancies. Over eighty per cent of the young people served by Mobilization for Youth were dropouts. The majority of applicants to all three programmes were Negro or Puerto Rican. The centres were, then, immediately successful in attracting many of the discouraged young high school failures, whose unreadiness for employment in an increasingly demanding technology was compounded by racial discrimination and, sometimes, a correctional record. But there was little to offer them.

Vocational Training

The Manpower Development and Training Act provided resources for two forms of subsidized training—individually, on the job,

[13] The New Haven Centres also catered for adults.

and institutionally, in groups of ten or more. The projects had to exploit these, if they were to satisfy the needs they had brought to light. But the institutional training proved very cumbersome to organize. Every course had to be justified by demonstrable employment opportunities, and have at least ten trainees. A preliminary survey of the local need of training had therefore to be undertaken. Once employers and recruits were secured, the course had to be approved by both state and Federal departments concerned with vocational education. Each application for a course had to pass up and down the bureaucratic hierarchy, at the mercy of departmental rivalries and congressional appropriations. A report to the Department of Labour recounts, for instance, the frustrations of a training project in Los Angeles: 'The next major obstacle posed was the need for "training need" surveys to be made by the California Employment Service, with findings of "a reasonable expectation of employment" after MDTA training. The net effect of this, according to Project Officers, was to bring almost all planned MDTA programmes almost to a standstill. And, even after the MDT-I is approved, there are other time-consuming steps necessary. Following a "favourable" Community Survey, the MDT-I is sent to the main office of the CES in Sacramento for approval. After approval there, the proposal then goes to the State Vocational Education Department, which goes over the proposal and develops the Course Curriculum Content (MDT-2). Following this, the Vocational Education Department picks a school to do the training and the school is then given the responsibility of setting it all up.' Even then 'another acute problem presented was the difficulty regarding recruiting and training qualified teachers . . .'[14]

When, after months of delay, a course was finally approved, the recruits might have drifted away. Since they could seldom be reached by telephone, and did not reliably answer letters, the minimum muster of trainees was hard to retrieve. Besides these frustrations, the Act originally paid training allowances only to those over nineteen, though the projects successfully negotiated a lowering of the age limit to seventeen.

Despite these obstacles, CPI launched its vocational training programme with a course in three skilled occupations for 47 inner

[14] Joseph L. Weinberg, 'Evaluation Study of Youth Training and Employment Project, East Los Angeles', (Department of Labour, August 1964, mimeographed), pp. 17 and 20.

city residents, devised in co-operation with two of New Haven's largest companies, each of whom set aside twenty jobs for those who completed the training. CPI was determined that its first venture should vindicate the viability of its policy: 'In choosing to train inner-city residents for "status" jobs never before open to them, CPI was taking a large, but calculated risk. Lack of motivation is the most salient characteristic of inner-city residents. In order to begin to overcome the effects of this characteristic, it was considered essential that the first training programmes succeed in terms clearly understandable to inner-city residents—in terms of "status" jobs with "real good salaries". If the programme succeeded, these trainees would give daily testimony that (1) the community was genuinely concerned about long-term unemployment and (2) it was possible for long-term unemployed to "make it". If the programme failed, however, it would add immeasurably to the sense of hopelessness and alienation so characteristic of inner-city residents.'[15]

The course was, in fact, highly successful. Forty-two trainees completed the training, and all but one were placed immediately in the jobs assigned for them. But it seems, too, that CPI had cut its risks in selecting the first recruits, to the point where their success was doubtfully relevant to the fundamental problem. If the course was to show that men who had been long unemployed could get good jobs, it was hardly a fair test, since two thirds of the successful applicants had worked six months or more in the previous year, and over half of them for several months in the year of the course. About a quarter could not be considered unemployed at all, and a few had previously held skilled, clerical or even professional and managerial jobs. Most had earned more than three thousand dollars in 1962. Nor did they lack ambition: a third aspired to white-collar jobs, mostly professional or semi-professional, and another third to skilled trades. As a whole, the successful applicants were better qualified than most employees, and much better than the unemployed. Sixty-two per cent had high school diplomas (fourteen per cent a year or more at college), compared with a national average of 54% for the labour force, and 37% for the unemployed.

By contrast, the unsuccessful applicants to the course included

[15] The New Haven Youth Employment Programme: The Six Month Report, May 1964, p. 5.

the same proportion of high school dropouts as the unemployed generally, none had previously held white-collar jobs, and more of them were Negro. Only a quarter of both groups were under twenty-one. It seems, then, that the success of the first New Haven course did not show how the problems could be solved, though it may have helped to establish confidence in CPI, especially amongst employers. Other courses in the early months, in autobody straightening and service trades, lacked even this appeal. The jobs were of low status, and since too many employers were involved to fit training to the specific needs of any of them, no promises of employment were pledged.

CPI had foreseen these difficulties, since a special training committee established by the Mayor had already tried to exploit the Manpower Development and Training Act. 'New Haven's earliest experience with MDTA was somewhat disappointing, but not unique; occupational skill training, throughout the country, was not having the impact intended. Many administrative problems beset the programme in the earliest days, but two observations in general are relevant: (1) too often training had little relation to the specific skill needs of local employers; and (2) too often the very individuals MDTA was designed to aid were ineligible for training because of such factors as poor scores on the General Aptitude Test Battery, minor police records, low level of education and lack of basic skills.'[16] CPI tried to meet the problems by a permanent working committee representing training institutions, unions and employers. But the delays remained frustrating, and the project's neighbourhood workers still complained that the courses related to the employer's needs, rather than to the abilities of the young people to be helped. The employment centres registered hundreds of applicants for whom no openings were available, while training courses were held up for lack of suitable recruits. CPI concluded that they might make better progress through individual training on the job.

On the job training is more adaptable to an economy of small employers with specialized needs, and involves fewer delays. Recruitment is less formal, and if the trainee completes his apprenticeship successfully, the firm is likely to employ him. But the negotiation of hundreds of individual contracts is a large undertaking. Action for Boston Community Development which, like

[16] *Ibid.*, p. 2.

CPI, had found institutional training frustrating, foresaw equally serious drawbacks in OJT:

> The programme design rested heavily on the availability of a wide variety of skill training projects for youth to be made available via the Manpower Development and Training Act . . . It should be acknowledged that it is not always easy to achieve complete co-ordination of available MDTA skill training projects with youth properly selected by the Intake Centres at the particular time that the training courses are available. The result has been that, even in the case of special youth projects, the Intake Centres have not been able to provide a full complement of youth to fill the available openings within a fixed time schedule . . .

> It was recognized early in the programme that placement of youth on one-to-one job training assignments with employers might provide a rapid and fruitful means of paving the way of disadvantaged youth into satisfactory working careers. ABCD arranged . . . to function as an agent of the Federal Government in soliciting OJT contracts with industry, supervising the placement and training of youth in such projects, and using Federal funds to reimburse employers for their cost of training (up to $30.000 a week for a maximum of 26 weeks). Such opportunities are not plentiful. Most of them must be uncovered usually one at a time, and most of them involve a considerable amount of red tape.

> The successful administration and development of an OJT segment in the Youth Training and Employment Programme requires special staffing and a generous amount of time, if it is to be carried out at all. Even then, not all youth will adjust readily to an OJT routine and not all OJT employers will be satisfied with the kinds of trainees that a special Youth Training and Employment Programme can provide . . .[17]

In the first few months, ABCD had registered twelve hundred at its centres, but had only been able to place 56 in MDTA courses, and 30 in on-the-job training.

In spite of their shortcomings, these training programmes did,

---

[17] A Report on ABCD Activities, September 1963–August 1964, *op. cit.*, pp. 236–7. ABCD's youth training and employment programmes involved direct relationships with eighteen other agencies, and with a further nine less specifically—apart from co-ordinating six related divisions of its own organization.

of course, extend opportunities to many who might otherwise have missed them. Between October 1963 and December 1965, New Haven, for example had received just over seven thousand applicants, and had found some form of training or employment for nearly half of them. Eighteen hundred had been placed directly in jobs: the majority were Negro, had not graduated from high school, and were less than twenty-two years old. By 1965, CPI was placing or training recruits with an average of only about 8th grade education, and their tested skill in reading, maths and spelling was at only 5th or 6th grade level. Three hundred and seventy two had passed through institutional training, and as a whole, they seem to have had many fewer advantages than the successful applicants to the first course: only 40% had completed high school and half were under 22. In this sense, the strategy of success had opened the way to less qualified recruits. But a survey in 1965 found that a quarter of those who had graduated from the institutional courses were once again unemployed. By contrast, only 11% of those directly placed in employment, and 7% of those trained on the job were out of work.[18] CPI was convinced that OJT was by far the more practicable programme, and had placed six hundred in it by the end of 1965. But successful as it was, the on-the-job training was not recruiting altogether comparable applicants. In the institutional courses (as in the direct placements), 59% of the trainees were Negro, 38% white, but amongst those trained on the job, the proportions were almost exactly reversed. The latter also included more men, more who had reached the higher grades in school, and their ages concentrated more in the early twenties— only 19%, as against 35% were over 25.

CPI seems to have exploited on-the-job training more success-

[18] CPI set out, in the Spring of 1965, to interview all the '4,597 New Haven residents who applied for employment related services at CPI neighbourhood offices between October 1963 and April 1965'. The survey was only able to contact and interview half of them, so the proportions quoted above may not be altogether representative. The report notes: '52% of all CPI applicants were contacted and interviewed. Because of the close association between poverty and mobility in the inner-city, it can be inferred that the population who could not be reached represented cases of equivalent or greater welfare severity than those persons who could be reached and interviewed. This inference is supported by studies conducted by CPI and The Community Council. This report will thus present a conservative picture of inner-city populations, their characteristics and their problems, and their response to training and employment opportunities'. Conservative here means optimistic. However, the figures for those who had been through MDTA or OJT training should be representative, as over 80% of these groups were contacted.

fully than any other project, though Mobilization for Youth's OJT programme had trained nearly a hundred between July 1963 and August 1964. The projects had also successfully pressed several changes in procedures: the age level for eligibility to MDTA courses had been lowered; testing was more flexible, and welfare payments to the parents of youths in training were no longer reduced by the amount of the trainee's maintenance allowance, a practice which had nullified any immediate economic incentive to enrol in courses. But set beside the demand employment centres had brought to light, these training resources were still too few, too cumbersome, and of too discriminating an entry standard.

Work Adjustment

The projects were therefore driven to provide more preparatory training, independent of the jobs immediately open, and within the grasp of very unsophisticated recruits. These programmes were less concerned with technical skills, than with adjustment to the demands of any employment. They set out to teach regularity, punctuality, neatness, how to approach a prospective employer, how to handle the conflicts and frustrations of work relationships, how to tolerate orders and respect the legitimate expectations of a boss. Mobilization for Youth, for instance, devised ten simulated work situations, such as a gasoline station, an automative repair shop, a shoe factory, a luncheonette, and a typing duplicating and mailing service, in each of which ten to twenty young people were to learn how to handle themselves in employment. The work was created, planned and managed by MFY staff, and not run for profit, nor the produce sold, but was otherwise real enough. To this were added several hours a week of basic education in reading and arithmetic. In New Haven, work-crews were organized in groups of about half a dozen under a foreman, and employed by City Hall, a school, a hospital, a boys' club, and especially the Parks Department for twenty hours a week. The rest of each day was spent in discussion with the foreman, individual guidance, and remedial education. Boston proposed, in 1964, to follow the New Haven plan. Other more institutional work-adjustment courses in Boston and Philadelphia seemed less promising: the skills taught were marginal, the schools failed to provide remedial education, and the guidance was directed more at serious personality disorders than everyday adjustment to employment.

The work-crew experience was designed by Mobilization and CPI to lead, after a few months, either to employment or vocational training. When each boy or girl finished the course, they would be 'employable'—in the sense that their self-discipline and realism would fit them for a worthwhile job, though they might still lack technical skills. Ideally, every applicant to the employment centres who, after testing and discussion seemed too immature for a job or skill training, could be eased into a career through this preparation—much as the physically disabled are rehabilitated through sheltered workshops. In practice, the transition from work-crew to a job proved unexpectedly difficult.

Although the Mobilization work-crews were trained in a situation very similar to unprotected employment, this did not save them from the difficulties of adjustment. 'The experiments last year', notes an OMAT review, 'demonstrated that in isolation on his first job, the trainee is likely to suffer what the project is beginning to call "employment shock". This seems to happen no matter how careful the effort to prepare him for the world of work, with the insistence of that world on personal anonymity, impersonal good manners, objective norms in performance and a quantity of expected behaviour which the culturally deprived have had no chance to learn in life . . . These things are hard to learn. If the trainee is docked for a day's absence, he is likely to be bewildered if the foreman is annoyed when he doesn't show up—"I'm not being paid for it, so what difference does it make?" If someone else drops tools or makes a litter, the isolated youth on the margins of the culture, unused to any sort of help-each-other activity, except perhaps to the strongly individualistic moments of a gang fight, may be amazed that he, as a junior man on the work team, is expected to clean up and do it cheerfully: "the other guy dropped it, why doesn't he pick it up?" The trainee is also likely to be amazed at the amount of travel time needed to go from the lower East Side to where the jobs are, at how dirty (in the sense of hand-soiling and clothes-soiling) many jobs are, and at how often jobs require odd-shift work, evenings and week-ends, which the trainee expects to have free to see his girl.'[19] So, for instance in the most

[19] '"Employment Shock" At the Top of the Job Ladder', (Manpower Monograph, Department of Labour, OMAT, August 1964), pp. 3-4.

publicized part of the work-crew training, the gasolene station, only one of the first 46 to complete the course went to work at a regular gas-station job, although a third had some job. Only married men, it seemed, could tolerate the travelling, the erratic shifts and week-end work demanded.

A more systematic evaluation of five work-training projects in New York State seems to confirm the ineffectiveness of this kind of preparatory course.[20] The five projects varied in detail, but they were all designed to help Negro and Puerto Rican high-school dropouts between 16 and 19 adjust to employment. The courses offered intensive counselling, work experience under supervision in workshops or a job, remedial reading and arithmetic classes, and assistance in placement. They concentrated on punctuality, personality, appearance and job-finding rather than vocational skills. The young people who took the courses were compared with a randomly selected group who were referred—on application to the projects—directly to the Youth Employment Service. The comparison showed, disappointingly, no difference between the two groups in their chances of employment, six to twenty months after the trainees left the course. Half of both groups were unemployed and a third had jobs. The rest, in very similar proportions, were either in school or military service. The courses therefore gave no obvious advantage to their students. Though there may be subtler differences which the study did not measure, and the later career of the trainees may bring latent advantages to light, courses of this kind seem surprisingly irrelevant to the immediate problem of employment.

In New Haven, CPI met a corresponding frustration in graduating its work crews into employment. Most of the crews had been formed about the beginning of 1964: by mid-year, only a quarter of the 88 entrants had been placed in jobs, 13 had left without trace, and 53 were still in the crews. It could point to several impressive histories of young people who—handicapped by emotional insecurity, family breakdowns and poor qualifications—had been guided into jobs. But these instances do not demonstrate so much the success of the programme as the disproportionate cost of the achievement. Here, for instance, is CPI's account of the rehabilitation of a young Negro:

[20] See the report of Youth Research Inc., New York State Division for Youth, July 1964.

B.J. and his family moved here from the South nine years ago. His early education took place as much in the cotton fields as it did in school. He never did well in school here and was considered an 'incorrigible' fighter with teachers as well as schoolmates. He eventually dropped out of junior high school in the ninth grade.

CPI's first contact with B.J. was made through a neighbourhood employment worker who is a Negro and a lifelong resident of the young man's neighbourhood. The worker learned that B.J. spent most of his time hanging around on street corners with winos, prostitutes, numbers' runners and, she suspects, dope addicts . . . Over time, she convinced him that he should see the neighbourhood co-ordinator at the community school and he did ask the co-ordinator to help him go back to junior high school. However, because of B.J.'s past record, and because there was as yet no special programme for boys like B.J., the school principal would not even consider his return.

The co-ordinator's failure to help B.J. return to school left him sulky and disgruntled. When he was approached later by the neighbourhood worker, B.J. told her that the co-ordinator was 'just another white man who doesn't give a hoot about kids like us'. He said that if he was white things would have been different. Eventually, over a two or three week period, the worker convinced B.J. that this wasn't true, and was able to get him to see the co-ordinator again. About this time, the work crew programme was getting ready to begin and B.J. joined the first work crew from this area.

In four months on the work crew, B.J. missed work only one day and that was arranged in advance with the foreman. B.J. showed slow but steady development in the area of self control. At first he had arguments and fights with the other boys and really put the work crew foreman to the test. Slowly but surely the foreman's skill and patience won out . . .

All of the time B.J. was in the work crew there were a number of people other than the work crew foreman giving him the support so necessary to sustain him in this difficult stage. Especially important was a group worker who ran a teen lounge programme at the community school. There was a good deal of ongoing communication with this worker who spent many, many hours in regular counselling sessions with B.J. Others constantly in the picture were two neighbourhood workers, the co-ordinator and the vocational counsellor.

B.J. presently has a full-time job as a stock boy and elevator operator in a downtown store. We are maintaining our contacts with B.J. and his employer on a regular basis. So far things have gone very well on the job. We know that B.J. is still a high-risk placement but we hope with our continued support it will be a successful one.[21]

Such cases evoke immediate sympathy with the programme's work. But they only prove that with enough time and patience, a team of understanding adults can sometimes support an adolescent through frustration and rebellion into a steady job. The cost of helping B.J. through 'many, many hours of counselling' by at least six adults must have amounted to something approaching the full salary of a professional social worker over several months. The New Haven neighbourhood co-ordinators admitted that they were altogether disproportionately preoccupied by a very few difficult but hopeful cases. The demonstration remains a moment of extravagant compassion unrepeatable on any larger scale. The OMAT review of Mobilization for Youth remarks, similarly, 'MFY possesses, of course, much rehearsed success stories, especially the hot-tempered youth who was placed as breakfast cook in a best-quality hotel where he found he could not cope with a dozen equally hot-tempered waiters clamouring for service, but who was counselled into a successful adjustment. This kind of continuous direct personal contact with each individual trainee, by both the field man and the counsellor back in the MFY office, is an expensive investment in expensive staff time. It costs a great deal of money … What Mobilization is seeking, however, is not successes for a handful of all the thousands of disadvantaged dropouts who live on the fringe of the American culture on the lower East side, but a *way* of success'.[22]

For many of the New Haven work crew, the experience became less a preparation for employment than an informal education which passed the time until they were old enough to compete more hopefully in an overcrowded labour market. As an alternative to the senior years in high school—rather than to other forms of

[21] The New Haven Youth Employment Programme: The Six Month Report, May 1964. Appendix B, *op. cit.*, pp. 7–8.

[22] ' "Employment Shock." At the Top of the Job Ladder', *op. cit.*, p. 7.

vocational training—the CPI programme had several advantages. Most of the crew foreman were themselves high school dropouts, skilled or semi-skilled manual workers unemployed through automation, who had originally approached CPI in search of a job. So the young people could readily identify themselves with their leaders, sharing a similar background. And for the boys, the work crew provided a more masculine setting than the school, where their own abilities appeared less contemptible. But the work crew had not been designed as a general education, and could not sustain it for long. After about four months, the experience became less valuable, as the trainee grew bored with its limitations. And instead of gaining self-confidence, he ran the risk of falling into dependence on his foreman, to whom he habitually turned for reassurance. The training lacked, too, a goal which the crew members could readily accept. They naturally did not recognize themselves as exceptionally immature, so the experience could not be offered as remedial. Discouraged by their schooldays, more education would not appeal to them. But to present hedging and ditching for the Parks Department as a directly relevant skill training would have been misleading. As the months went by in the work crew, without bringing the chance of a job visibly nearer, there were no intermediate goals to sustain a sense of achievement. As a form of further education, the experience lacked a graduated development with its own rewards, which would relate basic education to vocational aspiration without seeming too much like school.

If many young people are too immature at sixteen or seventeen to stand much chance in the labour market, and too poorly educated to qualify for scarce vocational training; if a few months in simulated employment cannot overcome these handicaps; if they are alienated from the high school, and cannot assimilate teaching in this unsympathetic institutional setting, then the logical evolution of the work crew is a new kind of junior college, shaped to the needs of high school dropouts. As it is, those with least knowledge and skill are paradoxically thrust most abruptly, unprepared, and youngest, into the impersonal, indifferent world of employment. The intelligent graduate of a suburban high school can count on another four years in an environment tempered to his inexperience, when his unqualified contemporary from a poor neighbourhood has already been trying for two years to find his way in a world

which makes few allowances for his youth. A boy who leaves
school at sixteen has no framework within which to work through
the lingering dependencies of childhood. Unable to qualify for a
recognized adolescent status, he is flunked brusquely into a working world of adult expectations. A junior college might turn the
limbo of these adolescent years into an imaginative initiation into
maturity, by integrating general education, practical experience,
and skill training under a liberal regime which respected the students' uneasy reaching towards autonomy. The New Haven work
crew programme, with the addition of a skill centre, seemed to be
developing tentatively in this direction.

The Integration of Training and Jobs

In planning their vocational courses, the projects had ignored the
technical high schools, and most did not attempt to substitute any
alternative institution. They reacted against a tradition which had
so often failed to integrate training with opportunities of employment. But since they were determined that each of their courses
should lead to jobs, they had to accept a continual, complex and
frustrating negotiation of opportunities, whose nature and timing
could only be determined by employers' needs. They could only
guarantee that they taught marketable skills by organizing their
programme about the limited demand, and so forestalled any
organization geared to the flow of applicants. Even so, their institutional courses could not always secure a specific promise of
employment. The work crews, in turn, were blocked by the scarcity of openings for them. A looser integration of training and
available jobs would have been more responsive to the demand
from the applicants without, perhaps, realizing any fewer placements. Only one experiment, in Philadelphia, began by trying this
alternative plan.

   Opportunities Industrialization Centre was conceived by the
Reverend Leon Sullivan, a Negro minister of North Philadelphia.
He rented an abandoned police building from the city at a dollar a
year, rehabilitated it, and begged equipment of local industry—
installing lathes in the basement, refrigerators in the cells. The early
planning was enthusiastic and haphazard, but with the support of
the Philadelphia grey area project, the technical provisions of the
scheme were revised and checked. The centre opened at the begin-

ning of March 1964, with one hundred trainees in drafting, electronics, power sewing, restaurant practices and cabinet making. Courses in sheet metal, machine shop, and chemical laboratory work were to be added soon after, and the centre planned to train seven hundred in its first year. This, in itself, was a more ambitious annual recruitment to skill training than Mobilization or CPI had achieved at the outset. But the Centre was also determined that 'no person applying for training will be passed by'. Since it had received more than four thousand applications even before its formal opening, this was a bold undertaking. A second building was acquired, where another two thousand or more would be offered preliminary training, using closed circuit television and programmed learning. From here they were to be directed into the Centre, or other vocational courses as vacancies arose.

It is hard to see how this promise to every applicant could be kept. The Centre, even with other courses in Philadelphia, could not absorb so many, and baulked by the scarcity of opportunities, the resources of the preliminary training programme must soon be overwhelmed. But even if the project could not secure any more jobs than the experiments in New Haven, or in lower Manhattan, its refusal to subordinate its intake to the demands of the labour market enabled it to plan more hopefully.

Though open to all races, the Centre was conceived essentially as an inspiration to the Negro community of North Philadelphia: 'the programme will prove to the world', its promoter said, 'that genius is colour-blind, and it will prove to Negroes that it is not the colour of a balloon that determines how high it will fly, but what it has inside it'. The spirit of this statement contrasts with CPI's sober insistence that 'testing and counselling functions actually reflect the realities of the local economy' and that counselling should' 'encourage or discourage a programme participant in the development of a skill, *in the light of New Haven's actual skill needs'*. Uninhibited by this cautious realism, the bravery of the Centre's promises made a more heartening gesture of faith—and risked a correspondingly sharper disillusionment. But if the Centre can train several thousand successfully, even though it cannot place them, it will at least have shown that the blame lies in the economy, not the incompetence of the unemployed. Caught in the dilemma of raising false hopes, or bending to the constriction of the labour market, the Centre's uncompromising assertion of the right to prove your worth was more challenging to the society that denied so many a livelihood.[23]

Job Development

All the projects were bound to recognize that their successes would be marginal, so long as they could not influence the number and nature of jobs open. Their original programmes seem to have assumed that unemployment was largely inflated by ignorance or indifference to training opportunities. But they met an overwhelming response to their offer of a new chance. Though the unemployed might be unrealistic in their expectations, they were not, after all, apathetic. They thrust their frustrated aspirations eagerly forward, but the jobs or training open were either too few, or too demanding of qualifications. The retreat towards more fundamental preparatory training seems only to have delayed the confrontation, without measurably improving their chances. The development of more jobs, fitted to the talents of the applicants rather than employers' needs, was therefore the crux of any viable programme. For this the original projects had been very inadequately planned. Boston, for instance, had only one man assigned to develop jobs for a programme foreseen to involve sixteen hundred young people—and he was also responsible for on-the-job training. Though CPI was encouraging new industrial estates

[23] The Centre's first report suggests that its recruitment and courses will, in practice, adjust more pragmatically to employment possibilities. By the end of December 1964, 546 people had been enrolled. Two hundred and forty six were still in training, about fifty had left for a job before they graduated, and about one hundred and twenty had completed a course. But over a hundred of these first graduates were trained in power sewing and restaurant practice—low paying occupations for which women, almost entirely, were enrolled. There were only about half a dozen graduates each from the electronics and drafting courses. Of the 246 still in training, three quarters were over twenty one—about a third of them over thirty. Amongst the day students, 37% had more than twelve years of education, and a fifth were currently employed; but two thirds of the evening students were in jobs, and nearly two thirds had completed high school. The first courses, then, had trained women for rather unattractive jobs for which there is a steady labour demand. The current courses had enrolled, as day students, as high a proportion of high school dropouts as amongst the unemployed nationally, but the evening students were much better qualified. As a whole, those enrolled included a slightly smaller proportion of dropouts, young people, and unemployed than the 1,234 unsuccessful applicants. Clearly, the Centre could not, in fact, take all who applied, by any means. But it does seem to have enrolled a representative group of applicants in its day courses, unlike CPI's initial recruitment of trainees. (The figures derive from the annual report of the Centre, January 1965.)

through the Redevelopment Agency, and planned a scheme to develop twenty-five small businesses, none of the earlier employment programmes challenged the logic of the economies in which they sought openings.

Some of the more recent proposals have begun to explore means of creating worthwhile careers within reach of the least qualified. In Washington, the United Planning Organization put forward a policy to downgrade some professional functions, and upgrade the most menial unskilled work, so as to enlarge employment at a middle level. It argued that gardening and domestic service, for instance, where the demand was unsatisfied, might become more attractive occupations if they were organized as agencies employing salaried workers. At the same time, UPO planned to promote a reclassification of professional employment in the Federal Government. 'Professional and technical levels of employment are expected to show the highest growth rate and to account for the most critical shortages in the next decade. It is not feasible to train the unskilled for the manpower shortages in professional and technical positions. But it is feasible to create a higher efficiency within professional and technical levels by eliminating functions not in keeping with professional standards. While increasing professional efficiency, such a process also creates new jobs at a lower level which can be filled by those who have or can absorb less training... The Federal Government, which employs more than 30% of all workers in the National Capital Area and is the most important starting point for this type of service, is receptive to the idea. UPO will work directly with the Civil Service Commission and with government agencies to restructure certain jobs and create others.'[24]

A small experiment in the recruitment of sub-professionals had already been undertaken. Ten high school dropouts, with a record of delinquency, were given training as research assistants, day care and recreation workers: all ten were assured permanent employment in these fields, with the opportunity of promotion. Though they had been judged very unintelligent at school, and suffered from many unresolved emotional conflicts, they seemed sensitive and intelligent workers, and were all still in their jobs after five months of practice. UPO hoped to expand the experiment to provide

---

[24] 'A Proposal for Developing Human Resources for the National Capital Area', (UPO, December 1963), p. 69.

training and employment for three hundred such workers in medicine and social services.

The Washington project enjoyed a special relationship to the Federal Government. Washington Action for Youth, which had pioneered the experiment in sub-professional training, was an outcome of the Kennedys' personal concern with the capital. And since the Government employed nearly a third of all workers in the area, it was a powerful instrument of reform in the employment structure. Elsewhere, community action programmes were much more limited to their own resources in opening new categories of jobs. They ran the risk of creating very artificial opportunities, if the salaries had to be provided by the project itself. No real change would then be brought about. Either an agency is merely asked to accept, at no cost to itself, assistants to its professional staff, or—as in the Harlem proposal—the recruits are to be employed in the project itself. Though this may demonstrate the usefulness of assistants to professionals in medicine, teaching, or social service, it does not institute an enduring career structure.

Of all the programmes only the North Carolina Fund was broad enough in its responsibilities to influence economic development. The proposals it had received from the rural counties, where agriculture was declining and increasingly mechanized, presupposed the attraction of new industry. In the face of the more sophisticated self-promotion of the principal cities, these counties were in danger of a mutually harmful competition with each other, unless their efforts could be co-ordinated. The Fund was therefore drawn into the planning of an equitable distribution of industrial growth. But this may prove to be an independent issue, only obliquely relevant to employment. Industry is attracted to the state partly by its lack of labour organization: here there is no union pressure against highly automated production. Heavy investment by the communities in subsidized sites and tax concessions may induce firms who bring their professional and technical staff with them, and employ few others. North Carolina will then have to face the paradox of a progressive economy in which unemployment remains high, or even rises. The logic of the market economy seems to increase the disparities of wealth, to the point where some are altogether excluded from a share in its fortunes. If this is so, only by diverting resources into public services less controlled by the market, and adapting their organization to the skills of those who need jobs most, can the ringing promise of a Leon Sullivan be more than a defiant gesture.

This review of the experience of action is necessarily tentative. The achievement of any programme of educational reform must take many years to mature. The first two or three years have revealed some of the frustrations; they cannot establish what progress has been made otherwise. The employment programmes were more amenable to interim evaluation, if data on applications, recruitment to training, and placement had been regularly collated, and analysed by the age and qualifications of each group. Here the reports of the projects provide few hard facts. What proportion of those who applied for help received it? Were the successful applicants better or worse qualified than the rest? How many were finally placed in jobs, and at what cost?[25] How far did the projects create new opportunities, or merely attract whatever opportunities there were from other organizations? Such figures as the projects published seem at times almost wilfully incomplete, as if the crucial analysis would reveal too disturbing a shortcoming.

The difficulty of objective evaluation from the current data is brought out by a debate in *The American Child* for January and March 1965. In the earlier issue Richard Cloward and Robert Ontell wrote of Mobilization for Youth: 'Between October 1962 (when the work programmes opened) and December 1963, approximately 1,700 young people applied for assistance. Of these, roughly one in four eventually achieved competitive employment as a direct result of the programme. For the bulk of those placed, the jobs are in marginal occupations at relatively low wages, and their subsequent job histories are not characterized by much stability or continuity ... And it is doubtful that programmes elsewhere dealing with a population comparable in composition and size are doing any better. Indeed, there is reason to suspect that many are doing much worse.' Melvin Herman, former director of

[25] The analysis of cost is admittedly very difficult. The extra expense of research, experiment, and the negotiation of innovation has to be allowed for. And besides the people immediately helped, the cost might fairly be distributed over the family, friends and neighbours who may derive indirect support. So it is perhaps unreasonable to look for such a necessarily complex analysis before a programme has run for several years. But some costs seemed unrealistic, as a requirement of widespread intervention.

the MFY work programmes, replied in March 'The authors, who do the MFY research, did not cite another statistic appearing in the same report, which they prepared, that "Of the 817 clients assigned to MFY programmes, 494 (60%) had at least one direct (job) placement".' Six hundred young people who applied to MFY never returned for intake interviews, and without knowing what became of them, and why they never came back, it is difficult to assess MFY's achievement. Herman adds 'All the work programmes that I have encountered report serious problems in the collection of reliable data.'

Such sporadic statistical data as we have been able to collate suggests that, while the projects could claim many individual successes, and may well have increased somewhat the range of opportunities, they did so at great cost, and without benefit to perhaps two thirds of those who sought their help. They were, we think, held back by a more deep-rooted problem than any they were equipped to handle.

In both their employment and their education programmes, the projects were cramped by their inability to supersede the limits of local action, and tackle the national problems which underlay their frustrations. So long as the apathy of the poor and the conservatism of institutions could be treated as prime causes, unrelated to the fundamental structure of society, a strategy of persuasion, encouragement, enlightenment and discrete pressure might succeed. And since such a strategy depended upon the manipulation of individual relationships, it was appropriate to community action.

The experience of the projects suggests, however, that apathy was not as crucial as they thought. As soon as the projects offered an opportunity that seemed genuine, they encouraged more response than they could handle. Young men and women crowded the Youth Employment Centres, in search of jobs and training. In New Haven, Boston, Philadelphia, on the Lower East Side of New York, the centres were scarcely opened before their facilities were overtaken by the demand they brought to light. After three years of continual expansion, CPI, for instance, was still able to provide some service to only half of those who applied. In the schools, remedial reading and regular bi-weekly tutoring improved performance, though they did nothing to change the demands of the system. Given a chance, pupils seemed ready to respond. Mothers brought their children hopefully to the nursery schools.

Indeed, it was not amongst the poor, but amongst the staff of the institutions which served them, that apathy and indifference more often frustrated progress. In March 1966, Sargent Shriver, director of the Office of Economic Opportunity, reported categorically to Congress: 'The experts said the poor are apathetic, inarticulate, incapable of formulating demands, assisting and diagnosing their own needs. They were wrong. The poor are only waiting for the opportunity to be heard on a subject only they understand.'[26]

Many who came forward, and had to be turned away, never returned. Many more, perhaps, were too cynical or despairing even to enquire. But while there is still such a frustrated desire for a chance in life, eager to overwhelm any promise of help, the preoccupation with apathy seems misguided. These young people suffered, not because they would not grasp at opportunities, but because they could not keep hold of them. They lacked the skills, the resilience, the tolerance or authority to meet the expectations of teachers and employers. The opportunities, for them, were too few, and too often spurious—designed for someone else with a different background, skin, and more amenable talent. The projects did what they could to overcome prejudice, and teach young people how to disarm it. But as each door they opened led nowhere, they were continually adding anterooms in which an appearance of hopeful activity disguised the ultimate frustration. The economy did not really want what these young people could offer, and therefore the schools only half-heartedly encouraged talents of so little potential use. The children of the slums responded to the projects, because they recognized the sincerity of the intentions; they became discouraged only as it became clear that the promise could not be fulfilled. Disillusionment is not apathy, and to confuse them only complacently displaces the responsibility for failure.

The poverty cycle seems, then, less intractably self-perpetuating than the projects assumed. Poor parents may give their children little encouragement and few amenities to learn, and fail worse than others to find an emotional security from which their children can draw confidence. But they do not seem to rob the new generation of a painful eagerness to test, once again, the possibilities of the society which their parents failed to master. If this is so, poverty cannot be dealt with simply in terms of overcoming apathy through more intelligent service.

[26] Quoted in *New York Times*, March 15, 1966.

However resourceful the projects' employment programmes, they could do little to influence the economy which determined how many usable skills were in demand. So, in turn, the education programmes could only buy more time and better techniques for the teaching of poor children: they could not influence the standards of performance which children would ultimately have to face. In the last resort the success of the programmes depended upon the creation of jobs to use the young people they were trying to help. Since even a buoyant economy was unlikely itself to create these jobs fast enough, at the right level of skill or in the right place, they could only be provided by deliberate policy—by the expansion of public services, the recruitment to undermanned professions like teaching or medicine of less highly-trained aides, the employment of local youngsters in community work. The projects themselves could only offer such jobs temporarily to a few. Nor could the cities themselves—desperately short of funds to maintain even their present services—finance such an expansion. Most of them were not even in a position to establish more permanently the innovations which the projects were demonstrating: if they were to raise more taxes, they stood to lose industry and prosperous residents to suburb cities with fewer social needs. Even a state-wide programme, as in North Carolina, could only attract jobs by inducements which undermined their social purpose. Thus the projects could only achieve their aims within the framework of a national redistribution of resources, which deliberately redressed the balance of opportunities between rich and poor communities.

Since the promotion of a national policy to reallocate services and jobs to benefit the poor lay beyond their scope, the projects naturally emphasized other aspects of poverty that lay more within their means. Any approach to reform must accept some practical limit to its aims, and work within a setting that partly frustrates its ideals. But by ignoring the wider issue, the projects risked deceiving both themselves and others as to what they could achieve, and provoking a corresponding disillusionment. The difficulties of young people from the ghettoes in mastering the demands of employment, or the insensitivity of schools and social agencies, only became crucial as the resources to provide decent jobs and training were assured. Forced to apply their remedies without the backing of complementary national reforms on which any wide-spread success depended, the projects could only act as pioneers, exploring the means to implement a policy that had to be undertaken. And even as pioneers, they were handicapped by lack of any foreseeable funds adequate to the need. The competition for scarce resources accentuated institutional rivalries; unemployment and the impoverishment of social services embittered relations between poor neighbourhoods and any official source of help. Thus the search for an enlightened, rational plan to promote change, endorsed by the whole community, set out to confront problems aggravated by a vacuum of national policy it could do nothing to fill.

IV

THE EXPERIENCE OF
PLANNING

W E have tried to show how a growing concern with the
decay of city life led the Ford Foundation and the
President's Committee to conceive a new approach to
community change; and how, convinced that slums, unemployment and juvenile crime could only be understood as the outcome
of many interrelated social factors, they concluded that any remedies must depend on correspondingly many-sided action. The
terms in which they understood the problem—the self-perpetuating
cycle of poverty, and the failure of social services to intervene
imaginatively or coherently to break it—emphasized those obstacles to change which a community itself could tackle, without
greatly increased resources.

The early experience of the education and employment programmes shows how quickly this approach came up against barriers
which could not be overcome within a community setting alone.
It would take us beyond the scope of this enquiry to argue the
relative urgency of a national distribution of resources, compared
with reform of the way these resources were planned and used
within cities and counties. Both were greatly needed. But in the
rest of our analysis, as we trace the struggle to find a leverage for
community change, it is important to bear in mind the broader
unanswered questions of national policy that were begged—
questions which the Economic Opportunity Act only later, and
very uncertainly, began to take up.

Against this background of the trends in American society
which provoked this movement of reform, its assumptions about
the causes of poverty, and the evidence of its own experience, we
turn now to the strategies of change themselves. In part, the
problems of promoting change are independent of the particular

maladies with which reform is concerned. In the negotiations of the Ford Foundation and the President's Committee, in the organization of the projects, in the interpretation of different kinds of intervention, one issue especially recurs again and again—the question of legitimacy. Where does the right to direct change lie in a diffuse democracy, whose power of veto has overwhelmed the enforcement of collective action? If reform depends upon a democratic mandate, who are the authentic spokesmen of the people's wishes? If it depends, too, on rational argument, how is the scientific analysis of social problems to accommodate the intellectually disreputable reasons of political life? Is it really possible to demonstrate, experimentally, the validity of reform: who waits in scientific humility to see the outcome?

In the chapters which follow, we will explore these questions in each aspect of the leverage through which community action sought to promote change—in the relationship between the funders and the cities, in the search for a coalition of leadership, in the organization of poor neighbourhoods and in the application of social science. But an account, first, of one city's experience will help to illustrate the dramatic complexity of the whole process through which the projects struggled to establish their viability. The conflicts were nowhere more pervasive and tenacious than in Philadelphia, and the Philadelphia Council for Community Advancement is perhaps the most comprehensive example of the difficulties which beset the realization of this approach to social change. It is untypical only in being, for a while, overwhelmed by them.

The Story of PCCA

After Paul Ylvisaker had visited Philadelphia in the Autumn of 1960 to promote a grey area project, his audience dispersed to prepare their responses to his invitation. The City, the Greater Philadelphia Movement, the Health and Welfare Council, the Citizen's Committee on Education each independently submitted their proposals, sometimes by merely adapting schemes already put forward to the new policy.[1] The Foundation rejected this uncoordinated response, indicating that it was looking for a

[1] The overtures of the Foundation, and later of the President's Committee, provoked in all five separate proposals and nine unrelated enquiries between 1960 and early 1962, as David Hackett reported to a committee of the House of Representatives: 'The Health and Welfare Council submitted a proposal for a Delinquency

concerted plan, in which all interests were represented. The search for a consensus began.

The organization of a new proposal seems, by general consent, to have fallen to the Health and Welfare Council. The Council, which had asked Temple University to prepare its own submission to the Foundation, now turned to the University again. The planning was assigned to an inter-departmental committee of social scientists, to whom the Council added its own consultant.

Temple, like other urban universities, was hemmed in by an impoverished Negro community with whom it shared no common interest. Its desire to expand threatened neighbouring residents with the loss of their homes, and provoked resentment. In its own interest, Temple needed to win the goodwill of the North Philadelphia community by a constructive concern with their problems. The Health and Welfare Council's programme director had originally chosen to involve Temple University with this in mind. The new proposal, therefore, was centred upon North Philadelphia.

Though the Council promoted this academic drafting committee, the final document was not sympathetic to the voluntary agencies. Leadership within the University group has passed to Herman Niebuhr Jr., the ambitious director of a new Centre for Community Studies, who represented the Temple administration's awakened interest in North Philadelphia, rather than the inter-departmental committee's preoccupation with co-ordinating the social sciences. A Programme for North Philadelphians[2] reflected Niebuhr's uncompromising criticisms of the school system and social services, and showed little tenderness for the susceptibilities of the Council's constituent agencies. Such a radical reappraisal was, he believed, what Paul Ylvisaker and the Public Affairs staff

Act grant. The Greater Philadelphia Movement submitted a proposal for a welfare survey to the Ford Foundation. The Philadelphia Department of Public Welfare submitted a youth work project for Delinquency Act grant. This programme requested $1 million a year for three years and would have employed 1,500 boys and girls. . . . The Department of Public Welfare also submitted a proposal for casework services to potential delinquents. This programme would have worked with 600 families in three years and cost $334,000. The Pennsylvania Department of Labour developed a project for a youth vocational centre for submission to the United States Department of Labour. During 1961 and early 1962, inquiries about the new Federal programme were received from the Big Brothers, the County Court, the Crime Prevention Association, the Goodwill Industries, the Jewish Employment Service, the Neighbourhood Renewal Corp., the school district, two settlement houses and the YMCA.'

[2] Prepared by the Centre for Community Studies, (Temple University, 1961).

had in mind. Under his influence, the new plan of action abandoned any attempt to integrate the original proposals submitted to the Foundation. The City's programme was casually dropped as irrelevant and unimaginative, the Health and Welfare Council's first ideas forgotten, while arguments inherent in the other proposals were developed into a coherent theory. The programme for North Philadelphia was thus inspired, not by the search for consensus but by a single-minded conceptual framework.

This conception emphasized the disparate structures by which state, municipal, school and private agencies organized their services, and which frustrated co-ordination. To reintegrate them, the programme proposed to decentralize administration, under the supervision of a district managing director. The improvement of services was to depend especially on strengthening the natural points of contact between the citizen and his institutions. If teachers, doctors, housing inspectors, policemen, related their tasks more sensitively to the neighbourhood in which they worked, their influence would be greater. The new decentralized administration would therefore promote such innovations as special language programmes for 'culturally deprived' schoolchildren, child rearing education for lower-class mothers in pre-natal clinics, and Spanish-speaking policemen in Puerto Rican neighbourhoods. Whenever, in the course of his life, the impoverished citizen came into contact with an institution, its professional staff should exploit the relationship to raise him from a dejected posture of resigned incompetence and mutual incomprehension.

The *Programme for North Philadelphians* was intellectually persuasive, unorthodox and challenging. The newly-formed President's Committee regarded it as an outstanding example of comprehensive planning for institutional and professional reform. And it seemed to meet also the Foundation's criteria of imaginative innovation. Though its critical analysis had offended both public and private agencies, it provided a conception about which to organize the project. Attention turned to the structure through which it was to be implemented.

The Creation of an Agency

Both the President's Committee and the Foundation were concerned to involve City government, believing that ultimately only the resources of the City could sustain their movement of reform. The President's Committee asked Stanley Brody—a Philadelphia businessman who had been active in both state and local welfare boards—to explore whether a structure could be established within the City administration. He tried first to place the project in the office of the Welfare Commissioner. But the Commissioner was single-mindedly interested in a proposal of his own for a youth conservation corps. At an embarrassing public luncheon, David Hackett reaffirmed the President's Committee's insistence on comprehensive planning structures—a commitment which precluded independent support for specific programmes. The Commissioner, whose proposal had been the only contribution from City government to the Ford Foundation's initial overture, felt himself rebuffed.

Undaunted, if somewhat shaken, by his failure to convince the Commissioner that a broader conception was needed, Brody continued his efforts to establish the project in City Hall. He met with the Mayor, Democratic City Congressman Green, and William Rafsky, the Development Co-ordinator. But Mayor Dilworth, though sympathetic, was preoccupied by his forthcoming campaign for the State governorship. Congressman Green was indifferent, and the Development Co-ordinator inhibited by a political transition in which his own future was uncertain. The incoming Mayor did not appeal to the civic reform movement which had backed his predecessor, and would not commit his support to the project. Thus the narrowness of the one city official who had an idea to put forward, and the uncertainties of a change of regime, left the initiative open to others.

The opportunity was grasped by three men, who shared a common vision of the potential influence of a new approach—Judge Abraham Freedman of the Greater Philadelphia Movement, John Patterson of the Citizens Committee on Education, and Herman Niebuhr of Temple. They represented the civic reform movement and the University, in the sense that each held an acknowledged position within his organization. But none could claim to control the source of their authority, nor commit it to their ideal. They were conspirators, using the name and tolerance of their organizations in the service of their cause. Their position was weaker than it publicly appeared, but meanwhile no one challenged their initiative.

Since Niebuhr was openly critical of both public and private agencies, and the others mistrusted the allegiance of the incoming mayor, they did not want to place a new organization under the control of either City government or the Health and Welfare Council. They proposed an independent non-profit making corporation, broadly representative of community interests. On January 10, 1962, at an unobtrusive meeting in Mayor Dilworth's office called by Judge Freedman, the Philadelphia Council for Community Advancement was formally launched. A Temporary Organizing Committee of 17, under Freedman's chairmanship, was formed to realize the new agency. This Committee was made up of four representatives of City government, two from the Board of Education, two from the Greater Philadelphia Movement, and one each from the Citizen's Committee on Public Education, the United Fund, the Health and Welfare Council, a local foundation, Pennsylvania and Temple Universities, the NAACP, organized labour and the business community. The Committee was, therefore, biased towards informal civic leadership: all the service agencies were represented by their board members, rather than their professional executives. As an interpretation of the power structure of Philadelphia, it gave less weight than the funding agencies had intended to City Hall, and left out three factors.

Firstly, the churches were excluded, though they never protested very vigorously against their omission. The Catholic Church objected when PCCA's educational programmes ignored the parochial schools; and Mayor Tate protested on behalf of the Catholic Universities, when the recruitment of the projects' planning staff appeared to overlook them. But this apart, the failure to involve the churches provoked little controversy. The other omissions were more damaging.

The North Philadelphia community was not represented. As the Deputy Managing Director of the City noted, in a critique of PCCA's proposed structure:

As far as North Philadelphia is concerned—presumably the prime target of this endeavour—the plan of organization of PCCA and the concept of the Prospectus provides for no participation of any kind, at the policy-making levels, of the people for whom the planning is to be done. Except for the recent addition of Mayor Tate, there is among the incorporators, officers and members of the Executive

Committee of PCCA, not a single elected or appointed official from North Philadelphia, in fact, there appears to be among them not one bona-fide resident of this area.[3]

Neither the residents nor their elected officials were invited to join the Temporary Organizing Committee, and their exclusion was all the more questionable, because the Civil Rights Movement was also neglected. Leon Higginbotham, as President of the NAACP, was invited on to the Committee, but he represented only the most moderate Negro leadership, and had no special commitment to North Philadelphia. Within a few months, he resigned the Presidency on appointment as a member of the Federal Trade Commission, and the Organizing Committee was left without even the nominal endorsement of any Civil Rights group. They were dangerously open to the change of white paternalism—a change which Higginbotham's successor on the NAACP was to exploit without scruple.

Between Paul Ylvisaker's visits, and the establishment of the Organizing Committee, the planning of PCCA progressed from a set of uncoordinated proposals to a boldly conceived master plan, and from there to a projected structure with wide community backing. But this progress had been made at the cost of growing resentment. Herman Niebuhr's conception had antagonized both public and private agencies. The Negro community remained uninvolved and suspicious. And the City administration, failing itself to grasp the proferred leadership, felt increasingly uneasy at the emergence of a new, independent structure, with a privileged relationship to Federal agencies and the Ford Foundation, which— as one city official put it—'would not only control planning, but also the execution of many of the programmes of its constituent agencies'.

The three men who had taken the initiative, and established the ascendancy of their conception, were thus very vulnerable. They advanced under the shadow of a political storm, which might break whenever the incoming Mayor chose to listen to the anxieties of his discountenanced officials. And the implementation of their programme of action would still depend upon the public and voluntary agencies whose jurisdiction they threatened, and

[3] 'Analysis of Prospectus of the Philadelphia Council of Community Advancement', (March 22, 1962, mimeographed), p. 4.

whose competence they openly attacked. At the same time, their own support was insecure. They had not won the confidence of the Negro community, nor could they even rely on the backing of the organizations they came from. Herman Niebuhr could not commit Temple University; Judge Freedman was not a member of the financial elite which dominated the Greater Philadelphia Movement. Their Temporary Organizing Committee was representative enough, but at best half-heartedly committed to their aims. Hence the first stage in PCCA's progress did not resolve the conflicts of power, but only postponed them.

The Task Forces

Soon after the Organizing Committee was formed, in January 1962, the City administrators who sat on it made a determined attempt to modify the proposed structure, so that the City and its agencies would retain a controlling influence. A new prospectus was prepared by the planning staff at Temple, which sought to satisfy the City's demands within the framework of Herman Niebuhr's conception. This structure proposed to organize planning around six fields of action: child development, community health, job training and placement, neighbourhood improvement, community planning, and specialized programmes. By organizing in terms of fields of action, rather than institutional functions, the institutions would be forced to co-operate across their jurisdictional boundaries. At the same time, an elaborate system of task forces was designed to reconcile competing claims for control over each field of planning.

The promoters of the PCCA structure felt that institutions could protect their interests at the board level, while the planning should not be inhibited by the intrusion of self-protective institutional concerns. But both public and voluntary agencies insisted on being party to plans which affected their own operations. By way of compromise, two task forces were to be created in each field— one professional, and the other of lay leadership.

The professional task forces were to include personnel from the service agencies together with university faculty. Their work was to define problems, evaluate services and develop experimental programmes. The leadership task forces would be drawn from the PCCA Board of Directors and the community at large. They were to

screen the work of the professional task forces for final approval
by the Board. Besides facilitating the work of the Board, this lay
involvement would leave Philadelphia 'the legacy . . . of . . . a
highly informed and sophisticated leadership group which would
persist far beyond the life of the specific action programmes'.[4]

This complex procedure, by which agencies evaluated their own
function, while the PCCA Board screened and selected the programmes which emerged, was a political compromise. But it was
also justified as a rational solution to the problems of institutional
innovation. Niebuhr argued that before an organization could
change, it had first to learn the thinking and practice of other
organizations, and acquire an innovative approach. The lay and
professional participants in the task forces would educate each
other.

The rationalization satisfied neither the City, nor the President's
Committee, for opposite reasons. The City objected that 'the separation of Leaders and Professionals into two different levels of task
forces destroys the blending together of lay people and professionals'. They feared that the professional task forces, on which the
public agencies were represented, would be relegated to technical
assistants, and policy would be controlled by the lay leadership.
The PCCA planning staff tried to reassure them that the lay groups
were intended only as advisers.

On the other hand, the President's Committee interpreted the
structure as conceding too much authority to the agencies to be
reformed. It believed that the professional task forces should
control the programme, and here agency representatives, who owed
allegiance to their own organization, held a dominating influence.
In March 1962, the field liaison officer for the President's Committee noted:

Our criticism arises from the fact that the organization is not
related to the functions of organizational modification or programme
development, but only addresses the learning function. The key
planning responsibilities are invested in the professional task forces.
These are persons assigned to the planning operation on release time
by their respective agencies, but remaining in the pay and accountable to the administration of these agencies. They will apparently

4 'Philadelphia Council for Community Advancement: A Prospectus', (February
1962), p. 14.

range from agency directors to staff persons supposedly knowledgeable in some aspect of service. Their selection will be largely in the
hands of the agency representatives, persons selected by the participating services structures, and functioning as the structures' administrative voice in the planning venture. This kind of structure can only
mean that the task force will not have 'planning authority' . . . At
most, the task forces constitute a kind of study group arrangement
and might contribute to a 'learning or training' task.[5]

The President's Committee objected vigorously to any structure
which would compromise the integrity of planning and lead to its
capture by the established bureaucracies. 'The planning group
should be given increased autonomy from the service structures
which their planning will address.' The key professionals should
be accountable to the planning agency alone. The Leadership Task
Forces would serve as advisers and consultants to the professional
task forces, in which the actual planning would take place.

This revision undermined the political compromise which had
been designed to meet the fears of city government and the voluntary agencies. By insisting that the members of the professional
task force be independent of established agencies, and that they
assume primary responsibility for planning, the President's Committee encouraged Niebuhr to revert to his original conception.
The Commitee's field staff only later realized that in criticizing the
integrity of the proposed planning structure, they had been insensitive to its political necessity:

> The series of second contacts revealed to the field person a factor
> which he had not previously been conscious of. The planning
> organizational model is apparently a compromise solution to two
> strong institutional pressures operating on the PCCA, one stemming
> from the Welfare Council and the other, perhaps less articulate,
> from the city government.[6] Both apparently encouraged, if they
> didn't demand, this study group approach to planning as a means to
> secure a containing voice in the outcome.[7]

But the President's Committee still obstinately held to the principle
that planning must have sufficient independence and authority to

---

[5] Philadelphia Active City Files, March 23, 1962.
[6] In fact, the City, rather than the Welfare Council, exerted most pressure.
[7] Philadelphia Active City Files, *op. cit.*

counter 'City Hall dominance'. It assumed, optimistically, that the City would not raise serious objection: 'the City is not sufficiently concerned about the prescribed changes, confident that they have sufficient power in the upper echelons of the structure to protect their interests'.[8]

The President's Committee was so concerned to protect the integrity of planning that it not only proposed a structure which ran counter to established institutional interests, but even extracted a promise from the Temporary Organizing Committee that, if the Ford Foundation made a grant before the planning was completed, the funds would be held in reserve until everything was fully worked out.

At the insistence of the President's Committee, then, a new structure was devised. The idea of parallel task forces was retained, but now the professional task force was to consist only of full-time members of PCCA's staff, while its leadership counterpart was replaced by an advisory task force of agency representatives. There were to be two associate directors of PCCA, one to work with the expert planners, the other with the agency advisers. Herman Niebuhr, encouraged by the President's Committee's support, inverted the advisory task forces' nominal role. They were to be educated by the planners, rather than advise them. He hoped that the associate director for community development would 'sell the programme, monitor the difficulties and hold hands with the advisory task forces when they were frustrated and disappointed'.

Naturally enough, city administrators continued to object that public and private agencies had too little voice in planning under the new arrangement. To reassure them, the Temporary Organizing Committee passed a resolution to redraw its organizational chart:

> In order to reflect accurately the importance assigned to the advisory committees, the box on the organization diagram will be the same size as the box representing the central planning staff . . . The advisory committees shall not be limited to the review of plans already advanced or developed by this central planning staff. The central planning staff shall be mindful that the advisory committees and agencies whose members serve on them will ultimately execute much of the programmes developed.[9]

[8] *Ibid.*
[9] Minutes of The Temporary Organizing Committee, April 26, 1962.

Thus there was no consensus as to how the new structure was to function. Were the advisory task forces to advise, or to be advised gently but firmly by their intellectual superiors? To compound the confusion, the Ford Foundation—eager to expand the role of City government, and less fearful than the President's Committee of planning by consensus—seems to have thrown its weight informally to a stronger advisory task force.

The Board of PCCA did not discuss in detail how this cumbersome and equivocal structure was to function, and left the planning staff to work out a viable interpretation. But in practice, the advisory task forces received little guidance, partly because the factual surveys which were to guide programme development were never completed, but even more because PCCA's staff resented the entire organizational structure. The task forces represented a political compromise, which could only have worked if all parties had accepted the need of it, and committed themselves to abide by the form devised. In any event, the task forces served only to cloud the unresolved power struggle with ambiguity, and the unwieldly structure finally collapsed. Meanwhile, conflict shifted to a new issue.

The Search for a Director

Early in 1962, PCCA was without an executive director. It was also without substantial funds. Twenty thousand dollars had been given by the Phoebe Waterman Foundation, and in May 1962 the President's Committee finally made a planning grant of $165,000. But the Ford Foundation grant of $1·7 million would not be forthcoming until an executive was hired. It took a full year to settle the appointment of the Project's director, and the process aggravated the struggle.

Herman Niebuhr of Temple University had been acting executive director, and Judge Freedman and John Patterson naturally supported him. The city—antagonized by his uncompromising criticisms of its institutions—as naturally objected. It doubted his ability to handle public and private agencies, and his competence as an administrator. Instead, it suggested Manuel Kaufman, the Deputy Commissioner of Welfare. But Freedman, Patterson and Niebuhr saw City Hall as controlled by a political machine hostile to their spirit of reform, and feared that if Kaufman were chosen, the project would be dominated by the City's interests. The appointment was deadlocked. As the months dragged by, and one compromise candidate after another was put forward without success, the future of the whole project was increasingly endangered. Finally the Ford Foundation, impatient to see the issue resolved, recommended Samuel Dash, who had served an enlightened six months as district attorney. He was appointed in December 1962, almost a full year after the search began. Even so, he suffered from all the disadvantages of a compromise choice. He was not fully accepted either by the City on the one hand, or by Freedman and Niebuhr on the other, and inherited a staff still loyal to Herman Niebuhr's leadership. Both Manual Kaufman and Niebuhr became associate directors, but their own candidacy rejected, it was hard to see how they were to work harmoniously with the less experienced successor who stood between them. The relationship was scarcely tenable, and both eventually withdrew. From the first, Samuel Dash was uncomfortably isolated, and without a basis for his programmes. He looked first to Temple for the results of their planning endeavour, but could make little of the academic discussion papers or the sketchy preliminary findings of their survey. The task forces were floundering without direction, and the Board provided no guidance on policy. And himself a lawyer without previous experience of social services, he lacked confidence to take the initiative in determining the programmes.

In the midst of these difficulties, Samuel Dash was faced with a new challenge to the legitimacy of the project, from the Negro leadership which had been largely ignored when PCCA was first established.

The Challenge from the Negro Community

On January 12, 1963, Cecil Moore—a lawyer recently elected President of the local NAACP chapter—opened a sustained and vitrioloic campaign against PCCA and its newly appointed director. In his inaugural speech before the NAACP, he attacked white liberal groups in general, and PCCA in particular. He accused the project of hiring a white director who knew nothing of North Philadelphia; of ignoring the views of the community, and slighting its representatives; of promoting studies designed to expose the weakness and inferiority of Negroes; and of serving the selfish interests of ambitious Temple University professors. Moore demanded instead an immediate programme of action in North Philadelphia, and threatened to picket all Ford dealers in the City if the Foundation continued to support PCCA. The vigour of the attack, with its blend of truth, fancy and threat evoked an enthusiastic response: one Negro newspaper likened Moore to Jesus Christ.

Though the accusations were histrionic and exaggerated, they had enough truth in them to be disturbing. Samuel Dash was, indeed, inexperienced; apart from an unsatisfactory meeting between the Temple planners and some Negro ministers, the people of North Philadelphia had not been consulted; there were only two Negro members of PCCA's Board, neither from North Philadelphia, nor identified with the Civil Rights movement; and Temple University certainly had interests of its own which PCCA could serve. Even the charge that the project was more interested in studying than helping Negroes could be made to stick, since after a year or more's planning there was still little sign of action.

The attack caught PCCA vulnerable and unprepared. Badly shaken, it hastened to prove its honourable intentions by expanding its Board, recruiting more Negro senior staff, and associating itself with two programmes already initiated in North Philadelphia by Negro leaders. None of these expedients was wholly successful.

At the time of Moore's speech, the Temporary Organizing Committee still constituted the project's Board. It had four representatives of City government, two of the school system, seven from volunatry agencies and civic groups, two from universities, one businessman and one Labour official. Only two were Negro, and none came from North Philadelphia. In February 1963, a new and more representative board was established with 48 members, 15 of them Negro—including one from the North Philadelphia community, one from the NAACP, one from organized labour, and three from State and City government. Even so, PCCA were unable to recruit any of the more militant Negro leaders to its Board. Though they dissociated themselves from Cecil Moore, they were not yet prepared to endorse PCCA. The North Philadelphia Board members were drawn from professional and businessmen, and the less influential ministers of local churches.

At the same time, two Negroes were recruited as associate directors—for community development, and public information and training. But both they, and the Negro representatives on the

Board, were subjected to a continuing campaign of vilification by Cecil Moore, who in the interests of his own position could not afford to relent. Moore was insidiously successful in harassing anyone associated with the project. When twelve Negro leaders published a letter in the press repudiating his irresponsible attacks on PCCA, and his right to speak for the Negro community, Moore's response not only crushed the incipient revolt, but impugned the writers' integrity. Hence the Negro staff and board members of PCCA were committed to a project which had yet to prove itself, and for whose sake they were personally and remorselessly discredited by an influential, and highly publicized, if unrepresentative Negro leader. They were therefore especially anxious to move from planning to action.

Partly in response to these pressures, PCCA began to seek for programmes it could sponsor without waiting for an overall design to be completed. The reverend Leon Sullivan, an influential Baptist minister who had led the selective patronage movement in Philadelphia, had conceived the idea of a vocational training centre in North Philadelphia, and was already organizing buildings, equipment and staff.[10] Sullivan had refused an invitation to serve on PCCA's Board, but he was willing to accept Ford Foundation advice, and a grant from the Foundation through PCCA. His Opportunities Industrialization Centre eventually became the most outstanding of the programmes with which PCCA was associated, though the project did not initiate it. PCCA also gave its support to the North City Congress, a community organization originally founded by a North Philadelphia leader with the encouragement of Temple University. By endorsing and helping to develop these two programmes, PCCA defended itself against the charge of academic ineffectuality, at the expense of the deliberate, co-ordinated planning in which the President's Committee put its faith. But since both programmes had backing independent of PCCA, neither provided a final justification of PCCA's existence. They could probably survive without it, as they had begun.

The Fate of Planning

From January 1962 when the Temporary Organizing Committee was formed, until the spring of the following year when the new

[10] See pp. 83–85.

Board was established, PCCA had been subjected to repeated challenges to its legitimacy. While the City's institutions had accepted the Ford Foundation and President's Committee's requirement of a new instrument of planning, they continually sought to contain and control it. The policy and procedures of PCCA remained ambiguous, as conflicts were only half-heartedly resolved in equivocal compromise. The relationship between the two sets of task forces was left undetermined, and the two original incompatible rivals for the directorship remained at first in the organization, as associates of the man chosen in their stead. At the same time, Cecil Moore's attack had unnerved the project, turning it from phased planning to the expedients of survival. But though the issues were not settled, from the spring of 1963 PCCA was for a year relatively free from external attacks. In this period, the project struggled to establish a viable planning procedure, that would reconcile the analytic bias of the original Temple University group with political realities.

As the Temple staff conceived it, planning was to be based solely on dispassionate empirical studies, carried out with scientific rigour. First, basic information must be collected for the target community, and interpreted according to a theoretical rationale. From this analysis, programmes would evolve, which were then to be carefully evaluated and reassessed. Step by step, the accumulation of research findings would determine viable solutions to social problems, which could be replicated in other communities. The research staff saw themselves not merely as responsible for the collection of data, but 'charged with a far reaching and comprehensive responsibility . . . All studies and consequent action programmes are to fit into the basic realities of the life styles of North Philadelphians as reported by the data collection operations of the baseline committee . . . *it is critical that all programme activities of the PCCA be integrally related to the assumptions of the conceptual scheme*'. This conception frankly repudiated the right of politicans or agency staff to obtrude their opinions upon the planning procedure.

The behavioural scientists of the PCCA (psychologists, sociologists, and social psychologists) have spent years learning and applying the method of science to the understanding of the individual and his interactions with others. *In any rationally structured organization of this type, such persons hold the prime responsibility and prerogative for 'making the diagnosis' and suggesting a series of alternate courses of action for 'treat-ment'.* Thus we are contending that from the standpoint of profession-al background, experience, etc., only a handful of persons in our organization can be officially conceptualized as 'planners'.[11]

Herman Niebuhr shared this view of the social scientist's exclusive competence, but he recognized that value judgements must enter into the analysis, and that politicians were not to be persuaded by science alone. Once the planner has developed his agenda for community action, he has to sell it. His plan of action must be based partly on a study of the most relevant empirical findings, and partly upon theoretical knowledge derived from the scholarly literature. Fact and theory are then interwoven with the planner's own social philosophy—his personal conception of how best to define and serve the public interest. Planning becomes the art of advocacy for a specific point of view, within a political context.[12]

In support of his advocacy, the planner can exploit the promise of funds, and the prestige of his backers. He identifies key officials who recognize the need for change in the institutions he seeks to influence. With them he bargains for as much as the money and prestige behind him can secure. Thus the planner, though he has no power himself, pre-empts the resources of his backers to manipu-late institutions to his own design. Though Niebuhr's conception of planning was as intellectually presumptuous as his university colleagues', he added an element of political shrewdness.

From both these points of view, the advisory task forces of PCCA were at best a political concession, which might be usefully exploited to explain the insights of social science to the workaday administrator. At worst, they were a tiresome irrelevance, which intruded institutional prejudices where they deserved no hearing. These bureaucratic preconceptions were to be dealt with only when the plan had been worked out. Whatever concessions had ultimately to be accepted, they were not to tamper with the con-ception however they might limit the extent of its implementation.

When Samuel Dash took office as executive director, this in-transigent idealization of scientific planning had already, as we have

---

[11] Memo from the Baseline Committee to the Planning Staff, October 1963.

[12] Niebuhr's own point of view seemed to derive less immediately from a concern with social justice than from principles of social order and efficiency. He argued for a kind of 'primitive comprehensiveness' in which as much co-ordination, integration and centralization is sought at the local level as is politically feasible.

seen, aroused some fear and resentment among administrators. Dash himself was unfamiliar with social planning—anxious to exploit expert knowledge, but uncommitted to the pretension of social science. As a compromise appointment under public attack, directing an unproved agency with doubtful backing, he needed above all to recruit support. To reassure the public and private agencies, and the residents of North Philadelphia, he promised that PCCA's programmes would be developed only with the participation of established institutions, and sensitivity to the wishes of the community to be served. PCCA was not out to compete in the provision of services, but would, rather, act as a broker, distributing funds to agencies for innovative experiments they themselves had approved. At the same time, Dash looked to Niebuhr and his colleagues at Temple to provide the research data and theoretical framework from which to derive informed criticism of accepted practice, and new ideas.

This approach restored the task forces to an influential role. The planning staff was to develop a series of working papers on education, manpower, neighbourhood development, drawing on the findings of research. These working papers would serve as the agenda of the task force meetings. The task forces would suggest programmes, adapting the ideas put forward by the planning staff to a practicable form which institutions could accept. The staff were then to work the suggestions into detailed programme proposals for the approval of the Board. Under this procedure neither social science, professional planners, nor agency executives were accorded any superior authority. The final decision rested with the Board. Dash, in effect, took PCCA's formal organization at its face value as a dialogue between intellectuals and practical administrators, whose ideas were to be mediated by the staff, and endorsed or rejected according to the overall policy of a broadly representative board.

This model of planning assumed that everyone was willing and able to play the part assigned to him. But the planning staff never accepted it, the research data was never forthcoming, the advisory task forces did not speak for their agencies, and the Board itself was too amorphous and uncommitted to initiate policy. The task forces floundered incoherently, lacking information on which to base their discussions. The planning staff—imbued with Niebuhr's intellectual hauteur—largely ignored them. Neither staff consultation with agencies, nor reviews of existing agencies were submitted for their views. And the baseline study of fifteen hundred young people was never completed, so the task forces were unable to draw upon a dispassionate analysis of research findings. Without expert guidance, they were equally without policy direction from the Board. Nor were the members of the task forces authorized spokesmen for the agencies from which they came, and hence could not even ensure the acceptability of whatever was suggested.

But even with more sincere goodwill, this deliberate procedure would still have been very hard to sustain. In practice, programmes evolved less from any process of planning than as a response to opportunity, or defence against attack. The task forces were frequently by-passed, in haste to take advantage of offers of funds. In March 1963, for instance, the Federal Department of Labour approached PCCA with an invitation to establish a youth training programme under a grant from the Office of Manpower Automation and Training. OMAT was eager to spend its current allocation before June, when unexpended appropriations would revert to the Treasury, with the risk that failure to exhaust its present funds would compromise its claim upon the next year's budget. PCCA had not yet formed an advisory task force in job training, nor hired a staff member to assume responsibility for it; and it had promised the President's Committee to avoid action until the planning process was completed. But the temptation of $150,000 in Federal funds overcame its planning scruples.

The nursery school programme was also put together over the heads of the appropriate task force. The task force was not convened until May of 1963, but meanwhile teachers had to be trained, if the programme—for which the Ford Foundation had promised support—was to start with the new school year in September. In practice, the details were negotiated between PCCA's planning director for child development and Henry Saltzman at the Foundation, and the task force apologetically presented with a decision that had already been taken.

Finally, there were the two programmes which PCCA adopted in defence against Cecil Moore's accusations—Leon Sullivan's Opportunities Industrialization Centre and the North City Congress. These, with the nursery school and the special training course, were in the event the only four programmes which PCCA ever funded. And not one of them had evolved from the project's planning procedure, as either Dash or Niebuhr conceived it. The ideas had been initiated outside PCCA, owed little to sociological theory, and even less to research in North Philadelphia. They had been developed into practicable proposals in informal discussion between the funding agencies, members of the project staff, and those who were to carry the programme out. If they expressed a coherent philosophy of reform, it did not derive from any articulate policy of PCCA's Board, but from a general understanding which pervaded the thinking of the President's Committee, the Foundation, and their associated projects.

For a while, the Board resisted the opportunism which was undermining its planning principles. The minutes of a meeting in May, 1963, record:

> Mr. Patterson voiced concern about the need to act on an emergency basis in order to take advantage of fiscal requests. Recognizing that PCCA has come through a trying period of organization in which it has been pushed by the nature of events and opportunities, he felt that it had now reached a point where it should look into programme possibilities by persons fully competent to judge them. The professional staff should move ahead full speed in making appropriate professional contacts and setting up Advisory Task Forces which will involve the community in the programmes and on a regular basis of relationships with our staff and professional consultants.

> Judge Freedman agreed that PCCA should set itself against organizing programmes on an emergency basis, even at the expense of passing up the benefits of year-end grants from government agencies or departments.

But by the end of the year, the attempt to formalize any planning procedure—whether of scientific analysis or consensual discussion —was finally abandoned. The task forces were abolished, and instead PCCA relied simply on informal consultation with agency representatives. By now, Herman Niebuhr and his colleagues at Temple had withdrawn altogether from the project, in mutual disillusionment, and the concern with a conceptual master plan faded. At last unencumbered by the ideals and rivalries of his predecessors, Samuel Dash was free to make a fresh start. But before any more programmes could be implemented, PCCA was undermined by a renewed crisis over its legitimacy.

The Experience of Planning

PCCA and the Poverty Programme

In March 1964 President Johnson presented to Congress his strategy for the war on poverty. Under the second title of the proposed legislation, three hundred and fifteen million dollars were allocated to urban and rural community action programmes. 'We intend to strike at poverty at its source' wrote the President '—in the streets of our cities and on the farms of our countryside among the very young and the impoverished old. This programme asks men and women throughout the country to prepare long-range plans for the attack on poverty in their own communities . . . These plans will be local plans calling upon all the resources available to the community—Federal and State, local and private, human and material.'

This proposal had been largely inspired and guided by the experience of the President's Committee and the Foundation's grey area projects. 'One crucial lesson has been learned from this community experience. Since the causes of poverty are complex, the solutions must be comprehensive . . . The most successful community action, therefore, usually includes the political, business, labour, and religious leaders, the schoolboard, the employment service, the public welfare department, private social welfare agencies, and neighbourhood houses in a co-ordinated attack on local poverty. Above all it includes the poor people of the community whose first opportunity must be the opportunity to help themselves'.[13] Clearly, such a comprehensive endeavour would exclude any rival organization in the same city. If the grey area projects were to survive, they would have to become the instrument of the new legislation. And since they had inspired it, they naturally met its criteria. At the same time, the greater Federal support promised under the new act revived the issue of control. A mayor who was content to see two or three million dollars spent in his city independent of his jursidiction might be less amenable when the funds were mutiplied. In March of 1964, therefore, Sargent Shriver asked Paul Ylvisaker to confirm that Mayor Tate proposed to use PCCA as the instrument of a poverty programme in Philadelphia.

[13] 'The War on Poverty, The Economic Opportunity Act of 1964.' A compilation of materials relevant to S.2642 prepared for the select sub-committee on poverty, 1964, pp. 3, 52.

The Mayor, however, refused to endorse any such assumption. Though, as a member of its Board, he had begun to take an interest in PCCA, he did not understand it in this sense. He resented the enquiry as an invitation to surrender his authority to an autonomous agency, to which city government must subordinate its policies. Paul Ylvisaker, realizing that he had provoked a reaction which threatened PCCA's whole future, wrote urgently to the Board asking that it clarify PCCA's aims, and work out a relationship with the City that would integrate its development with the poverty programme. If this proved impossible, the project would be left dependent upon Foundation grants, without prospect of federal or city funds, or an accepted co-ordinating function—and in these circumstances, the Ford Foundation itself would withdraw. In the face of this challenge, the Board revised its leadership. While Judge Freedman remained as Chairman, Richard Bennett—director of the local foundation which had given PCCA its first funds—became its President. Bennett was readier to confront the Board with the issue: PCCA was either to re-establish itself, with a clear conception of its purpose and a mandate from City government, or wind up its affairs.

Throughout the summer, Bennett and his executive committee struggled to secure the Mayor's endorsement. But torn between the advice of his officials, Tate vacillated. Commissioner Wise, who had not forgiven the repeated rebuffs to his proposal for a Youth Conservation Corps, wished to treat PCCA like any other voluntary agency, which might submit programmes for the City's approval. Other city administrators were more conciliatory, acknowledging the project's claim to a co-ordinative planning function. Each time PCCA was ready to despair, the Mayor surprised it with an offer of co-operation. But whenever the Board sought to confirm the new agreement in writing, the Mayor refused to sign. From week to week, PCCA swung between dissolution and revival.

In truth, no one was enthusiastic about the project's future. Bennett acknowledged that its record had been disappointing, and its Board was even now only half-heartedly committed to the purposes for which it had been created. The Mayor was out of sympathy with the civic reform movement from which its leaders came, and his officials still resented the intellectual arrogance of its original approach to public agencies. The Health and Welfare Council was not reconciled to the surrender of its responsibility for social planning. The influential members of the Negro community were hostile or warily neutral. As for the funding agencies, the President's Committee was uncertain of its own future in the setting of the new legislation, and the Ford Foundation was prepared to write Philadelphia off if no really satisfactory agreement could be reached.

Yet, equally, no one wished to assume responsibility for PCCA's collapse. The Foundation could not afford to antagonize City Halls throughout the nation by appearing to dictate terms to the Mayor of a great city. Nor did Mayor Tate want to lay himself open to the accusation that he had lost Philadelphia several million dollars of Foundation money. Fearing that PCCA might cause even more trouble dead than alive, he finally endorsed a structure which Dash and Bennett had negotiated with the City's managing director.

Under this organization of the poverty programme, PCCA would co-ordinate, review and initiate the development of social services, while a parallel committee would handle economic services. Each would report directly to the Mayor and his task force, while the City's managing director would co-ordinate the programme as a whole. A public meeting of over a hundred community representatives was called to introduce the new proposal. At a similar meeting, less than two months before, PCCA had been pointedly ignored. It was now to be recognized, very much on its own terms, though more clearly subordinate to the Mayor's ultimate authority. But at this point, the Health and Welfare Council chose to intervene.

The Council's director announced at the meeting that it would refuse to be represented in the poverty programme through PCCA. Cecil Moore, who was also present, seized the opportunity to renew his attack: what claim had the project to influence, if even the Health and Welfare Council repudiated it? Thoroughly embarrassed by this turn of events, the Mayor started to read the name and affiliation of everyone present. After half an hour of this exercise, the meeting was adjourned.

A few days later, July 27, the Council explained its position in a memorandum to the Board President:

The Council believes failure to use Council resources or to attempt to duplicate them in another organization would be inefficient and wasteful and would lead to substantial misunderstanding and possible conflict. Should PCCA decide upon a course of action that would tend to duplicate existing council resources it would then be necessary for the Health and Welfare Council to re-evaluate its position and make this known to its constituents ... No matter what the structure of the city's programme to eliminate poverty, the council would expect and hope that its services would be utilized fully—directly by the city of Philadelphia or through PCCA.

The Council insisted that PCCA contract the review of poverty programmes to the Council, and abolish its own planning staff, using instead the Council's services. PCCA, in effect, was to be a mere broker, through which the Council was restored to its traditional responsibility for social planning. Bennett responded with a forthright attack on the Council's pretentions. He wrote to its President on the fourth of August:

It assumes for itself rights, roles and expertness which labels may support but experience does not justify. It imagines that not being exclusively in the 'poverty' driver's seat means that its principle responsibility will be destroyed.

The statement's ultimatum indicated that if its terms are not accepted the Council will re-evaluate its position ... and 'make this known to its constituents'. This flexing of muscles and inflexibility of position is reflected in the fact, while 'it is imperative that agreements be reached at the earliest possible time', any agreement other than on the terms demanded by the Council seems precluded by the public taking of position and the apparent private discussions of them.

... The Council can and should ultimately be the instrument for service *and* change as regards the human needs in Philadelphia. But it appears to be wedded to traditional means of serving the status quo. It seems to have little sense of time—or of the needs of the times.

In the face of this vigorous counterattack, the Council withdrew its open challenge. Though it might have been relieved to see the last of PCCA, it was no readier than any other interest to assume the responsibility of an executioner. Conciliatory in public, it continued to press, more discretely, for an independent function in the poverty programme. Within three months, it had won its case by default. On November 5, 1964, PCCA voluntarily withdrew from the poverty programme, worn down by the long summer of indecision.

'Thou shalt not kill but needs not strive officiously to keep alive' wrote Arthur Hugh Clough in his new decalogue. PCCA—as it was originally conceived—died of attrition from the unresolved conflicts which had dogged its history. But no one in Philadelphia was ostensibly to blame. Only the Ford Foundation was manoeuvred into a position where it had to take a firm decision. Was it to continue its support, when the project's future status remained so equivocal, and the commitment of the City's leaders to it so half-hearted? A compromise was discussed, whereby PCCA would, while withdrawing from the Mayor's community action programme, continue to review social policy, promote experimental innovations, and provide a channel of communication between officials and the people they served. But the Foundation's senior executives were finally persuaded that this was too doubtful a proposition to deserve their support. At a gloomy meeting in late autumn, Paul Ylvisaker announced bleakly that PCCA must wind up its affairs. Two hundred thousand dollars remaining from the development fund was to be distributed to Sullivan's Training Centre, which the Foundation would continue to support. The balance of four hundred thousand would enable PCCA to phase itself out gradually, through a number of small scale terminal programmes.

Looking back, the story of PCCA suggests that both the Foundation and the Presidents' Committee approached reform with too hopeful a rationality. The Committee's idealization of planning as a scientific process, uncontaminated by political compromise, presupposed an intellectual authority which the project never enjoyed. Expediency and theoretical rationality could never, in practice, be separated. The more the distinction was insisted upon, the more the planners alienated the officials on whom their proposals depended, and weakened their influence. Instead of informing the policies of politicians and administrators, the social scientists challenged them, as an alternative government bent upon power, and Philadelphia was not ready to accept so drastic a revolution.

The Ford Foundation was less constrained by any planning dogma, but it overrated the power of money to enforce lasting agreement. It could negotiate a compromise as a condition of support, but could not ensure that the bargain was honoured. Institutions formally accepted undertakings to which they were not sincerely committed, or interpreted them to suit their interests. This equivocation left the unresolved issues continually nagging at the project's authority, and exhausting its energies. The search for a consensual programme of community action can lead to a stalemate, all the more damaging because the failure to achieve anything is masked by the project's continued existence. Just as a neurotic evades his problems in self-stultifying defences, so a city may be unable either to confront or ignore the need for concerted action, and sustains a PCCA while denying it effective co-operation. The Foundation's strategy did not allow for such an outcome. If the President's Committee trusted too much to scientific rationality, the Foundation assumed too unguardedly that a political compromise would at least represent a rational accommodation of institutional interests. When PCCA became imprisoned by the struggles for control, the Foundation was unable to rescue it. Tired of paying the gaoler's expenses, it could only put the project out of its agony.

Yet there was an alternative which, under Richard Bennett's resilient leadership, and using the insight Samuel Dash had derived from his experience, PCCA finally adopted. The project's future only depended upon the Mayor's poverty programme, and the support of all the community's leaders, so long as it was uncritically accepted that 'since the causes of poverty are complex, the solutions must be comprehensive'. But however complex the causes, it did not follow that they could only be tackled through a single organization. Bennett foresaw, as both the Office of Economic Opportunity and Ford came later to recognize, that no one structure could comprehend every promising approach to the needs of the poor. The authenticity of the Mayor's programme would depend, not only on general agreement, but upon independent initiatives which challenged City Hall to match them in boldness and imagination. In the Autumn of 1965, PCCA reconstituted itself, under a new director, as an independent agency of reform.

The experience of PCCA suggests the common dilemmas of community action. This approach to reform argues from the interrelatedness of social needs, and the incoherence of the means by which they are handled, for an instrument of policy that will at once exploit the resources of social science to unravel their complexity, and integrate leadership behind the proposed innovations. At the same time, sensitive to the concentration of power inherent in such an instrument, community action tries to confront the expert planner and his political backers directly with the views of those they serve. Scientific objectivity, political consensus, democratic participation—each without the others, would lead to ineffectuality or overbearing authority. 'Planning is people' as Clifford Campbell, one of the Foundation's consultants, continually reminded the Public Affairs staff: you must plan with people, not for them. But, equally, planning is politics, and the determination of a rational purpose. Ideally, then, community action enables people to use politics for a purpose. But it does not explain how these principles are to be more effectively integrated than in the present structure of local democracy. The first abortive attempt in Philadelphia shows how hard a task it was. All the projects had great difficulty in reconciling systematic planning and evaluation with political realism; none succeeded in remaining equally responsive to both institutions and the people they served; some were even less able than PCCA to hold together a viable coalition of support. The promoters of community action hoped that if each principle were acknowledged and insisted upon, a means of integrating them would evolve. But in practice, the pursuit of consensus, rationality, or direct democracy led in different directions. The projects only stultified themselves if they remained faithful to them all, yet could not subordinate one to another without seeming to invalidate their right to intervene.

In retrospect the aims of PCCA seem impossibly ambitious. The interests it was seeking to reconcile were too powerful and too much at odds with each other to submit to its arbitration. But the Ford Foundation and the President's Committee had to establish some base in the community from which to promote innovation and co-ordination. To understand why they were led to support organizations as inherently unstable as PCCA, we need to consider the constraints under which they themselves manoeuvred.

V

THE DILEMMAS OF THE
FUNDING AGENCIES

'IN a political system where nearly every adult may vote but
where knowledge, wealth, social position, access to officials,
and other resources are unequally distributed, who actually
governs?' asks Robert Dahl at the outset of his study of New
Haven.[1] He concludes that a few professional politicians—who
share, despite their competing interests, a common understanding
of the rules and procedures of political life—direct affairs within
the limits of public tolerance. This tolerance may extend even to
policies which, if they gave them thought, most citizens might not
approve. The professional therefore holds the initiative, so long as
he does not arouse public opinion from its apathy. He can manoeuvre amongst his peers, who are usually better informed and
more coherent in their interpretation of democratic principles
than most of their constituents. Government is a sophisticated
game of professional players, who abide by the same rules, and
react to each other according to the same understanding of the
latent democratic constraints upon their freedom of action.

Like the politicians, the Ford Foundation executives who
promoted the grey area projects, the staff of the President's Committee, and their consultant sociologists were also professionals.
Their vocation was reform. And their freedom to initiate reform
was similarly circumscribed by an indefinite mandate, whose
limits they tested, but which they had ultimately to respect. They
too were a small, sophisticated group who knew, or came to know
each other, and who—though they did not always agree—
thought in the same terms. Within the context of their democratic
ideals, and guided by a wary sense of the length to which they could
push the authority they represented, they staked their money on

[1] Robert Dahl, *Who Governs?* (New Haven: Yale University Press, 1961), p. 1.

a bold initiative. But neither the Foundation nor the Committee was well placed to protect its stake—one because it was unrepresentative, the other because its own standing within the Federal Government was precarious.

The Dilemma of Philanthropy

As the largest of all philanthropic foundations, Ford faces most uncomfortably the crucial dilemma of private giving: it is an exercise of power without responsibility. 'With the exception of major governments, the Ford Foundation possesses the largest fund in the world specifically designed for the advancement of mankind. The Foundation therefore should analyse its role . . . with reference to the full depth and breadth of the problems and prospects of mankind.'[2] On these terms it is preoccupied with the same broad issues of policy which are already the chief concern of government. How is it to deploy its funds effectively, when—in comparison with government—its resources are, after all, meagre? Since there would be little point in adding marginally to the money government is already spending on a particular policy, it has to find something to do which government does not. How then, as an autonomous organization without a democratic mandate, is it to justify its intervention? Unless it innovates, it wastes its opportunity to advance mankind beyond the scope of political leadership: but whenever it does so, it lays itself open to the charge of unwarranted interference. Philanthropy treads a narrow path between redundancy and presumption.

The Ford Foundation has tried to resolve this dilemma by an emphasis on education, in the broadest sense—demonstrating possibilities, evaluating achievements, but never asserting or institutionalizing purposes of its own. 'The Ford Foundation is essentially an Educational Foundation', wrote the President in the 1957 annual report. '. . . In these terms, education extends beyond the academic world, and into the atmosphere of society, which is the composite of the beliefs and ambitions of its members.' Even here, he disclaimed any directive influence. 'This is where Foundations have an appropriate role to play, not in shaping those beliefs and ambitions but in encouraging competent, serious-

[2] 'Directives and Terms of Reference for the 1960's', (Ford Foundation, June 1962).

minded people to understand, maintain and realize them'. Philanthropy is, as it were, a rain-maker—seeding the atmosphere of society to precipitate a latent flood of productive ideas.

In negotiating the grey area projects, the Public Affairs staff tried to act according to this conception of their proper role. They did not begin by putting forward any specific proposals. To impose their own prescription would have seemed both illegitimate and self-defeating. The grey area projects were designed to revitalize community leadership, not to overwhelm it. The Foundation did not want to cut short a thorough reappraisal of the cities' problems by revealing at the outset too much of its own thinking. It defined its aims in very abstract terms—human betterment, opening opportunities, 'harnessing the urban-rural reaction'. Poverty, unemployment, delinquency were taken as symptoms of a pervasive hardening of the social and bureaucratic structure. The first step, therefore, was to break out of this constricting framework in any promising direction. Once the institutions of the city came together, and saw the problem as a whole; once they examined their performance in the light of this understanding; once the leaders everywhere in the community committed themselves to seek authentic solutions, then the logic of this commitment would drive institutions towards experiment and co-operation. It did not so much matter where they chose to begin.

In principle, then, the Foundation sought to play only a catalytic part. As Paul Ylvisaker wrote modestly of the first grey area grant: 'Foundation prospects have expanded and hopefully improved the Oakland project, they did not create it.' But in practice, the Public Affairs staff could not seriously pretend to themselves that they were merely crystalizing the ambitions of community leadership. In a less formal memorandum he was franker: 'The Foundation is in most cases "out in front of its customers",' he admitted, and went on to remark generally on the narrowness of most plans cities had put forward, the vested interests, the lack of hard thinking, the publicity seeking 'and worse, the object of human betterment usually gets lost in this morass, replaced by more tangible concerns such as physical monuments and agency survival ... If nothing else the Foundation has shown—and temporarily filled—a vacuum of constructive criticism and leadership which exists in most American communities, and in which the problems of the grey areas have thrived.'

A note in the file on the original Oakland proposal includes the revealing phrase: 'Foundation bargaining position to be agreed upon by September 15th.' In the drawn-out negotiations with Oakland, New Haven, Boston, Philadelphia, the Foundation was obliquely setting out terms which it was inhibited from openly declaring. In all its dealings with the cities, it was torn between reluctance to prejudice the communities' own conception of their needs, and insistence on meaningful reform—displaying, according to one's point of view, hypocrisy, humility or inconstancy of purpose.

The Public Affairs negotiators resolved the dilemma by leaving the initiative in drafting proposals to local leadership, while guarding their intentions in the revisions they imposed as a condition of support. In part, this simply reduced the negotiations to a guessing game, in which the cities arrived by elimination at the answer the Foundation had first thought of. Even in the specification of programmes, where the Foundation was genuinely open-minded, the fertility of human invention could not match the opportunity. In search of fresh ideas, the drafters of the proposals in the cities could only turn, after all, to the Foundation itself, to discover what it would accept as relevant and new. The programmes which gained currency came to look very much alike, and they bore the stamp of the Public Affairs staff's analysis, more than the communities' first thoughts.

But the ambivalence of the Foundation's negotiating posture also gave rise to a confusion of purpose, which damaged its chances of integrating community leadership. By surrendering the initiative, it left the field open to rival interests in the city to compete for the right to co-ordinate the master plan. And this emphasis upon institutional aggrandisement was the one thing, above all, that the Foundation was trying to prevent.

The breakdown of coherent social planning had arisen, not so much from a 'vacuum of constructive criticism and leadership', as from inability to agree on who should fill it. Local reformers in the councils of voluntary agencies, urban renewal authorities, schoolboards and city halls had long recognized their growing problems, and begun to search for solutions. Everyone recognized much the same needs, and the inadequacy of present means to solve them. To Redevelopment Authorities and Health and Welfare Councils alike, to the settlement houses, Youth Commissions, Welfare departments, schools, city managers or universities which in one city or another initiated proposals, more cogent planning, closer co-ordination and imaginative innovations were unexceptionable aims. But at the same time, everyone was also committed to the interests he represented, and could plausibly argue that urban renewal, or social work, or city hall was the natural focus of a new approach. The Foundation was convinced of the need for a broadly representative coalition of leadership to implement reform. But the institutions which responded most purposefully to the Foundation's invitation were often also those with the most urgent problems of survival, and so least willing to concede any part of their faltering authority. They hoped to reinforce their own functions by assimilating the new resources for social development. They certainly did not expect to subordinate these functions to a new agency.

Edward Logue, for instance—director of urban renewal first in New Haven and then Boston—illustrates the progressive disillusionment of some of the Foundation's most vigorous supporters. Logue shared, and had helped to form, many of the principles of Ylvisaker and his team—co-ordinated development, the reform of education and the broadening of its function through community schools, the participation of poor people in plans for their own welfare. He gave much of the original impetus to the planning of grey area projects in both cities: CPI was worked out in his office by his staff, and ABCD was prompted by the discussions he initiated with voluntary agencies. But his concern with social planning was not disinterested. The relocation of the first families to be displaced in New Haven had brought to light social needs which the Redevelopment Agency had no resources to tackle. Unless the slum dwellers could be convinced that clearance would no longer cause them hardship, all the redevelopment plans might founder in the face of popular outcry. In New Haven, the Mayor's skilled non-partisan leadership had helped to forestall a crisis of confidence. But in Boston, Logue faced a more complex and conflict-ridden community, where renewal had aroused bitter resentment. He saw in the grey area project a chance to consolidate the Yankee business elite, who dominated the voluntary agencies, with Irish Catholic political leadership, behind a programme that would restore popular backing for renewal and associate it with immediate social benefits. The proposal centred on a plan of community organization, which would foster neighbourhood leadership to understand, support and contribute to the Redevelopment Authority's plans.

Logue was determined that redevelopment should be the pivot, about which the whole grey area programme would revolve. He kept faith with an ideal of renewal as an essential instrument of social justice. He had once accused the Foundation of 'not knowing that there were any Negroes in the United States': to him, slums stood, above all, for racial inequality. Here Negro Americans were condemned to live in a degrading setting, whose meanness stunted the growth of stable relationships. So long as the slums remained to perpetuate discrimination, American civilization was dangerously flawed. Although renewal could not, in fact, do much to improve the fortunes of those it displaced—indeed often left them worse off—and seemed merely to brush the problems aside, distracting attention by its new office blocks and luxury apartments, Logue was too deeply committed to renewal to concede that the instrument of his ideals had failed. To prove the truth of his vision, he was driven only more impatiently, more ruthlessly to manipulate support for his solution. Aware of all the shortcomings, and faced with mounting resistance to his plans, he still held that slum clearance and rehabiliation were fundamental to reform. The unpopularity of renewal only proved that it confronted the hard conflicts of interest which purely social programmes could evade. Unless the grey area projects, which he felt he had done so much to bring about, reinforced and facilitated his redevelopment plans, they would shirk the uncomfortable issues.

But neither the voluntary agencies, nor the Mayor, nor the Ford Foundation were willing to tie the Boston project so exclusively to urban renewal. In the protracted negotiations from which ABCD evolved, the aims became confused. As we shall see in Chapter VII, community organization—which did not much appeal to the Foundation—had a different meaning for Logue and the settlement houses whose support he had recruited. By its equivocal neutrality as a promoter of reform, the Foundation encouraged Logue to take an initiative which it was not, when it came to the point, prepared to back. As the grey area project captured public attention, and established its own independent purposes, Logue felt increasingly betrayed. Gazing from the picture window of his office on the rising frame of Boston's new government centre, he brooded on the bad faith of those to whom he had once shown the way.

With less passion, this pattern of disillusionment was repeated in the voluntary agencies. Their planning and fund-raising councils had come to recognize, like urban renewal authorities, the need for a new impetus in social planning. And like the Ford Foundation, they were concerned with the co-ordination of public and private welfare services. But they, too, were more immediately preoccupied with a crisis in their own survival. While costs were rising, their resources remained much the same. Higher taxation and the growth of public services had dulled the response to charitable appeals, especially as the well-to-do abandoned the central city. At the same time, many of the voluntary agencies supported by the United Fund no longer seemed to perform any very essential service. Some had abandoned those in greatest need in favour of a more prestigeful and less frustrating middle-class clientele: some had failed to change with the neighbourhoods they served, and existed only for a few, no longer typical residents. Others had outlived their function. A thorough re-distribution, reorganization and rationalization of the voluntary agency structure would deploy the limited resources of the United Fund to much better effect.

This reconstruction had been in mind for several years. In 1949, for instance, Boston's United Community Services had published a survey of the Greater Boston Community, designed to show the future need for services. Unfortunately, it preceded by a year the City Planning Board's Greater Boston Plan, and there seems to have been no communication between the two.[3] But apart from this rift between public and private thinking, the plans did not result in action. A council which represented a federation of agencies found itself the captive of its constituents. It could not impose reorganization on them, nor repudiate without risking the loyalty of its financial support any agency it had traditionally supported. A rationalization which weakened the United Fund

[3] See Robert Perlman, 'Social Welfare Planning', (Ph.D. dissertation, Brandeis University, 1961). He discusses the evolution of the United Community Service's concern with urban renewal in Boston.

would be self-defeating. In this dilemma, the prospect of Ford Foundation intervention suggested a way out.

The Foundation enjoyed national prestige, and was independent of community attachments. A study financed from this source would have the weight of impartial authority, and strengthen the arguments of local reformers. If, besides, the Foundation would support the recommendations of the study, the prospect of grants would encourage reluctant agencies to redirect their services and co-operate more effectively with each other. In Philadelphia especially—where for years the United Fund had failed to meet its already inadequate target of contributions—the initial response to Paul Ylvisaker's overtures was largely in terms of agency reorganization. The early development of the Washington grey area project was also influenced by dissatisfaction with the incoherence of voluntary agencies. A health and welfare council for Greater Washington only came into being in 1959, and at once initiated a long-range planning study. But two year's work produced only a very unsatisfactory document, and it began to look for a more effective instrument of planning.

Yet, although the councils of the voluntary agencies were amongst the most active promoters of the grey area projects, they were also the first to resent them. The health and welfare councils saw their prerogative of social planning usurped. The new organization, with its smart, bustling offices and well-paid staff, flourishing under the patronage of city hall, philanthropy and the Federal Government, became a dangerous rival. Instead of helping the council to reconstruct the pattern of voluntary services, and revive the council's function, the project's staff set about to manipulate public and private agencies to their own design, as if the council were an obsolete and ineffectual body. This was all the more painful since the council, in promoting the project, had indeed confessed its weakness. Like Ed Logue, the voluntary agencies found they had hatched a cuckoo, who swallowed all the grants, grew prodigiously, and left their own starvelings disconsolately chirping at the bottom of the nest.

The disappointment of the Redevelopment Administrator and the voluntary agencies expose the inherent weakness of the Foundation's position as a disinterested innovator. Whether the response to its invitation originated in concern with relocation or the plight of the United Fund, with the quality of public education, the control of delinquency, or the underlying fiscal crisis of the centre city caught between a shrinking tax base and an increasing population in social want, the proposals were all designed to retrieve the viability of the institutions which sponsored them. The needs they described, and the remedies they put forward, did not contradict the Foundation's analysis. But there was a fundamental misunderstanding. The Foundation wanted the plans to arise from a comprehensive review of the problems of grey areas, in which agency services were ruthlessly subordinated to the interests of their users, and reorganized without regard for conventional jurisdictions. But since it was inhibited from taking charge itself, and the authoritative leaders in the cities all had institutional ties, there was no one who could dominate the planning from this detached point of view. Nor did the most active participants represent the most directly relevant institutions. The Public Affairs staff thought in terms of education and vocational training rather than community organization, case work, or the relocation of alcoholics and problem families. At their insistence, the plans shifted their emphasis. But the school system, which now became the centre of attention, had not itself taken much part in the initial discussion. In spite of the great cities schools programme, the pressure for school reform came from outside the system: in Philadelphia, for instance, from the Citizens Committee on Public Education; in New Haven, from the Mayor, his Redevelopment Administrator, and the School Board they had appointed; in North Carolina, from the Governor. So the proposals came to depend very heavily on an institution whose co-operation was only sought when the planning was already advanced.

The Foundation was also worried by the professional or academic bias of the initial planners, who tended to be recruited from the staff of redevelopment authorities, voluntary agencies and their councils, or from universities. It pressed for a wider involvement of public officials, community and political leaders. So, as boards for the new agencies were set up, and task forces and communities ramified to develop programmes, responsibility became shared by people who were less committed to the endeavour, and sometimes only vaguely aware of its aims.

By insisting on a broadly representative coalition of leadership, the Foundation was able to prevent ambitious institutions having their way unchallenged. But the outcome was often—as we saw in Philadelphia—a confused compromise in which the issues were unresolved, and the project was left without a constituency of committed supporters. Its originators in the community had been edged from control, while those who displaced them were less sure of their purpose, and less involved.

At the outset no one wished to push his claim so far as to frustrate the negotiations, even if he saw how his interests might be threatened. But from the first there were signs that an impending power struggle lay in wait for the projects, as soon as they were funded. When, for instance, the Oakland City Manager forwarded the Oakland community's proposal, he wrote to the Foundation that 'the individual agencies involved in the development of the programme proposals are . . . autonomous. They have agreed to involve themselves voluntarily in the integration and co-ordination of the work to be done. For this reason, we have exercised only limited persuasion and control in the development of the plan'. This warning seems to have gone unheeded. Six months later, the grant was announced in a mood of general optimism at the success of voluntary co-operation. Yet within another three months, the project was falling apart. The Director of the project had run foul of some of his colleagues in City Hall, and antagonized the Associated Agencies. Neither the research committee nor the programme development seminar had met. Communication had broken down. The Council of Social Planning was attempting to profit by the confusion to assert its leadership, and involve the Foundation in an independent conference. It took Oakland nearly two years to recover any coherence.

The disintegration of the Oakland project is the most immediate, and least complex instance of a characteristic reluctance to resolve the power struggle before the new organization was in being. Elaborate organizational charts were, indeed, prepared: they spread across the pages of the proposals with a reassuring precision. Interlocking circles and ranks of boxes are neatly articulated with lines and arrows, drawing everyone from the President of the United States to the office typist into a Hegelian unity. But the diagrams all suffer from a crucial ambiguity: the connecting lines do not indicate the nature of the relationship. Orders, advice, information, money might equally flow along them. This evasion of the realities of power was at once shrewd and self-deceiving. It held together an alliance of community and national interests long enough to bring the projects into being. But it left the projects to face the postponed struggle while they were still scarcely organized, and unguardedly trusting to the illusion of support.

Hindsight throws the unresolved ambiguities and tenuous assumptions into sharp relief. Yet without this ambiguity, the projects would not have been negotiable. Neither by its philosophy, nor its posture as a reformer, could the Foundation impose its remedies. At the same time, it was, in Paul Ylvisaker's phrase, so far 'out in front of its customers', that it had to prepare its own criteria of relevance. It had, then, at once to seize the initiative, and advertise its aims, and yet to appear responsive and open-minded. The abstraction of Paul Ylvisaker's conception of the urban problem, its appeal to moral purpose and the commitment of concern, rather than detailed institutional or social analysis, gave him room to manoeuvre. A subtle balance between the exploitation of means, and the assertion of ultimate ends made the projects possible. And as they evolved, so the interpretation of the problem evolved with them. But this saving ambiguity also entangled the projects in a confusion of purpose from which some never fought themselves free.

The Dilemma of Government

The dilemma of philanthropy arises from its lack of a base within the political structure, from which to organize reform. It must work discretely through those who have, easily finds itself at cross-purposes with its allies, and has little power to assert policy once its grants are committed. The dilemma of Federal Government arises from the multiplicity of overlapping agencies, each with its own political constituency, through which its policies must be implemented. A coherent plan of reform depends upon co-ordination. But the instrument of co-ordination rarely finds its authority accepted, and tends to become yet another agency competing for power, adding still further to the confusion of rival jurisdictions. The right of the President's Committee to initiate reform was therefore as open to challenge as the Foundation's.

Juvenile delinquency concerns the administration of justice, the welfare of children, the treatment of mental illness, education and vocational training. The President's Committee entered a field where, over the years, many Federal departments had claimed interest or special competence. Of these, the Children's Bureau of the Department of Health Education and Welfare and the National Institute of Mental Health most consistently asserted their claim.[4] The rivalry between them is reflected in their different approaches. For while the Bureau was preoccupied with policy for the treatment of offenders, the National Institute set delinquency in a much broader context of social frustrations, and sought to prevent it.

On the eve of President Kennedy's inauguration there were, then, two federal bureaucracies competing for funds from a Congress increasingly alarmed at the rise in delinquency, and increasingly dissatisfied with conventional measures against it. NIMH was seeking to develop a policy of comprehensive community action research projects, aimed at the complex social causes of delinquency, of which Mobilization for Youth was the model. The Children's Bureau hoped that new legislation would grant it a statutory authority equal to its rival, through which it could promote technical assistance, studies and demonstrations of new methods of correction. It had been campaigning since 1955 for Federal grants-in-aid against delinquency, and a higher status as an Office of Children's Affairs. But when legislation was

[4] The Children's Bureau was created in 1912 'to investigate and report on all matters pertaining to child welfare and child life'. But only in 1952, as the number of such crimes attracted growing national attention, did it establish a juvenile delinquency branch, which became two years later a separate division of service. The Bureau had also, at least in principle, a co-ordinating function. In 1948, President Truman created an Inter-Departmental Committee on Children and Youth, covering the work of thirty-four government agencies, chaired by the chief of the Bureau and staffed by its personnel. The Bureau could claim, therefore, to be the appropriate instrument to co-ordinate and implement a policy for delinquency. In practice, the Bureau has suffered a progressive attrition of power and influence ever since its inception. At one time it reported directly to Congress, then to the Secretary of HEW, today it is only a division within the Bureau of Family Service. It could not effectively discharge its role as a co-ordinator, and never succeeded in mastering the ramification in other departments of activities related to delinquency. Its own expenditure on delinquency programmes was, besides, meagre—about a third of a million dollars in 1962, mostly spent on technical assistance to states and communities. Unlike the National Institute of Mental Health, the Bureau had no authority to give direct financial support for community projects. At this time, the Institute was spending ten times as much on delinquency, and the largest part of its expenditure went on sixty or more demonstration and research projects. Thus the Bureau, which held a recognized claim to organize and direct delinquency policy, lacked the resources to fulfil its mandate.

at last enacted, an instrument of policy was contrived which overlaid these rivalries with the ambitions of new men, uncommitted to established bureaucracy.

The President's Committee on Juvenile Delinquency and Youth Crime is misleadingly named. It never met as a working committee, derived its authority from the Attorney General rather than his brother, and was never primarily concerned with delinquency and crime. It was less an instrument to advance the study and control of a threatening social problem, than a movement of reform, attacking within both Federal and local government the bureaucratic fragmentation and conservatism which the Ford Foundation had also seen as a crucial obstacle to progress. The struggles of the Committee in Washington parallel the jurisdictional conflicts, the resistances and confusion of aims which beset the community action programmes. The Foundation had to justify the democratic legitimacy of its intervention: the Committee had to justify its organizational legitimacy, within the competitive structure of Federal Government.

The creation of the President's Committee and the provisions of the Delinquency Act both rebuffed the Children's Bureau. Under Lloyd Ohlin's influence, they inclined more towards a preventive strategy, involving the widest range of agencies, than to measures of professional training or experiments in the treatment of delinquents. The authority to make grants for demonstration projects, which the Bureau had long sought, was qualified by the obligation to take the Committee's advice. And the Bureau had lost to the Committee its claim to co-ordinate all Federal programmes concerned with delinquency. The reformers were determined to circumvent an established bureaucracy whose competence they mistrusted, and keep the direction of policy to their own instrument.

But the new structure was encumbered by an awkward fiscal arrangement. The Committee, since it was created by executive order, was not entitled to a direct appropriation from Congress, and so depended upon contributions from the Departments into whose jurisdiction it intruded. Each of the departments of Justice, Labour and Health Education and Welfare were to contribute forty-five thousand dollars annually for the Committee's own expenses—and HEW a further eighty-seven thousand. Its policies were to be carried out by a staff spread amongst these departments, to act as co-ordinators and innovators. The personnel was assembled by distributing functions between five branches of the Federal bureaucracy, which would meet the cost between them. Thus the administration of the act was delegated to a Special Assistant for Juvenile Delinquency, with a staff of nine, lodged in the Office of the Secretary of HEW. Direct services and technical assistance to community demonstration and training programmes were assigned to the Children's Bureau, for which twenty-two additional workers were requested. Six professional and four clerical positions were allocated within the Office of Education, to develop school programmes and work with field staff in demonstration programmes. Finally, three professional staff were to be assigned to each of the Departments of Justice and Labour, to co-ordinate their youth and delinquency work with Committee policy. The plan assumed that these departments and offices, eager to expand their resources, would be prepared to surrender some of their autonomy for the sake of co-ordination and an increase in manpower. As a formal structure, it failed almost entirely.

The Department of Justice refused to accept the money for its three professionals. Instead it reallocated its grant to the President's Committee, expanding the Committee's budget, and permitting it to hire its own staff. The Justice Department thus straightforwardly dismissed the use of personnel hired by HEW to co-ordinate its own youth and delinquency activities, and effectively blocked liaison between its own operating units and the Committee. Though the Attorney General vigorously supported the new legislation, and the viability of the Committee rested on his influence, he did not use it to effect co-ordination and innovation within his own department. The Office of Education was extremely suspicious of the new positions allocated to it, and successfully blocked the recruitment of staff who would have promoted the Committee's ideals. The Office itself proposed to hire retired school superintendents anxious to qualify for a Federal service pension. The negotiations dragged on for months, and the full complement was never recruited, nor did those who were hired fulfil effectively their co-ordinating function. The Department of Labour accepted its funds, but refused to allow the Committee or the Special Assistant for Juvenile Delinquency to participate in the recruitment of the staff. The new personnel were absorbed into the Department, and no one was assigned permanently or consistently to work with the Committee.

The strategy of co-ordination by liaison therefore failed. The established bureaucracies generally either ignored, blocked or circumvented the Committee's intentions. The staff who were to broadcast its policies owed their primary allegiance to the department which paid them, or risked being mistrusted. As an administrative organization, the structure broke down even before it was formed.

But it did bring into the federal bureaucracy several able young men who shared the President's Committee's ideals. David Hackett himself put more faith in an informal network of like-minded people than in formal arrangements, and so long as the personal power of Robert Kennedy lay behind it, the Committee staff could still put together a workable system of alliances. In the pattern which evolved, policy development, administration and the implementing of programmes became separated, and were precariously held in line by the overriding influence of the Attorney General's office.

Although the President's Committee was conceived as an inter-departmental committee at Cabinet level to promote co-ordination, it never officially met, and remained a polite fiction. Since it was not integrated with the administration of the Justice Department either, it functioned as an arm of the Attorney General's personal authority. As such, under David Hackett's direction, it exercised considerably more power than it was formally granted. Technically, the administration of the programme was the responsibility of the Secretary for Health Education and Welfare, who was required to consult the Committee in making grants, but not (as in an earlier draft of the legislation) to act only on the Committee's recommendation.[5]

[5] The earlier draft limited the secretary of HEW to making grants 'which have been recommended' by the President's Committee, but this was too much for HEW and the Budget Bureau. They substituted merely a right of the Committee to be consulted. As the Deputy Attorney General remarked, this changed 'the basic concept of the role of the Attorney General and the Secretary of Labour in this legislation. Since the Secretary of HEW could . . . overrule or disregard their advice'. In practice, the Secretary never did so. The original intent of the bill was followed, and its administration was widely but inaccurately regarded as lying with the President's Committee. Members of the Technical Advisory Committee, for instance, believed that they were responsible to the President's Committee rather than directly to HEW. The projects in the communities also mistook the President's Committee's formal authority.

In practice, Hackett, with the Attorney General's backing, was able to assert the authority which the law denied.

The influence of the Committee was extended by informal understandings with departmental divisions. The staff of the special section created within the Children's Bureau, for instance, worked closely with Sanford Kravitz, the Committee's programme co-ordinator. The Office of Juvenile Delinquency relied on the Committee's support in the face of opposition or indifference from the Children's Bureau, and critics in the Secretary's office. And in the Labour Department, the Office of Manpower, Automation and Training was led by similar internal rivalries into alliance with the Committee—though the Department as a whole remained indifferent to the programme, and failed even to honour its financial obligation.[6]

The delinquency programme operated, then through an unstable alliance of Robert Kennedy's personal authority with internal departmental rivalries, and the mutual understanding of a small group of idealistic innovators within the bureaucracy. The interlocking cadres of professional staff, who were to represent the President's Committee policies in each department and co-ordinate Federal resources, were never satisfactorily established. As a formal administrative rationalization within the Federal Government the plan failed. The direction of policy and its implementation were never integrated, and the politically-minded staff of the Committee maintained at best an uneasy relationship with the more professional departments. And OMAT apart, departments were unwilling to commit their own resources to supplement grants under the Delinquency Act in jointly-planned community demonstrations. 'While we have encouraged co-ordination in the local level, we are constantly

---

[6] Responsibility for vocational training under the Manpower Development and Training Act was assigned to the Bureau of Employment Security, but the Bureau did not want its function to be confused with the special problems of young people from the urban ghettoes. So OMAT sought to promote experimental and demonstration programmes of its own for disadvantaged youth, from other sources. Here its interests converged with the Committee, which recognized the crucial importance to its own policy of vocational training. The Committee hoped that the employment programmes financed by the Department of Labour would become an integral part of their community projects and enlarge their resources; while OMAT was anxious to develop programmes apart from the state employment offices, and used funds under the Juvenile Delinquency and Youth Offences Control Act to pay some of its programme staff.

hampered by the lack of a corresponding co-ordination of Federal programmes,' David Hackett remarked in a memorandum to the Attorney General. 'Fortunately, we have been able to develop informal arrangements with some of the Federal agencies to help meet the needs of our seventeen cities. But such arrangements are tenuous, are not carried on within an overall commitment to comprehensive programming, and often are endangered by bureaucratic haggling . . .'[7]

The President's Committee possessed, therefore, very slender resources. It did not formally control the approval, administration or implementation of any Federal grants, and its attempts to establish a rational co-ordinative structure within the government had been rebuffed. Despite the Attorney General's personal backing, and President Kennedy's interest, the Committee's right to direct policy was open to challenge. Powerful critics in Congress repudiated its emphasis on planning and social reform.[8] Powerful bureaucratic interests questioned its intrusion on their jurisdiction. State officials resented being by-passed through a direct relationship between cities and the Federal Government. But even while the Committee could, in fact, determine the distribution of demonstration grants under the delinquency act, these resources were too meagre for a comprehensive programme. The plans it promoted depended upon further Federal and local grants, and it had failed to secure any prior commitment of these funds. It could act only as a facilitator, assisting communities to put their case before the Federal departments.

Like the Ford Foundation, therefore, the legitimacy of its intervention as a reformer was vulnerable, its funds and power inadequate. Its manoeuvres within the Federal Government had succeeded no better than the Foundation's diplomatic obliqueness in disarming the jurisdictional rivalries they sought to override. In answer to their difficulties, both followed essentially the same strategy. Instead of asserting any specific programme or reform, they tried to stimulate a process, by which communities would

[7] Dated November 6, 1963.

[8] Congresswoman Green, chairman of the Special Education Subcommittee of the House Labour and Education Committee, was strongly against the President's Committee's emphasis on urban reform, which she regarded as a flagrant departure from Congressional intent. For a full account of this conflict see John E. Moore, 'Delinquency: Presidential, Congressional . . . and Juvenile', in *Cases in Urban Legislation* (Washington D.C.: Brookings Institution, 1967).

spontaneously arrive, through the same logic, at the policies the reformers foresaw. In this way, the outcome would not depend upon the legitimacy of any authority the originators of the process might claim. Professional expertise, community leadership, the people to be helped were to be brought together to work out a new approach which they themselves would control, and whose worth was to prove itself by empirical evaluation. The Foundation and the Federal government would then finance a core of programmes, on which the communities could build.

We have already seen how, in Philadelphia, the process faltered. But if the Ford Foundation and the President's Committee were prevented by their questionable mandate from ensuring a constructive outcome to their intervention, they were fundamentally no worse off than any other agent of reform. In a society which guards against the abuse of power by diffusing and fragmenting it, any authority to direct change is necessarily confined within a single jurisdiction. If discrete, uncoordinated reforms within the scope of particular agencies could not match the complexity of the problem, it followed that no one held any unchallengeable right to order the priorities of change. The administrative and political structure of the United States explicitly intends that no power, at any level of government, shall claim an authority broad enough to control all the social institutions of a community—and this principle is upheld by radicals and conservatives alike. Any concerted social policy had, then, to rest on a consensus, and the creation of a consensus involves, like any compromise, conflict, intrigue, ambiguous accommodation.

But could the projects reconcile the diverse interests of society any more effectively than the conventional processes of democracy? They tried, in effect, to hasten these processes by confronting the agents of reform more immediately with their shared responsibility. In the offices of community action projects— where, away from the harangue of public debate, the rational determination of a common purpose set the agenda—politicians, professionals, intellectuals and popular leaders were to come together to resolve their differences. Could such an agency force the pace of democratic accommodation?

In the next chapter, we discuss the inherent difficulty of

integrating institutions about a common plan, even without introducing the claims of popular participation or research. By seeking to co-ordinate all three, the projects were faced with the task of reconciling very disparate conceptions of reform, each with its own inherent strength and weakness, its own kind of authority, and each at odds with the others.

VI

IN SEARCH OF A
COALITION

A CONFERENCE. Hot coffee expires in paper cups. The project director switches restlessly from pipe to cigar to cigarette, seeking to appease at once his fear of cancer and the tension of the meeting. Soft-footed secretaries insinuate pink telephone messages and airline bookings before the foundation representatives who, even as they talk, tirelessly weave their web of influence. The tone of the discussion is bland: the city is to be congratulated on its progress, the funders on their far-sighted support. But the air is heavy with unspoken reservations. Only the foundation staff are disinterestedly committed to the project, and they are beginning to wonder what they will see for their money. Beside them is their most powerful ally in the community, who recognizes in the project a chance to extend his influence beyond the limits of his formal jurisdiction. Across the table sits the representative of a public agency, indifferent to the project's wider aims, but determined to secure from it funds for his favourite scheme. Another participant is neutral. He is there because nothing can be done without him; he has no quarrel with the project, so long as it makes no serious demands upon his overburdened administration. But one is hostile: he sees in the project a fundamental threat to his authority. He is not for this reason any less genial than the rest, merely vaguer. The disagreements are marked only by a subtle pause in the meeting's unruffled urbanity. Ideas will be worked on, rather than accepted; proposals redrafted, not submitted; decisions postponed. Later in the day, the members of the meeting will exchange, in private, obliquely collusive telephone conversations, prepare memoranda to their boards, draft letters. And around midnight, after a reception and a formal dinner, the foundation representatives will gather in a hotel bedroom to analyse the springs of conflict—prizing up the platitudes of mutuality to confront the implacable face of power.[1]

From the first tentative explorations to the negotiation of a renewed grant, the reformers were continually preoccupied with the intractable rivalries which underlay the agenda of every meeting. Lacking the means to coerce agreement, they sought to turn their weakness to advantage, manipulating a commitment to change more enduring and widespread for being voluntary. But unless institutions could be persuaded to subordinate their policies to a master plan, the whole strategy of reform would be abortive. Without some concession of autonomy, no project could be organized at all; and only if the concessions were made in good faith could the project promote an integrated programme of innovation.

The reformers therefore had to subvert a traditional principle of American government, which holds that, since all power corrupts, it is wiser to corrupt many people somewhat than a few altogether, and contains the temptations of authority by an elaborate counter-action of many limited and often overlapping responsibilities. 'The major problem of American systems,' remarks the French sociologist Michael Crozier, 'concerns the strictness and arbitrariness of jurisdictional delimitations of competence ... This system has great advantages. It makes it possible to tap many kinds of human resources which would otherwise remain indifferent or hostile. Very diverse kinds of initiative flourish, and citizens participate at all levels of the decision-making machinery ... On the other hand, the detours imposed by the mere existence of all these different authorities, the difficulty of co-ordinating them and of harmonizing possibly conflicting decisions, call for an extremely complex strategy of procedures that is the focal point of American administrative disfunctions. Wilful individuals can block the intentions of whole communities for a long time; numerous routines develop around local positions of influence; the feeble are not protected so well against the strong; and generally, a large number of vicious circles will protect and reinforce local conservatism. The American system may also be viewed as a system that cannot correct its errors easily.'[2]

---

[1] This is not, of course, an account of any particular meeting, but a synthesis of impressions from many.

[2] Michael Crozier, *The Bureaucratic Phenomenon* (Chicago: The University of Chicago Press, 1964), pp. 235–6.

The reintegration of institutional functions was, then, not only a prerequisite of any other action, but a reform in its own right, designed to rescue cities from the jurisdictional conflicts which frustrated rational adaptation to changing needs. 'We wanted to provide a framework,' as Lloyd Ohlin, consultant to the President's Committee, explained, 'where we could concentrate a whole series of programmes together in the same area. This would show greater impact. We felt that the problem was not just one of providing new services here and there, but of trying to reach a new threshold by an integrated approach.'[3] Here both the President's Committee and the Foundation faced the problem of a community structure adequate to the purpose. Since they believed that city hall and the school system should assume the leading responsibility for an imaginative social policy, and yet were mostly poorly prepared to provide it, they wanted to create a structure which the mayor and public agencies would accept, but which could not be controlled by narrow political or bureaucratic interests. The Ford Foundation relied mostly on its promise of money to negotiate a workable structure. But the President's Committee was led, for a whole, into a more ambitious attempt to secure an intellectual commitment to reform through a highly articulated planning procedure.

In Search of a Structure

At first, the cities had responded to the opportunity with a clamour of competing applications from their public and private agencies. In its first year, therefore, the Committee's staff was much preoccupied with the promotion of structures able to organize a comprehensive, innovative plan of action. William Lawrence, as the Committee's consultant to some of the cities, was concerned to bring together city hall, the school system, and the private agencies in a coalition of leading institutions. This structure was not to be so broadly representative as to inhibit challenging innovation—though it might be served by a more inclusive advisory committee. On the other hand, it would have been futile to exclude such major institutions as the schools which, however conservative, necessarily limited innovation to what they would accept.

[3] In an interview with the authors.

But the Committee did not seek to impose a single organizational model. At the outset the Federal staff seem to have had four possibilities in mind, suitable to differing local circumstances, which set out a range of institutional and unofficial representation:

—a government elite, comprising key officials of state and city departments;

—a power elite, where non-government leadership—including the Negro community—joined key agency staff in a small board;

—a larger board, responsible to the mayor, representing voluntary agencies, senior professional staff of public and private services, and community leadership; or

—a coalition of public and voluntary agencies, such as the mayor's office, the welfare department, the juvenile courts, schools, voluntary foundations and welfare councils.

At this stage, the staff was preoccupied with marshalling established power, and the participation of those to be helped by the projects was overlooked.

By March 1962, it had become clear that any such structure would need time to establish itself as an effective instrument. The cities had not organized their social services according to any comprehensive, integrated plan, and could not immediately meet the Committee's criteria. The Committee would either have to revert to the funding of isolated projects, or provide resources for extensive preliminary planning and regrouping. To rescue the integrity of a comprehensive approach, it therefore decided to institute a policy of planning grants, to precede any funding for action. Here Mobilization for Youth, which provided a model for so much of the Committee's thinking, provided a precedent. It had been pressed by NIMH to undertake two years of preliminary planning, and the Committee had been influenced from the first by this example.

A comprehensive programme depended, then, on planning. But what did comprehensive mean—a programme which tackled all the causes of delinquency? which involved every institution? or which simply integrated every aspect of a particular service— as a youth employment programme might integrate counselling, training and placement? 'We act as if we really have something in the concept', a member of the Committee's staff confessed, 'but we really do not. I talk with glib generality about these ideas, but when pressed to pin down the meaning of them specifically, I'm at a loss.' But the Committee continued to assert that the concept was crucial, however vaguely defined. 'The point at which a programme would qualify as comprehensive must be related to the particular set of conditions and institutions in the given community. But always proposed action will be examined in the light of Federal policy of supporting these programmes which have identified many sources of the problem and have proposed to seek changes in many institutions.'[4]

By the end of the first year, the principles underlying the conception of a comprehensive programme had become more explicit. Firstly, delinquency arose as much from social frustration as personal maladjustment, and the demonstrations should concentrate upon changes in the social environment rather than in personality. Secondly, the planning organizations must, therefore, possess the authority and community influence to bring such changes about. Thirdly, successful planning depended upon advanced knowledge, and 'should utilize and integrate the theoretical and research skills of ... universities and research organizations'.[5] Finally, action must be integrated with evaluative research. One other principle was not officially endorsed until a year or two later, but became increasingly influential—the participation of the residents in the demonstration communities. This was seen both as a means of legitimizing the reformist aims of the programme, and of repairing the disintegration of community self help.

Taken together, these criteria placed the emphasis upon social reform through rational planning. The vested interests and conservative prejudices of bureaucracy were to be overborn by an alliance of academic experts with political innovators. Since the Committee lacked power to force change against the will of established community leadership, everything depended upon the persuasiveness of the planning process. If the analysis of the problems were only thorough enough, if the authority of specialists were sufficiently recognized, if the aims of the programme were

[4] 'Policy Guides to the Presentation of Proposals for Funding under Public Law 87-274', (September 1963), p. 3.
[5] 'The Federal Delinquency Programme. Objectives and Operations under the President's Committee on Juvenile Delinquency and Youth Crime and the Juvenile Delinquency and Youth Offences Control Act of 1961', (November 1962), p. 5.

given a truly rational justification, the forces of enlightened understanding might prevail. The President's Committee staff conceived this as a radical departure from conventional social service planning, where tradition and conformity to upper class interests were dominant. But to achieve it, the planning had to be protected against the contamination of expediency; it must precede action, defining its aims, and never concede the right of institutional interests to distort the logic of fact. 'We have to hold this line at all costs,' Lloyd Ohlin insisted, 'maintaining the integrity of planning by keeping action out of the planning phase. We couldn't get an effective co-ordination of effort unless we forced the planning processes, where they would be forced to dig into the facts of the situation and to justify their programme together.' Ohlin and some of the Committee's planning staff were perhaps more single-mindedly committed to this conception of policy than David Hackett himself, who had to bear in mind the political needs of the Kennedy administration: Hackett also employed political trouble-shooters to negotiate on a more political level when projects ran into difficulties. In the end, Lloyd Ohlin's line proved after all untenable, under pressures within both federal and local government. But in principle, to place goals before means, thought before action, fact before programme was compellingly rational.

The Foundation had taken a different line, stressing leadership and consensus rather than rational planning, but it was equally convinced of the need for a new organization to receive the grants, work out the programme, oversee their performance, evaluate their success and develop new ideas. Both funders rejected the existing public and voluntary planning structures. Welfare councils were accused of ignoring public agencies. 'They have laboured under an illusion of community inclusiveness that hampers their capacity to recognize and deal with problems in the public and political sphere.'[6] Publicly-sponsored Youth Commissions, as in Chicago, St. Louis, Los Angeles, New York, were passed over because of their traditional bias. The funders preferred a broadly representative structure, which would include both the major public and voluntary institutions, and established community leadership—

---

[6] Sandford Kravitz, 'The Implications of Governmental Participation in Health and Welfare Planning—Possibilities and Problems', (Speech to the New York State Association of Community Councils and Chests).

financial, political, religious and racial. Political government, the funders believed, must play a crucial role. Only government could command the resources to implement the demonstrations on a larger scale and co-ordinate functions. Social planning was becoming too important and costly to be left to the councils of voluntary agencies. Against the tradition that democracy was best protected where government was least intrusive, they put forward a new principle of political responsibility.

A variety of structures were created to adapt these criteria to local circumstances. In New Haven, Boston, Philadelphia, New York, Washington and North Carolina a quasi public agency was incorporated with an independent board. In Los Angeles a new district government was created under state legislation which authorized governmental bodies to develop formal relationships by a joint powers agreement. Oakland administered its project from within the city manager's office, under the guidance of an advisory committee. Cleveland created an incorporated structure comprised of city, county, schools and courts, and community representation. Chicago and St. Louis formed unincorporated planning bodies appointed by the Mayor, but administratively responsible respectively to the Youth Commission and the Welfare Department. Occasionally, the projects adopted different structures during different phases of operation. In St. Louis, for example, an unincorporated body had been created to work out plans, but they were implemented through a non-governmental, privately incorporated organization—the Human Development Corporation.

In Search of Commitment

To invite the participation of established power in a new coalition, and win their allegiance to the need for reform, the funders relied on the inducement of money. In the recipe of social change, seed money was the crucial ingredient. Seen as a proportion of the total budget of the institutions they were attempting to reform, the grants were meagre. But the scarcity of local funds made the promise of several million uncommitted dollars a worthwhile prize; and Foundation support also lent prestige. As Paul Ylvisaker remarked to a gathering of philanthropies: 'You have discovered, and I have discovered, that we are usually wanted not for our money but for what we supposedly represent: society's seal of approval; the hallmark of rationality; the symbol of personal disinterest.'[7] The process of bargaining for funds, the visibility of much-publicized grants, the encouragement of national sponsorship to insurgents within the established bureaucracies, all gave the seed money a power for change much greater than the services it could buy. It could show what needed to be done, and stimulate a new spirit in social policy committed to co-operative innovation. But it clearly could not meet the cost of reform. The Federal legislation called only for demonstrations, it was not conceived as a grant-in-aid programme. The Foundation had allotted only limited funds, and did not intend to continue its support indefinitely. Sustained reform must depend, in the end, upon an investment by the local community. The strategy needed to ensure that adequate local resources would be committed when the demonstration period ended.

Two interrelated principles were adopted to achieve this aim—matching funds and participation. The initial planning grants were to be matched by local contributions, and the programmes were to be jointly financed. The amount and the form of the local contribution was not specified, as the funders recognized the difficulties. They did not wish to insist rigidly on criteria which could defeat the project before it was launched. But they were equally convinced that it was crucial to bargain for local matching, because a contribution had the symbolic value of a pledge. Institutions would be eager to protect the capital they had invested, and make it yield dividends.

Participation meant sharing in decisions. Lay leaders representing community interests were to join in determining final policy, while professional agency staff were to be drawn into programme development. The more they were engaged in the formulation of policy, the more they would abide by the outcome, while conflicts of interest would be worked out in open discussion. At the same time, they were to design their programmes within an experimental framework, and submit political expediency to the test of scientific analysis. If the programmes succeeded, institutions would be impelled by the logic of empirical demonstration to establish them more widely.

If the reformers' theories were right, bureaucrats were con-

[7] Paul Ylvisaker, 'Private Philanthropy in America', (Speech to the National Council of Community Foundations, May 1964).

tinually distracted from their true function by pressures within their organization towards a rigid, protective conformity. By laying down a challenge and some funds to meet it, the funders hoped that mere conformity would be discredited. Now the agency executive with imaginative ideas would stand to win more for his organization than his conservative colleagues, and he would find his natural allies amongst innovators in other agencies. The strategy assumed, then, that if you offered enough money to excite attention, by the process of self-education, shared responsibility, and growing financial commitment you could reintegrate a divided bureaucracy and commit it to a demonstrably rational programme of innovation, procuring a new reasonableness at little cost. Institutions could hardly reject a programme of change which was at once based upon knowledge, supported by a prestigeful coalition and in which they themselves had participated fully.

The Frustration of Commitment

But this manipulation by the power of money suffered from the equivocal position of the funders. As we have discussed, their right to intervene depended on the tolerance of the communities with whom they were bargaining, and they could not press their criteria too forcefully. Though they held a power of veto in the negotiations, once the bargain was struck they had few sanctions to uphold its terms. And in practice, they were virtually committed even before the negotiations were concluded. The more prolonged the discussion, the more difficult it became to repudiate expectations. The promise became insensibly more specific and more embarrassing to withdraw, until the funders could no longer withhold their approval, though much had still to be resolved to their satisfaction. The Committee hoped that the preliminary planning, by sheer force of logic, would constrain the projects from betraying its intentions, while the Foundation reserved a large part of its grant in a development fund, to be released as acceptable programmes were put forward. But the first expedient presupposed a much tighter theory of reform than any social scientist could confidently provide, even without politicians and administrators looking over his shoulder. And the second merely postponed a part of the negotiations until later, when the Foundation's bargaining position would be largely undermined by the prior commitment of the funds.

Because of these weaknesses, the strategy succeeded most where it was needed least. When a community had already formed a coalition committed to reform, the added funds of the President's Committee and the Foundation could be used to best advantage and with least controversy. Where no integrated, progressive leadership stood ready to exploit the grants, the funders faced continual frustrations. They returned from their visits to the cities discouraged by unresolved jurisdictional wrangles, indifferent performance, delays and inconsistencies. And to much of this, they could only reluctantly acquiesce. The principle of matching funds, for instance, was relaxed until it lost its point as a community commitment. Matching in kind was accepted, so that cities were able to meet the requirement by offsetting a part of their current costs. The President's Committee was even driven to accept the Ford Foundation grant as local matching, while Ford reciprocally accepted Federal money. In the end, the cities seldom made any substantial contribution from their own resources. And after the projects were funded, innovative ideas tended to relapse into conventional practice, or were simply ignored; undertakings were not honoured; or programmes which should have reinforced each other were, for administrative convenience, implemented without co-ordination.

These frustrations arose because, so often, institutions would not in practice commit themselves either to the sacrifice of autonomy implied by the project's structure, or to its innovative spirit. The reformers supposed, for instance, that if the school system took part in the planning of changes in curriculum and teaching practice, it did so out of genuine interest. But its participation seems often to have been merely defensive. To have rejected a grant, and refused its co-operation in a progressive community venture, would have incited a public opinion already critical of school performance. But it did not at heart believe that shortcomings sprang from unimaginative administration and insensitive teaching; it preferred to lay the blame on inadequate resources. To the school system, the projects were a fund-raising resource, whose independent views on education practice were a tiresome impertinence, directing money into peripheral experiments.

The strategy of intervention depended upon the authority of

the project itself to sustain the ideals of reform. In principle, this authority was protected by the endorsement of community leadership, whose prior commitment was a condition of the grant. But since the momentum of negotiation forced the funders to release their funds before the conflicts had been truly settled, the project itself could become a non-man's-land over which more powerful interests fought for supremacy—an executive without a constituency of its own. Even where its authority was not so wholly demoralized, it might still find that agency participation had not, after all, educated officials into any enthusiasm for self-critical innovation.

The experience of PCCA has already shown how hard it could be to establish an effective authority behind the project, and how, in its absence, endemic conflicts inhibited a coherent programme. Not that the failure was necessarily final. Coalitions which seemed at the outset hopelessly divided amongst themselves, sometimes— as in Syracuse for instance—were once more pulled together. But though the breakdowns may be only stages in a long drawn out process of reintegration, they demonstrate the vulnerability of the funders' strategy.

Characteristically, conflicts arose—as in Philadelphia—over the balance of authority within the planning process, the appointment of a director, or the exclusion of powerful interests. Sometimes they frustrated the project from its inception, blocking any agreement acceptable to the funding agencies; more often, it distracted attention from the development of programmes, or insidiously undermined the project's ideal to save an appearance of community action. The experiences of Chicago, Cleveland and Los Angeles illustrate the breakdown of the strategy at each of these stages. In all these cities, the issue turned essentially on the control of the project, not the nature of its proposed reforms.

Chicago: Citizens Against Politicians

In Chicago, an elite group, formed at first as a neighbourhood advisory committee, was led to challenge the political control of the project. They were determined enough to force a stalemate, and the project was virtually abandoned at the end of the President's Committee's planning grant.

The district selected for the Chicago project adjoined the Gold

Coast, and most of the members of the local community advisory board were not drawn from the slum residents, but their wealthy neighbours. The bias of the Community Board was conservative, and its attitudes towards racial segregation divided. But it was united in its hostility to overweaning political control. 'Politicians don't want citizens to help themselves,' the Chairman protested, 'they want citizens to be beholden to them, especially at election time. People are taught to be beholden to precinct captains. Elected officials fear that citizen participation may grow in such a fashion so as to be competitive with their political interests.' Upon this fundamental issue, the project eventually foundered.

At the outset, the project's planners had not intended to involve citizen's groups as a challenge to the political establishment. The neighbourhood panels and the Community Board were to inform the Joint Youth Development Committee—to which the project was responsible—of their understanding and experience of the 'area's youth-related problems', suggest programmes, and 'develop attitudes of receptivity and support for the demonstration plan'. But as the planners became increasingly alienated from public agencies, they turned to the Community Board for more militant support.

The project's professional staff and its technical advisers had based their plans on school reforms. The schools were 'a key focal point of entrance into community life to affect fundamental change'. 'If the school's goals can be restructured beyond academic achievement to induce socialization, it then offers an effective basis for social change.' But the School Superintendent rejected this conception of community schools, resenting the implied interference of the community in the management of education. The Director of the Youth Welfare Commission, an influential member of the Youth Development Committee, also interpreted the encouragement of neighbourhood organization as a threat to the Mayor's control, especially as its leaders included political opponents. The project's planning director, caught between the President's Committee, which supported his conception, and the powerful public officials of Chicago who rejected it, turned to the Community Board.

The Chairman of the Community Board, misled—as he later complained—by the project's staff, overestimated the authority assigned it in the planning structure. But when the Youth Development Committee and the School Superintendent sought to curb it, the Board came together in a determined stand against an overbearing bureaucracy. 'There is some irony in the situation,' as a newspaper report remarked. 'YDC staff members tried hard to get the Near-North Lincoln Park residents interested and involved in planning the project. They succeeded so well that now the citizens have come to think of the project as "ours"—and want to keep it that way. They fear that recent action placing it under the control of a city agency, the Commission on Youth Welfare, means their voices will be cut down to a whisper, if not stilled altogether . . . The issue of how citizens should participate—as doers or as mere endorsers—goes to the very heart of the Federal delinquency control programme.'[8] 'This issue,' noted a President's Committee staff report, 'has become a wide open fight between the representatives of the City and the Community Board . . .'

The Board finally repudiated the city altogether. Armed with the sympathy of the local newspaper, and a community organization of its own, it went in search of funds for an independent project. The President's Committee, unable to accept either a city programme without citizen support, or a community programme divorced from public agencies, extricated itself from Chicago with a token grant.

The planning of the Chicago project was also inhibited by another characteristic source of breakdown. The competition for control may be disguised under an involved organizational structure which does not resolve rivalry. Charles Livermore, Director of the Commission on Youth Welfare, saw the project as falling under his jurisdiction. But the Mayor assigned responsibility to his deputy commissioner of City Planning, who was also co-chairman of the Commission. Though the Commission became the nucleus of a new, more comprehensive planning committee, its director was by-passed. Such a compromise between jurisdictional claims within City Hall was not really viable. When the deputy planning commissioner resigned, for personal reasons, Livermore was able to secure control. But by then, the professional planning staff was already committed to a conception which Livermore mistrusted, and the conflict with the local community began to evolve.

We have seen in Philadelphia how an elaborate system of task

[8] *Daily News*, January 16, 1964.

forces was devised to reconcile conflicting interests, and how the ambiguity of the compromise left the issues unresolved. The reformers' manipulation of the power structure was most often frustrated by the instability of the coalitions they engendered. The boards of the new agencies might be broadly representative, the planning procedures drawn out. But when crucial decisions were to be made, the forms of co-operation were too vaguely delineated, and too half-heartedly endorsed, to arbitrate an agreed solution. The basis of the project's authority might thus never be clearly established.

Cleveland: The Mayor Against the School System

In Cleveland, a struggle between City Hall and the School System eventually destroyed the tenuous consensus on which the project had been founded. Cleveland Action for Youth was constituted under a board on which—besides the Welfare Federation and the Juvenile Courts—the County Commissioners, City Government, and the Board of Education were equally represented. At the end of the planning period, the Board became locked in a conflict over the appointment of the director for the demonstration phase. The controversy had political overtones, pitting the Mayor, who stood for the Independent Democrats, against his natural enemies, the Democratic School Board and County Commissioners. The Chairman of the School Board was seriously thinking of running against the Mayor in the forthcoming elections on a white blacklash platform.

If the School System and the County Welfare Service were not to withdraw from the demonstration, a director acceptable to all parties had to be found. The Mayor supported the director of the project's planning phase, while the schools presed their own man. By way of compromise, the deputy superintendent of schools received the appointment, while the current director was relegated to his assistant. This division of responsibility between an experienced planner, who was politically unacceptable, and an inexperienced compromise candidate proved as unworkable in Cleveland as it had in Philadelphia. After much contention the associate director resigned.

The Mayor regarded the compromise as a personal defeat, and opposed it when a formal vote was taken by the Board. Local resident organizations protested that they had not been consulted in the appointment, and circulated a letter at the Board meeting expressing their sense of betrayal. Later, before a congressional sub-committee, they accused the Director of being anti-Negro. The project's staff were also out of sympathy with their new chief, who had no previous experience of the project, and owed his loyalty to the School System—he retained his title of Associate Superintendent, and saw the project essentially as a political asset in his bid to secure the Superintendent's post when it fell vacant. Thus even the School System, once it had won control, continued to mistrust the project, since it recognized the disunity of the director and his staff. It refused, for instance, to supply information about its pupils, for fear that members of the project staff, actively engaged in the Civil Rights Movement, would use the information against them. Its leadership was cautious and constraining, and did not encourage a vigorous, innovative programme. Finally, it threatened to abandon the project altogether, unless it diverted more of its resources to the schools' own, independent, compensatory education programme.

The compromise appointment failed, then, to satisfy any interest. It alienated the Mayor, the local residents and the project's staff, leaving control to a school system which sought only to exploit it for their own ends, and never trusted it. The Board which should have lent their authority to the new agency remained uncommitted, and acted chiefly to protect their own interests. A Federal report asked in despair: 'does anybody really feel loyalty to the project, as an entity, apart from its instrumental use in funding and in personal and institutional ambitions?'

Wherever community action bases its authority on a coalition of institutional power which is not already secure, the project seems to reach a point at which it can no longer contain the rivalries it has stimulated. At the outset, the proposal appeals to every interest frustrated by scarce resources and constricted function. But as the project takes shape, it begins to appear as a new jurisdiction in its own right, and not merely as a means to escape the limitations of the old. It threatens those who cannot control it, provoking rather than appeasing latent conflict. The project's original aims then become unrealizable. If no interest is strong enough to capture the project, the plans break down in stalemate; if one succeeds, it alienates the others. Either way, the project is no longer viable as an expression of community action. When such an outcome threatens, the project may try to save itself by abandoning its pretentions to integrated reform. So for instance, by conciliating powerful interests, the Los Angeles project survived and even grew. But it no longer fulfilled the ideals for which the President's Committee had supported it.

Los Angeles: All Against Co-ordination

The Los Angeles Youth Opportunities Board formally constituted a limited metropolitan government, without the power to tax, created under the Joint Powers agreement. It brought together five separate jurisdictions: City, County, their two School Systems, and the State. The City was represented by the Mayor's Executive Assistant, who served as chairman, the County by the Probation Department, and the State by the Employment Service. Of these, only the Mayor was eager for the Board to evolve a co-ordinated programme. Since the probation, health and welfare services of the city were controlled by County, not City government the Mayor hoped to secure a voice in the development of the city's social services through his representation on the Board. The Board might also be able to implement policies which his own City Council had rejected. The Council were generally conservative, and suspicious of Federal or foundation grants as potentially subversive. They had voted against a community renewal programme, and were unsympathetic to research on the city's social problems—'we don't need to have information on how many niggers are moving into my district'. The Mayor's Executive Assistant hoped to go round their opposition by funding, through the Youth Opportunities Board, a comprehensive data collection system. This store-house of knowledge was to provide the basis of an integrated policy, despite the Council's hostility to any systematic study of human needs.

The other jurisdictions represented on the Board were, however, indifferent to these larger issues. The County treated the Board as a personal interest of the County Supervisor, whose constituency lay in the city's Mexican American community. The County Administrator believed the Board was primarily to deal with school dropouts—which was not a concern of County government—and associated it so little with wider problems, that he made his own independent study of delinquency prevention. The County's official representative on the Board, the head of the Probation Department, was more interested, but out of sympathy with the broadly preventive approach to delinquency which the President's Committee had promoted. Finally, the County had earlier established a Community Services Department which, though it was not highly regarded, might be revived as an alternative to the Youth Opportunities Board whenever it was politically convenient.

The City School System had its own agenda of reform. It had already established a special unit for compensatory education, and had unsuccessfully approached the Ford Foundation for a grant under the great cities schools programme. It wanted to use the Board as a source of funds for its own plans, without interference. The County School System was less involved, since its role in the City was not administrative: it merely ensured that State educational standards were met.

If the other members of the Board were largely indifferent to its aims, the Employment Service was even hostile. It was solely concerned to protect its own jursidiction, and prevent a direct relationship between the Federal Government and the Board's employment project. Not that the Employment Service had made up its mind to start a special programme for disadvantaged youth itself. It did not want to become still further identified with jobs of low prestige; and since it was compensated by the Federal Government according to the number of placements, it might suffer financially by taking on difficult applicants who preoccupied the time of its staff for little reward. At the same time, it was unwilling to surrender any of its responsibilities.

In these circumstances, the parties to the coalition could not be expected to subordinate their interests to the new agency. Though the Mayor was seeking an intrument of co-ordinated planning, his hopes derived from the very factors which made them insubstantial—the weakness of his own position, and the limited jurisdiction of City Government. The project never, for instance, risked antagonizing the schools by putting forward educational proposals of its own. An administrator from the City School System was co-opted as the project's deputy director, and the programmes which evolved, while acceptable to the schools, were scarcely innovative. 'The City schools programme will be a problem,' observed the

President's Committee, more concerned with reform than political accommodation, 'because of the Deputy Director's lack of programme skills and his rigidity about change'. Its fears were confirmed: the programmes were later described in a Federal report as 'discrete and remedial services with little emphasis on classroom or curriculum revisions'.

As another concession to the self-interest of established power, the project placed its youth employment service in the Mexican American community of East Los Angeles, where the County Supervisor sought his votes, rather than in the Watts section—the project's target area. The Employment Service was not, however, reconciled, and once it became clear that the training programmes were not to be conducted under their auspices, as their programme, they raised a series of obstacles. The training programme could only be approved after the Employment Service had surveyed the labour market to prove 'a reasonable expectation of employment'. By a rigid interpretation of this criterion, the Employment Service brought the planning of any training programme to a standstill for several months, until the State Governor and Congressional leaders intervened. Even after half a year, the only course approved was for clerical training, which seems especially unsuited to a Spanish-speaking neighbourhood where half the young job-seekers could reportedly neither read nor write.[9]

By its conciliatory tactics, the Youth Opportunities Board escaped destructive conflicts, and reconciled jurisdictional rivalries more successfully than many projects. But, though it ran several programmes of its own, it was essentially a broker, channelling Federal funds to support institutional ambitions. The inadequacy of this bland evasion of more fundamental reform was tragically underlined, when in 1965 the project's target area was overrun by five days of rioting in which thirty-four people lost their lives.

The experience of Los Angeles, Cleveland, Chicago and Philadelphia suggests that community action projects, as the Ford Foundation and the President's Committee conceived them, could not after all master the jurisdictional rivalries which pervade city government in America. In practice, institutions remained stub-

[9] See Joseph L. Weinberg, 'Evaluation Study of Youth Training and Employment Project, East Los Angeles,' (U.S. Department of Labour, Office of Manpower, Automation and Training, August 1964, mimeographed).

bornly self-interested, and their formal endorsement of the project did not guarantee any commitment to its aims. The new agency merely provided another setting in which to deploy the struggle for power, and generated, not a self-sustaining process of reform, but a self-sustaining conflict over the control of reform. This was a profound and disturbing issue which no one was in a position to resolve, but which could not be ignored so long as the project remained true to its innovative spirit. Sooner or later, it found itself forced to choose between its principles and survival.

The evidence of less conflict-ridden projects does not contradict this disappointing conclusion. Community action seems nowhere to have brought into being a more unified power structure than had already been created. It could only extend the resources of an established coalition. In New Haven, Oregon, and some of the North Carolina communities, a concerted leadership already held effective control. In New Haven, for instance, before CPI came into being the Mayor had already established the Redevelopment Agency, and reinvigorated the School System, by appointing a progressive schoolboard under the chairmanship of Mitchell Sviridoff, later Director of CPI. Community Progress was thus one further component in an executive-centred coalition under the leadership of City Hall. CPI did not create a new consensus, its success was a reflexion of consensus which had earlier been achieved. When it ventured outside the Mayor's sphere of influence it succumbed to the same conflicts which the other cities encountered. Its legal programme, for instance, ran against the opposition of the Bar Association. Under this attack the members of the Bar co-opted on to CPI's planning committee retreated into neutrality, and the programme waited upon the reconstruction of a viable consensus of legal support.[14]

Similarly, if Oakland achieved more than Los Angeles, this was partly because the City Manager had previously brought county, city and schools together in the Associated Agencies, and partly because the settlement houses had been deeded to the city in the 1920's, establishing in the Recreation Department a tradition of co-operation between social work, recreation and the schools. Even so, the Oakland Interagency Project nearly foundered in conflict in its first two years, and recovered only by compromising

[10] The programme was finally launched without the Bar Association's endorsement.

the funder's intentions. The programmes remained encapsulated within their departments, with little relationship to each other, or even to their own administrative system; some were merely an extension of conventional practice; and the City Council never came to endorse the project's aims with any enthusiasm, or to vote any substantial financial support. In Boston, the project reflected the position of an independently-minded mayor, who was not beholden to a political machine, and sought a broader basis of power through the Redevelopment Authority and ABCD, whose professional administrators were influential in their own right, yet owed their opportunity to him. But faced with the ethnic and religious tensions of the city, the independence and power of the voluntary agencies, and the difficulty of reconciling social and physical planning, Mayor Collins had not yet established an underlying unity. He could protect ABCD from attack upon its legitimacy as an instrument of social planning, he could not ensure it the authority to realize its plans. ABCD therefore promised more than in its first few years it was able to fulfil—its reports a reasoned apology for continual frustrating delays.

As a means of reintegrating community leadership about a concerted programme, the strategy seems, then, to have proved ineffectual. The projects depended upon whatever unity had already been achieved, and could only nominally enlarge its scope. Where did the fundamental weakness of the strategy lie?

Were the grants too small? If the funding agencies had offered more, they would, of course, have given communities a greater incentive to meet the criteria of concerted action. But they would also have raised the stakes in the competition for control of the project's resources. As the experience of Philadelphia shows, once the poverty programme opened a prospect of much larger grants, the conflicts became sharper. Mayors everywhere began to assert the authority of city hall, and even state government was alerted to look to its interests. If the grey area or delinquency projects had been put forward on a larger scale, they might have been forced, from the first, to accommodate even more to institutional pressure. A marginal addition to the city's resources stood at least a chance of insinuating an influence for change, without intruding a challenge to bureaucratic authority too obvious to overlook.

Were the funding agencies too impatient? If they had guaranteed support for six years, instead of three or less, the projects could have worked gradually towards a viable place in the structure of community power, secure at least in their immediate future. But the funders would then have left themselves with even fewer sanctions to protect their intentions: as it was, they were virtually helpless to insist upon their principles, once they committed their support. They could reject a specific programme proposal, or return drafts for reconsideration, but they could not ensure that the spirit of their grant was honoured. If larger grants would have provoked more unmanageable conflicts, longer grants might only have enabled more projects to survive to confound their promoters' ideals, as they drifted into uncontroversial programmes subservient to institutional ambitions.

The crucial flaw seems to have lain, not in the financial inducement, but in the insistence on formal co-ordination as a prerequisite, rather than an outcome of changes in the power structure. Independent authorities were to commit themselves at the outset to the principles of a planning procedure which none of them could individually control. The plans were to evolve from an analysis which deliberately disregarded established boundaries of service, and none could know whether, if he were to allow the logic of the procedure to take its course, he would end up with greater responsibilities or less. In assuming that participation in an innovative agency would lead to a sacrifice of sectional interests, the strategy misjudged institutional motives. The project opened an opportunity to advance all manner of institutional claims: it did not follow that those who were disappointed would gracefully subordinate their ambitions to the plans which evolved. When it comes to the point, no one voluntarily surrenders power. Personal ambition apart, loyalty to the organization he serves makes any agency director honourably reluctant to compromise the responsibility entrusted to him. Where the pressure to co-operate is strong, he safeguards his autonomy by seeking to control the policy making, or if this fails, subverts its intentions when they threaten his own. These tacit reservations and manoeuvres for control undermine the co-operative endeavour.

The realignment of power and policy must, then, be achieved first, and this depends as much on new men as new ideas. No formal procedure for integrated planning can persuade independently powerful executives to abandon their prerogatives. Reform must await the opportunity to promote its own supporters to positions of authority. So, for instance, to realize his educational plans, Mayor Lee had first to get his own nominees on to the New Haven Board of Education, and they in turn had to wait for an opening to appoint a new assistant school superintendent.[11] The authority of cpi's programmes rested on ten years of patient recruitment, through which a group of like-minded reformers had been gradually insinuated into key positions.

The experience of community action suggests that there are no short cuts. A project board room is no magic circle, where long standing conflicts dissolve under the spell of planning. On the contrary, it introduces new hopes and fears, new ambiguities, which can harden resistance and complicate intrigue, embittering old rivalries. In any city where the foundations of a viable coalition have not yet been laid, innovation from within the power structure can only make ground by manipulating vulnerable institutions one by one, not by confronting all at once the issue of jurisdictional autonomy. This alternative strategy has, in fact, been supported by the Ford Foundation in Kansas City, and succeeded where a grey area project would probably have failed.

The Kansas City Association of Trusts and Foundations was formed in the 1940's to combine the resources of four local philanthropies, and redirect their grants from the relief of symptoms to a concern with the roots of social problems. Under its executive director, Homer Wadsworth, the Association built up a network of influence which did not depend on any formal structure. The office itself consisted only of the director, his assistant, and two secretaries. But through staff in agencies it supported, through its board members, through the committees on which Homer Wadsworth sat, the Association established its own constituency for reform.

Its strategy typically exploited the weakness of a potentially valuable institution. A charity hospital, for instance, is in difficulties—out of date, and short of funds. At this point, Wadsworth or one of the Association's supporters is likely to turn up on the Board of the failing agency, and suggest an evaluative study. The Association offers to meet the cost of the analysis, which—naturally enough—is contracted to Community Studies, a research organization founded and subsidized by the Association. The evaluative report sets out a sweeping plan of reorganization, which

---

[11] See Robert Dahl, *Who Governs?* (New Haven: Yale University Press, 1961), pp. 205–14.

rescues the institution from its financial embarrassment, replaces its administrative head, and adapts it to the Association's conception of the City's needs. Re-established on a new footing, the agency may become a corner stone of the Association's larger plans.

Perhaps the most ambitious of the Association's schemes concerned the University of Kansas City. Founded unluckily in 1933 by the Methodist Church, the University had become increasingly indebted, and its Board of Trustees were at a loss. Homer Wadsworth appeared on the Missouri Council of Higher Education, equipped with a plan prepared by Community Studies. The University was to become a campus of the University of Missouri system, while the present Trustees were to remain as a fund raising body, with the task of finding one and a half million dollars every two years for faculty salaries and improvements. The plan was approved, and the Trustees have already raised over a million dollars, agreed to a higher salary for a new chancellor, and encouraged new departments. The University is growing in both size and quality, and appeals no less to local pride for being now a branch of the state system. At the same time, it has been drawn into the Association's plans for a new medical complex to be built on one hundred acres cleared under urban renewal. The Association's schemes have been, at times, as comprehensive as any grey area project's programmes: and just because it must manipulate without any formal power, the outcome seems often more radically integrative.

In 1961, encouraged by a grant of one and a quarter million from the Ford Foundation, the Association began to develop a series of experimental demonstrations in the public schools—over whose Board Wadsworth presided. These programmes have been very similar to the grey area projects—work-study for likely dropouts, tutorials by college students, special scholarships, visiting teachers, nursery schools, curriculum changes, upgraded classes—but depended far more on the school budget and local financing. The Association also helped to promote a reorganization of vocational education, and, on a small scale, ways of finding jobs for high school dropouts.

As a means to institutional change, the Association has engineered reforms as innovative as any grey area project. As a means to overcome the handicaps of poverty, its educational programmes have been as imaginative. As a stimulus to community concern, it has recruited more local resources in support of innovation. Yet it has never sought to institutionalize a consensus of community leadership, nor to incorporate its reforming spirit in an operating agency.[12]

The Association's experience in Kansas City does not prove that its strategy would work elsewhere, or with another executive. But it does suggest that—in a city which has traditionally lost most of its ablest talent, where leadership has often been lethargic, and segregationist attitudes still covertly widespread—the aims of the grey area projects may be better realized by discrete political opportunism, than by attempting to induce a coalescence of power. Such a strategy does not create leadership, but unobtrusively supplies it, manipulating the existing structure. It demands no prior commitment, and threatens no jurisdiction. It does not predetermine the targets of reform, or theorize its plans, but exploits its chances. This flexibility makes it less vulnerable, more resilient under attack, and surer of its goals.

But such a strategy takes time, and though the Ford Foundation could perhaps afford to work gradually, here and there, through agencies like the Kansas City Association, the President's Committee staff had to seize the moment of their political opportunity. By insisting on the creation of an instrument of comprehensive planning, they hoped to force the growth of a will to use it. Where, as in New Haven, a coalition of leadership was ready to absorb it, the new organization had scope to deploy its professional talent. But wherever the rivalries within the power structure had not been resolved, the intrusion of fresh resources to exploit only aggravated the conflicts. It seems then that very different strategies may be appropriate to different communities, and the search for a leverage for change must adapt very sensitively to time and place, without putting its trust in any one prescription.

Community action which rests upon the combined authority of elected officials and established institutions may have to be content to limit its scope to those cities whose power has already coalesced, or to that part of the power structure which had been brought

---

[12] When Kansas City came to put together a proposal to the Office of Economic Opportunity for a poverty programme, this became a liability. The preparation of the proposal was bogged down in long-drawn-out negotiations, which suggests that the Association's work had ingeniously circumvented, but not resolved the city's bureaucratic rivalries. The requirements of the poverty programme may make its position altogether more difficult.

under unified leadership. If neither of these alternatives is acceptable, it must turn to a less structured opportunism, patiently infiltrating positions of leadership. If this, too, cannot satisfy the urgent idealism of reform, community action must abandon the security of bureaucratic endorsement, and seek a different kind of authority to legitimize its intervention.

VII

THE VOICE OF
THE PEOPLE

A POLICY of institutional reform clearly could not depend
for its mandate only on the support of the institutions
to be reformed, however powerful their influence. Mayors,
school superintendents, public-spirited bankers, representatives of
organized labour, pastors of churches, were not the accredited
spokesmen of the poor. They stood rather for that established
power whose rivalries and mutual accommodations had always
vitiated the good faith of the concern they expressed. Some
countervailing authority was needed to protect the programmes
against the encroachment of institutional self-interest upon
genuine service.

Both the Ford Foundation and the President's Committee
had already devised safeguards against the abuse of their aims—
through the criteria by which grants were approved, control of
development funds, the requirement of rigorous preliminary
planning. But these sanctions, which relied on money and
expertise, appealed to principles of rationality rather than democracy, and could be challenged as intellectually or politically
presumptuous. The reformers believed that the people of the
slums, too, must have a voice in any programme of their behalf.
The grey area projects were to 'plan with people, not for people',
and the President's Committee insisted upon 'evidence that
individuals and organizations in the target community recognize
in the project a legitimate force for change. Part of such evidence
will be their involvement in the project's planning process'.[1]
Thus the programmes were not only to be dispassionately rational,
and endorsed by community leaders, but also an authentic expression of the wishes of the programme's constituents.

[1] 'Policy Guides to the Presentation of Proposals for Funding under Public Law
87–274', (September 1963).

To draw the institutions of a community together in a concerted plan of action, without compromising intellectual integrity, was arduous enough. But this further principle compounded the difficulties. The participation of the residents in the neighbourhoods to be served was likely to interfere as much with the rational priorities of the funding agencies, as with the more political interests of institutions. The reformers believed that programmes had failed in the past for lack of co-ordination, consistent effort, and thorough analysis of the nature of the problems. Their own thinking was intellectually sophisticated and disinterestedly experimental. The leaderless, ill-educated, dispirited people of a city slum, if they could find their voice, would hardly speak to the brief of a nationally-minded elite of university professors and foundation executives. Research, planning, co-ordination, must seem remote answers to a rat-infested tenement, the inquisitorial harassment of a welfare inspector, debts and the weary futility of killing time on the streets. Yet, at least in principle, the reformers were ready to jeopardize their carefully laid strategy for the sake of this grass-roots participation.

Perhaps only in America would this have seemed so self-evidently right. The funders' mistrust of their own authority as an intellectual elite, and faith in the power of spontaneous, local democracy, reflect a peculiarly American tradition. 'No sooner do you set foot upon American ground than you are stunned by a kind of tumult,' observed de Tocqueville, over a century ago, 'a confused clamour is heard on every side, and a thousand stimultaneous voices demand the satisfaction of their social wants. Everything is in motion around you; here the people of one quarter of the town are met to decide upon the building of a church; there the election of a representative is going on; a little farther, the delegates of a district are hastening to the town in order to consult upon some local improvements; in another place, the labourers of a village quit their plows to deliberate upon the project of a road or a public school . . . The great political agitation of American legislative bodies . . . is a mere episode, or a sort of continuation, of that universal movement which originates in the lowest classes of the people and extends successively to all ranks of society.'[2] De Tocqueville noted both

[2] Alexis de Tocqueville, *Democracy in America* (New York: Vintage Books, 1945), p. 259.

the inefficiency and inconsistency of all this democratic bustle—
'gross instances of social indifference and neglect are to be met
with; and from time to time disgraceful blemishes are seen, in
complete contrast with the surrounding civilization'.[3] But he
also recognized its overriding strength. Reflecting on the rival
merits of democracy and enlightened despotism, he touches upon
the abiding dilemma of the elite reformer in American society.
'When the opponents of democracy assert that a single man
performs what he undertakes better than the government of all,
it appears to me that they are right,' he admitted. 'The government
of an individual, supposing an equality of knowledge on either
side, is more consistent, more persevering, more uniform, and
more accurate in details than that of a multitude, and it selects
with more discrimination the men whom it employs . . . Democratic liberty is far from accomplishing all its projects with the
skill of an adroit despotism. It frequently abandons them before
they have borne their fruits, or risks them when the consequences
may be dangerous; but in the end it produces more than any
absolute government; if it does fewer things well, it does a
greater number of things. Under its sway the grandeur is not
in what the public administration does, but what is done without
it or outside of it. Democracy does not give people the most
skilful government, but it produces what the ablest governments
are frequently unable to create: namely, an all-pervading and
restless activity, a super-abundant force, and an energy which is
inseparable from it and which may, however unfavourable circumstances may be, produce wonders.'[4]

The reformers in the Foundation and the President's Committee were attacking just those features of American life which
de Tocqueville saw as the liabilities of a democratic creed—the
gross social neglect, inconsequential policies, uncoordinated
effort, carelessness of skilled application—and yet they were
deeply committed to it. To Paul Ylvisaker the grandeur was
indeed not in the public administration—nor in any philanthropic
administration—but in what was done without it or outside of it.
The strategy of reform was somehow to accommodate both the
analytic precision of a carefully staged experiment, and the
extension to its furthest limit of democratic participation. Neither,

[3] *Ibid.*, pp. 94–5.
[4] *Ibid.*, pp. 261–2.

without the other, could have proved the fundamental assumption upon which the strategy was based: that a talented elite, with enough authority to deploy seed money, could generate a self-sustaining, democratic impulse towards reform.

But how was the principle of citizen participation to be inter-preted in practice? Who truly represented the people of the neighbourhood to be served by the programmes—the ward leaders of the political parties, civil rights groups, pastors, settlement houses? Anyone who enjoyed an identifiable status was already, for that very reason, partly assimilated to middle-class American society. Anyone who could hold his own in a committee of public officials, business leaders, the mayor and project directors, was unlikely to be still poor and uneducated. 'Most efforts to organize lower class people attract individuals on their way up the social-class ladder,' observed the prospectus for Mobilization for Youth. 'Persons who are relatively responsible about participation, articulate, and successful at managing organizational "forms" are identified as lower-class leaders, rather than those who actually reflect the values of lower-class groups.' Mobilization proposed to encourage instead more truly indigenous leaders. But this alternative has paradoxical implications, as the Assistant Secretary of Labour rather unkindly pointed out to a conference on poverty: 'Note what is to be remedied: instead of getting hold of local people who are "relatively responsible about participation, articulate, and successful at managing organizational 'forms' ", Mobilization for Youth is going to get hold of a lower level of true and genuine leaders who are—what?—inarticulate, irresponsible, and relatively unsuccessful? I am sorry, but I suspect that proposition. I was raised on the West Side of New York, and I must report that those are not the principles on which Tammany Hall, the International Longshoremen's Association, or the New York Yankees recruited indigenous leadership.'[5]

The formal organization through which the projects authorized their decisions inevitably precluded the effective participation of unsophisticated people. Faced with the inherent contradiction of vesting a joint authority of leadership in those you perceive as leaderless and alienated, the project boards do not, in fact, seem

[5] Address by Daniel Patrick Moynihan to the Conference on Poverty in America, Berkeley, California, February 26-28, 1965.

to have included a single poor man or woman. Only the Office of Economic Opportunity, in the more recent projects promoted under the poverty programme, has seriously considered the formal representation of the poor. It proposes that several board members—even a majority—might be directly elected by the people of the neighbourhoods served.[6] But the difficulty remains that if these representatives can make their influence effective in so formal a setting, they may lose their understanding with their constituents. By achieving influence itself, such a representative of the poor loses many of the characteristics which identify him as one with those he represents.

If it was impracticable to invest the beneficiaries of the programme with the same kind of authority as a board of directors, the projects looked then for other means of keeping the board and its executive responsive to the demands of those it served. It was assumed that in any neighbourhood, however disrupted and demoralized, potential leaders could be found to articulate needs, and organize the expression of local feeling. But the projects would themselves have to identify these leaders, and encourage them to rouse their neighbours to make their influence felt. Participation presupposed some programme of community organization, by which the process of democratic consultation could extend its reach.

It proved, however, very difficult to establish and sustain an unambiguous purpose for community organization. It could mean the polite formality of block committees, deliberating by Roberts' rules of order: or the clamour of protest marches on city hall, rubbing raw the sores of discontent. The intention was to distribute power—to extend to the people of the neighbourhoods a measure of control over the projects which served them. But since they were not organized to assume such power, control remained with the project staff, as a responsibility to foster whatever organization seemed appropriate. And as the devolution of authority was postponed, more paternalistic aims of community organization began to intrude: to promote self-help and social control through social cohesion, to facilitate the assimilation of middle-class values, to disseminate understanding of project policy. At the same time, in reaction to this insidious manipulation, organiza-

---

[6] OEO's policy is discussed more fully in Chapter IX.

tion might turn towards a more militant, but equally manipulative strategy of protest against established institutions.

Community organization could, then, be interpreted with a very different emphasis, according to the standpoint of the organizer. It could be used to encourage the residents of a neighbourhood to come to terms with the demands of a wider society, or conversely to force the institutions of that society to adapt more sympathetically to the special needs of a neighbourhood. Or it could be seen rather as a form of therapy, to treat apathy and social disintegration. And it might take an individual bias—promoting the social mobility of potential leaders, championing cases of personal injustice—or a communal bias more concerned with the neighbourhood as a mutually supportive community. To a redevelopment administrator like Edward Logue, community organization meant, essentially, a way of persuading a neighbourhood to understand and accept a redevelopment programme, and contribute constructively to it. To the settlement houses, it meant an education in the conventions of democratic participation, as middle-class society practiced them, more for its own sake than for any particular purpose. To the social theorist, it meant the reintegration of those informal community functions which in the past had mediated the assimilation of urban newcomers. To the reformers, it meant above all, a new source of power to reinforce their pressure for institutional change.

Neither the President's Committee nor the Ford Foundation successfully clarified these issues. In 1960, in a discussion paper for the Foundation,[7] Lloyd Ohlin explored the different aspects of community organization, and saw that the sponsorship of any movement would largely determine its course. But he did not resolve the problem. 'It seems to be a common experience that whenever existing organizations are used to sponsor indigenous social movements, the primary interests of the sponsoring organization tend to affect the selection of members, the form of organization, the specification of objectives, and determination and control of the implementing activities. This apparently universal tendency raises a very basic issue, "What types of conditions can be developed so that restraints on the growth of new

[7] Lloyd Ohlin, 'Issues in the Development of Indigenous Social Movements Among Residents of Deprived Urban Areas', (October 1960, mimeographed), p. 17.

indigenous movements are minimized and the articulation of indigenous interests, rather than those of the sponsoring organization, are maximized?" . . . The solution is not easy to see.' The Foundation was sure that the settlement house tradition of community organization would not serve its purpose; nor was it prepared to support the manipulation of neighbourhood opinion in the interests of urban renewal. But it was much less sure how the projects, with their commitment to institutional co-operation, were themselves at the same time to encourage an independent challenge to the autonomy of institutional decisions. Nor was it always clear whether the influence of community movements upon institutions, or upon the community itself, was uppermost in the reformers' minds. Both Lloyd Ohlin and Leonard Cottrell, Chairman of the technical review panel, were preoccupied with the demoralizing effect of impotence and frustration: any form of community action which restored a sense of competence to handle the demands of city life would promote the aims of the projects, whether or not it also induced institutions to change their practices. Speaking at appropriations hearings in 1960, Cottrell advocated community organization as a means of reintegrating the disrupted culture of migrants, and so reviving their confidence to regulate the behaviour of their children. When the newcomers arrived in the city 'meat-grinding begins—their cultures, their churches, their standards and their norms—the authority of the parents deteriorates and you get a community of people who have lost the competence to act in a community problem . . . the way to attack it would be to restore the community's confidence to act and to control its children and to support one another in maintaining some kind of standards . . . whenever you could do that effectively you would lower the rate of delinquency'.[8] Four years later he predicted 'A concept of the competent community will emerge that will increasingly define a major objective of such social welfare efforts as the control and prevention of delinquency.'[9] Thus the justification for promoting indigenous movements seemed to equivocate between an argument that social reform depended upon the self-

[8] Hearings before the Sub-Committee of the Committee on Appropriations, House of Representatives, 86th Congress, and Session 1960, pp. 93–6.
[9] Leonard Cottrell, 'Social Planning, the Competent Community and Mental Health', in *Urban America and the Planning of Mental Health Services*, Vol. V, Symposium No. 10, (November 1964).

The Voice of the People

assertion of the disadvantaged, and a concept of community rehabilitation through concerted action.

The projects were, then, committed by the funding agencies to a democratic ideal of citizen participation, but were left with little guidance as to the form it should take, or even its essential purpose. They were bound to be held responsible for the consequencies of any movement they stimulated, yet they were not, in principle, to defeat their own democratic idealism by controlling the direction which the movement chose. How the projects would come out, if the people of the neighbourhood were drawn into conflict with civic leadership, remained obscure. Pledged to both sides, they could only hope to be allowed a benevolent neutrality. In practice, the three projects which had, by 1964, attempted some form of community organization, each experienced a serious crisis, and each resolved it differently. CPI accepted the limitations of its loyalty to the Mayor of New Haven; Mobilization for Youth was drawn into alignment with the people against institutions; and ABCD largely withdrew from the risks of neighbourhood movements.[10]

The crisis in New Haven arose out of a programme of legal aid, rather than neighbourhood organization itself: but legal protection, broadly interpreted, merges with the ideals of democratic participation. Both seek to assert the rights of the least privileged against richer, more powerful, and better organized interests. Court actions may serve as demonstrations of protest, just as marches, boycotts, or petitions may serve as an alternative to legal redress. The law lends itself impartially to manipulation by militant radicals or repressive conservatives. The interpretation of a legal service in a poor neighbourhood is therefore controversial, and in New Haven it brought CPI to near disaster.

In its original programme, CPI proposed that 'a plan be worked out, with the co-operation of the New Haven County Bar Association, to provide legal assistance at the community schools. Lawyers would look at all legal problems of the family, would provide legal advice on simple matters, and would make referals on more complex cases'. The intention was certainly not radical,

[10] The Oakland Inter-Agency Project, perhaps because it was organized within city government, never seriously experimented with citizen participation, though its programmes included support for conventional community organization through the Urban League and the Council of Social Planning. The other projects are too recently funded to have had much experience of action by the end of 1964.

171

and the lawyer's task intended to be merely advisory. One of the two lawyers hired was Jean Cahn, a young Negro graduate of Swarthmore, married to a Yale law student. Both the Cahns were deeply committed to the cause of civil rights, and to their sense of a lawyer's responsibility in that struggle. From the outset, she interpreted the legal adviser's role more positively than Mitchell Sviridoff, Director of CPI, thought was prudent, given CPI's dependence on the Mayor, and the Mayor's dependence on a broad consensus of support within the City. She also felt that, as a lawyer, her first duty was to the furtherance of justice, not the interests of her employer. The issue came to a head over a case, of all cases most emotionally charged: in February 1963, three young Negroes were accused of brutally assaulting and raping a white nurse.

Two of the accused pleaded guilty. The third eventually pleaded innocent, and through his mother, who consulted her, Jean Cahn became increasingly concerned in his defence. It seemed to her that the Public Defender, to whom the case had been assigned, was inexperienced and out of sympathy with his client, and evidence which might have aided the defence was being ignored. In this, she was supported by two other lawyers—a Yale consultant to the Ford Foundation, and the Mayor's Human Relations Assistant. Together they organized Yale students to gather witnesses to the victim's character, to establish a case that she had consented. They harassed the Public Defender, more and more convinced that New Haven was proving itself at heart as prejudiced as any Southern community, and that the proceedings were a travesty of justice. Meanwhile, Mitchell Sviridoff became alarmed at the risks to CPI in Jean Cahn's involvement, and insisted she withdraw. He also strongly discouraged his staff from attending the meetings in the Negro community, where the question of injustice was being raised with growing concern. Jean Cahn refused and three of his staff persisted. Principle would not yield to prudence.

But Sviridoff was equally convinced that he should not jeopardize the future of CPI for a doubtful cause. The Mayor was being harassed by anonymous letters and abusive telephone calls. If this public outrage found its target in CPI, his whole programme was in danger. Summoned to New York, he rejected Paul Ylvisaker's urging to identify CPI with the cause of justice for the poor, and support Jean Cahn's stand. He was ready to resign, rather than commit what he sensed would be a fatal political mistake. And CPI never did become publicly associated with the defence. 'The only good thing about it all,' remarked Mayor Lee in retrospect, 'is that we kept the Ford Foundation and CPI out of it—at some cost to my own hide.'

The three accused were all finally convicted, and sentenced to fifteen years imprisonment—sentences which were upheld on review. Even if justice had not always been seen to be done, the convictions were probably inevitable, and it appeared afterwards that there was little sympathy in the Negro community for the three men. But miscarriage of justice was not the crucial issue. A young Negro, faced with a charge where racial prejudice was most likely to contaminate a fair hearing, had sought help from CPI, and CPI had refused to identify itself publicly with his defence. Though its neighbourhood lawyers had not been intended to provide more than advice, Jean Cahn's insistence on a lawyer's overriding duty to his client precipitated an issue which could not then be evaded by pleading the programme's limited aims. Could CPI at once champion the disadvantaged, in the face of public outrage and the embarrassment of its political allies, and maintain the coalition of institutional support on which its programmes depended? Mitchell Sviridoff believed not. Forced to choose, he sacrificed quixotic idealism to the practical politics of effective reform. Jean Cahn resigned, and the legal programme was temporarily laid aside.

In an influential paper, written about a year after she had left New Haven, Jean and Edgar Cahn set out their criticism of the CPI strategy. 'The War on Poverty: a Civilian Perspective' develops the military analogy to suggest that agencies like CPI will seek, like an army in time of war, to monopolize initiative. Resources are mobilized in a totalitarian organization that buys off or intimidates independent criticism: 'The most disturbing defect of CPI, viewed as a military service operation, lies in its record of ennervating existing leadership, failing to develop potential leadership, undercutting incipient protest, and manipulating local organizations so that they become mere instruments of the comprehensive strategy . . . Criticism can be stilled or ignored by token responsiveness and publicity. A half-dozen rehabilitated persons make good photographs, good news stories, and good research material. Local leaders who feel that the programme is doing too little too slowly can be silenced, undermined, discredited—or hired. And in such neighbourhoods, the leadership is unlikely to be so rich or so secure as to withstand the temptation of an honorary appointment or a job with prestige and a salary of several thousand dollars. Should a potentially powerful neighbourhood organization prove bothersome, it can be rendered ineffectual by absorption, by being given official status, or by setting up a rival dummy organization. Finally, something approaching a show of support and endorsement can be compelled by communicating to the target population the probability of temporary curtailment of programme operations, rent increases in public housing, welfare crack-downs and a variety of other consequences . . . Embarrassing revelations about the programme's deficiencies are not likely to be welcome, particularly around election time. To the extent that deficiencies in existing programmes or questionable practices by governmental and private authorities are uncovered, the alliance upon which the programme is founded is threatened. Thus, not just the Mayor but the employment service, the retraining programmes, the police, the recreation department and school officials all may be anxious that their colleagues not be criticized for fear that such criticism will in turn reflect on them, resulting in investigation of their performance . . . the reputation of the whole programme, its future, and its potential for good should not be jeopardized simply because defects show up and because dissatisfaction is engendered by certain "minor" and "temporary" deficiencies. The individual and his complaint, the neighbourhood and its grievances must be sacrificed to the greater good.'

At the same time, the prestige of the organization takes precedence over the interests of those it was created to help. Impressive manoeuvres are undertaken with the least possible risk. 'Projects initially undertaken must yield quick, dramatic results with a minimum of controversy and investment of resources. The job retraining programme may thus utilize an elaborate screening process to select as its first crops of trainees the most promising and able applicants, having the highest qualifications in terms of skill, motivation, acculturation and past experience . . . Risk avoidance is, at least in the initial stages of the programme, likely to play a particularly important role. The definition of controversy, moreover, is likely to grow to embrace any situation which might possibly antagonize any interest in the community, including such activity as the vindication of legal rights, which are by definition a legitimate form of controversy . . . In sum, the decision as to whether or not any single demand or criticism is heeded will depend upon . . . the institutional costs of granting assistance, such as inconvenience, internal friction, political danger, expenditure of staff, alienation of allies, and estrangement of potential allies. Then the individual's plight and ability to mobilize community criticism will be reckoned and weighed against the potentially vast institutional repercussions which might flow from rendering assistance. And so, "enterprises of great pith and moment . . . lose the name of action".[11]

The analysis does not distinguish clearly between the behaviour of CPI, and a speculative projection of the actions such an agency might be expected to follow. Carried away by the logic of their analogy, the Cahns seem to overstate their case, implying accusations for which they offer no evidence. But their argument sets out essentially the same theory of bureaucratic introversion by which the grey area projects themselves understood the incapacity of other institutions. As CPI strove to establish itself, self-protection and internal cohesion threatened to displace its original aims. The Cahns were not alone in questioning the way in which it had, by its energy and self-confidence, pre-empted the initiative in social reform. So able an instrument of executive authority seemed by its nature unsympathetic to any independent expression of community demands. How long, then, would it remain responsive to those demands, in the face of other, more articulate claims?

In a semi-official reply to the Cahn's paper, a member of CPI's staff challenged—besides their specific criticisms—the whole philosophy of citizen participation. As a 'partisan defender of the "faith" of Community Progress', he claimed that the search for such participation rested on a misunderstanding of the realities of leadership in a complex society:

There is a dangerous tendency for middle-class persons to over-estimate the potentiality for leadership in the poverty group. In

[11] Edgar S. and Jean C. Cahn, 'The War on Poverty: a Civilian Perspective', *Yale Law Journal*, Vol. 73, No. 8, (July 1964).

areas of deep poverty, such as public housing projects, the potential for leadership is minimal . . . But there is also involved here, what I call the 'Democratic Fallacy'. This fallacy assumes that every man is motivated to participate in political activity. I would, on the contrary, maintain that there is a hierarchy of motives, in which other needs usually precede the need for political participation . . . there can be an exaggerated 'democratic' bias which lies behind the concern for participation in planning by the poor. The Founders of the American Republic did not suffer from that bias; they believed that 'pure democracy' was an impossibility, especially in a country of this size, and they further believed in the wisdom of representation. So too, in a complex urban context (given the limitations of full participation by any citizen—not only the poor), I personally do not see any substitute for the planner.

At the same time, the writer recognized that CPI could not represent the interests of the poor, without also being sensitive to the counter-pressures. 'In essence, Community Progress Inc. is a *public* programme with, for the most part, *public* funds to spend on a programme to relieve poverty. The programme depends upon the co-operation of *public* officials . . . It is not the Civil Rights Movement, and to confuse the two, or to judge one another by a common standard, would be disservice to both. Since Community Progress Inc. must be responsive to the whole community, it must balance community claims.'[12]

This defence alligns CPI unequivocally with the enlightened self-interest of established power. So frank a scepticism towards grass-roots democracy made the New Haven project, for all its accomplishments, widely mistrusted as a model of community action. Yet given its political commitments, and the nature of effective action in a highly structured society, Mitchell Sviridoff may well have followed the only practicable policy. The fate of Mobilization for Youth suggests what might have happened if he had chosen otherwise.

The Mobilization for Youth conception of community organization evolved, over five years, from a conformist tradition to a radical challenge. In its original request to the National Institute of Mental Health, the Henry Street settlement house had proposed

[12] Richard Oliver Brooks, in an open letter to Mr. James O. Freedman, circulated by CPI, July 1964.

a programme of community organization based upon the settlement houses which, under the guidance of elite leadership, would help people to help each other. But this approach did not survive the two years of planning imposed by NIMH. The planning committee of Mobilization, dominated by the thinking of Richard Cloward and Lloyd Ohlin, argued that the settlement houses were unsuitable sponsors for any organization of the poor. The style of their council (The Lower East Side Neighbourhood Association) was too formal, and would intimidate the unsophisticated. It was, besides, largely controlled by middle-class white leaders, who might resent the intrusion of newcomers upon their power. The controversy reached the point where the planners threatened to resign, rather than see their community organization programme left in the Neighbourhood Association's hands. A compromise was finally agreed, whereby the Association was given some money for its more middle-class approach, while Mobilization pursued another strategy.

At this time, Mobilization was more concerned with encouraging and training genuine local leaders, than with defining issues. It proposed—like CPI—to recruit these leaders as full or part-time workers in its programme, but unlike CPI left them free to take part in community affairs as independent citizens. In this way, it hoped to promote organization, without over-influencing the organization's aims. But in the event, the stimulation of leadership, and the issues about which leadership might develop proved inseparable, and Mobilization was driven to take a political initiative. Organization needed a purpose, and Mobilization began to take up causes which might be served by collective action, as they appeared from the problems which people brought to the agency. It hired the team for a voter registration drive, organized a local contingent of the March on Washington, encouraged rent strikes, and—as we have seen—supported Mobilization of Mothers in their protest against a local school principal. At the same time, it developed a legal aid programme, through which the people of the Lower East Side could defend more effectively their rights—challenging, for instance, the legality of adverse decisions of the State Welfare Department.

Mobilization never committed itself unambiguously to the issues it had helped to raise through its community organization programme. Pressure from militant neighbourhood groups might help promote institutional changes in which Mobilization itself was interested, but the support of protest was also justified on more neutral grounds. 'We believe that the personal sense of powerlessness felt by low income people is a major cause of their isolation and apathy,' explained George Brager, the programme director. '. . . To encourage education and social learnings, therefore, it is necessary to decrease the sense of powerlessness. To achieve this end requires the organization of isolated individuals and unaffiliated groups to take action. It means that MFY must give active assistance to Lower East Side residents who feel, justified or otherwise, that their rights are being violated.'[13] The phrase 'justified or otherwise' seems to disclaim Mobilization's ultimate responsibility for the actions taken—and in principle, unless the sponsors of community organization surrender control of the organization they promote, they defeat their own purpose.

Unfortunately, the targets of popular protest seldom discriminate between the sponsor and the actions taken by the movements he encourages. As George Brager admitted, 'This programmatic direction has caused strain in MFY's relations with important persons and institutions.' The campaign of a small group of Puerto Rican mothers against a school principal provoked, as we saw, a counter-attack which went far beyond the immediate issue to impugn the motives of Mobilization itself. As a whole, Mobilization was not a militant radical organization, but an experimental application of a theoretical analysis of the roots of delinquency. It never attached crucial importance to its programme of militant self-assertion, which was small scale and doubtfully effective. More concerned with economic than political deprivation, it invested most of its resources in youth employment and training. Yet Mobilization became the victim of a sustained and powerful prosecution which all but destroyed it, and which would probably never have arisen, if important persons had not been ruffled by its encouragement of protest.

In August of 1964, the *New York Daily News* published a story containing three principal charges against Mobilization for Youth—that the agency employed a large number of Communist sympathizers; that there had been serious financial irregularities; and that Mobilization had helped to inspire the Harlem riots earlier in the summer. The charges were at once

[13] Director's First Annual Report to the Staff, October 1963.

reported by the other New York papers, and were soon under official investigation by a bewildering harassment of public scrutineers. The City, the State, the FBI, the National Institute of Mental Health, even Mobilization itself in self-defence, anxiously pulled the agency apart in search of subversive employees and misspent funds. By the following year, weary and disillusioned, the senior staff whose ideas had inspired the project began to disperse into university life, while the investigators published their disparate reports. The charge that Mobilization had abetted the Harlem riots was seen to be spurious, but its book-keeping was open to question, and either nine, or twenty, or maybe some hundred employees with sinister political sympathies were darkly hinted at. The *New York Times* reported on November 10th:

> The Antipoverty Operations Board, headed by City Council President Paul R. Screvane, denounced Mobilization for Youth yesterday for 'loose and shoddy' administrative practices, 'lavish and improper' spending and indications of Communist infiltration. In a unanimous report to Mayor Wagner, the nine-member board said that a quarter of a million dollars in expenditure was subject to challenge. It also said it had found other irregularities which caused deep concern . . . Investigation of the agency will continue on several fronts, the report said, with one of the most thorough involving allegations of Community activity . . . The Federal Bureau of Investigation's un-classified files contained the names of nine individuals 'who allegedly had present or past subversive or Communist affiliations or had engaged in subversive activity'. Commissioner Fischel reported that eleven other names had come from 'confidential sources' . . . James E. McCarthy, retired administrative director of Mobilization, received the harshest individual criticism in the report . . . His 'lavish and improper spending', an accompanying report by Commissioner Fischel declared, involved an outlay of $23,204.89 'for dinners, hotels, restaurants, etc.' . . . Also challenged were Mobilization activities 'in the areas of school boycotts and rent strikes' that were approved by administrative leaders.

Though the findings were inflated by the pompous language of official rebuke, they proved to be very insubstantial. No evidence was suggested that any of the elusive Communist sympathizers had, in fact, abused his position for political ends. Nor had any of the funding agencies required that MFY investigate the political sympathies of candidates for employment. Public Agencies are debarred from employing Communist sympathizers, but it was not clear that the same rule applied to a non-profit agency receiving public money. MFY could not, then, fairly be criticized for ignoring the political affiliations of its employees, so long as their work was not affected. Even Mr. McCarthy's notorious $23,204.89 for bed and board turned out eventually to be a gross exaggeration. The City investigators had, as they lamely confessed much later, 'confused various columns' in their public report. McCarthy's own expenses had only been a quarter of the sum originally charged—$7,000 of which was actually attributable to the Mayor's Office, not Mobilization at all.[14]

James McCarthy commented on the report: 'I wonder if our identification with the fight against slumlords, our battle for better schools and our participation in the March on Washington could figure in the pressures behind this investigation?' It seems that so vicious, sustained and highly publicized an attack must have been inspired by more than mere concern with administrative laxity in a government supported agency. Mobilization had made influential enemies, and by August of 1964 it had lost its most powerful backers. Robert Kennedy had left the Attorney General's office to run as senator in New York, taking David Hackett with him, and reorganization within the City administration had displaced Mobilization's chief support amongst senior officials. The President's Committee on Juvenile Delinquency, which had always been closely identified with Mobilization, was losing its position within the Federal bureaucracy. Compounded by departmental conflicts in both Federal and City administration, the resentment against Mobilization's militancy chose its moment, and struck with deadly effect.[15] Though, under new direction, the agency has survived—and carried forward many of Mobilization's original aims—it will be more closely circumscribed by discrete official sanctions. The brave paradox of government backing for programmes which challenge government seemed,

[14] We are grateful to Frances Piven for an extract from an unpublished paper by herself and Richard Cloward, which explains the details of this financial misunderstanding.

[15] At least some of the information on which the attack was based had been reported to City officials several months before the *Daily News* published its story. The timing of the public attack was, then, probably no accident. But we do not know how the information reached the *Daily News*.

at least for a while, to have been hounded out of New York City.

Mobilization's experience of community organization suggests that when institutions are provoked by community protests, they will react against the sponsoring agency, rather than meet the protest on its own terms. And since an agency like Mobilization for Youth inevitably arouses jealousy amongst other agencies whose function it has displaced, or upon whose jurisdiction it has intruded, the reaction will find willing allies. All the community action projects rested upon a delicate balance of power. Even though their administration might be less vulnerable to criticism, probably none could have withstood the kind of attack to which Mobilization was subjected. It seems, then, that Mobilization's conception of community organization could only withstand the opposition it must arouse if it were wholly independent of resources under the control of such opposition. As Lloyd Ohlin had recognized at the outset, the fate of community organization is inseparable from the nature of its sponsorship. The Boston programme foundered on the same issue.

Since Edward Logue, Administrator of the Boston Redevelopment Authority, had initiated the plans for a grey area project in Boston, ABCD's conception of community organization was at first closely related to urban renewal. Each neighbourhood was to be encouraged to take an active part in the planning of its own redevelopment. Through this participation, the proposals could be refined more sensitively to the resident's needs, and the resources of the community mustered to meet the social problems raised by physical reorganization. And since ABCD had committed itself to work wherever possible through existing agencies, this community organization programme was implemented through settlement houses and voluntary councils, to which ABCD assigned its own professional staff. In this way, the programme acquired three sponsors—the Redevelopment Authority, the settlement houses, and ABCD itself—whose interests were not compatible. The Redevelopment Authority was seeking a constructive contribution to its plans, hoping above all that community organization would promote a local leadership committed to the Authority's aims, and influential enough to swing opinion in the neighbourhood behind them. ABCD was groping for a relationship with the people it served, through which they could articulate their needs, and share responsibility for programmes ABCD was planning. The settlement houses were more concerned to encourage the procedures of democratic organization than to guide it towards any issue. The confusion might not have mattered, if urban renewal had been popular. In the event, the community organizers not only failed to achieve a consensus of local support for the renewal plans, but hardened opposition. When a public meeting was called in Charlestown to discuss its redevelopment, the spokesmen of the Redevelopment Authority were shouted down.

From the standpoint of traditional community organization, the outcome was a successful demonstration of democratic self-assertion. To Ed Logue, it was a betrayal of the whole purpose of the programme. ABCD was caught in an uncomfortable conflict of loyalties. It could not keep the confidence of the people it served if it identified itself with renewal plans which they had rejected, and which they believed would contribute to the social hardships ABCD had been created to relieve. Nor could it openly challenge the Redevelopment Administrator, who had done so much to promote it, and who enjoyed, as much as ABCD the Mayor's confidence. ABCD therefore extricated itself as best it could, shifting the emphasis of its approach to the education and employment programmes in which the Ford Foundation and the President's Committee were chiefly interested. In December 1963, ABCD reported in its proposal to the President's Committee:

> During its early months, ABCD's activity was concentrated on the development of citizen participation in urban renewal planning. Community organization workers were assigned to the high-priority renewal districts to participate in the planning of renewal projects and to begin to develop guidelines for social planning.

> The receipt of the grants from the Ford Foundation and the President's Committee turned ABCD's efforts towards the research, planning and financing of programmes. This emphasis was one of the factors that lead to a reassessment of the earlier, heavy involvement in local community organization. From the outset the value of this activity has been difficult to measure. In one area of the city ABCD efforts seemed to be in competition with existing agencies which considered themselves responsible for community organization work. In other areas, ABCD staff were caught in the cross-fire between pro-renewal and anti-renewal partisans.

Community organization workers were withdrawn by ABCD from some parts of the city. The function of those who remained in Roxbury and Charlestown was redefined with greater emphasis on working with local organizations and agencies on programme planning . . .[16]

This redeployment was not a really satisfactory solution to any but the agencies which had resented the competition of ABCD's programmes in the first place. Ed Logue believed that ABCD had deserted its true function, and the Ford Foundation staff—who had never admired the settlement house approach to community organization—remained worried at the lack of citizen participation. A year later, ABCD had still not worked out how, obliged to plan with the Mayor, the Redevelopment Authority, the School Superintendent and United Community Services, it was at the same time to plan, in all humility, with the people it served.

Each of the projects was forced to choose between its institutional alliances, and its sponsorship of a challenging redistribution of power within the City. Only Mobilization for Youth dared to risk antagonizing public agencies, and disastrously miscalculated their power to exact retribution. It seems unlikely that any programme of community action, so dependent upon a consensus of established leadership and public funds, could be at the same time an effective champion of radical democracy. If the sponsors of community organization cannot disclaim responsibility for the organization they create, and if at the same time they defeat their own purpose in seeking to control it, only a sponsor free from other commitments can afford to support his organization in whatever course it chooses.

But even had the projects been at liberty to risk the consequences of aligning themselves with the poor, was it practicable for a sophisticated professional staff to work out programmes in equal partnership with the people they served? Planning with people raised a conflict of intellectual as well as political loyalties. Only one project seriously attempted it, and the experience suggests the mutually frustrating ambivalence of such a relationship.

[16] 'The Boston Youth Opportunities Project: a Report and a Proposal', (ABCD, December 1963), pp. 8–10.

Early in its planning, Harlem Youth Opportunities Unlimited was approached by two young men, President and Vice-President of an organization of young people in Harlem, who wanted 'to improve the community in which we live and to better the responsibilities of our youngsters—you know, fifteen to sixteen'. From this initiative grew the HARYOU Associates, a group of over two hundred young people, who shared for a year in the development of HARYOU's plans. HARYOU felt the experiment had been a qualified success. But its staff took a lot of punishment, as the Associates adroitly drove them in both mind and body to the wall:

> There were many problems, frustrations, and risks involved in the realities of involving a large group of young people between the ages of fourteen and twenty one in the day-to-day planning operations of a professional staff. Not the least of these problems was the fact that these young people, encouraged by those staff who were assigned to them, took seriously the invitation to participate and to contribute their ideas in the planning. They understandably interpreted this invitation to mean that they would be welcome in the HARYOU offices not only on Saturdays and Sundays, but also during the work week. The limitations of office space generally made for a type of chaos when groups or committees of Associates were around. They often seemed to take over the HARYOU offices. The patience of some of the members of the professional and secretarial staff was often stretched to the breaking point and beyond . . . As the interest, excitement, enthusiasm of the Associates increased and reached a crescendo, they tended to dominate more and more of the office and the activities of HARYOU . . .

> During this period, the group held the adult staff team in a 'heads I win, tails you lose' bind. A programme faltered either because the staff had not given the group its head and had not really shown faith in the group, or because the staff had allowed the group to go off half-cocked.

> Alternation between feelings of respect, affection and loyalty, and hostility, suspicion and a contempt for the authority or competence of the adult staff, has characterized not only the youth leaders of the Associates but also some of the rank-and-file members. The adult

consultants, on the other hand, have also alternated between over-enthusiastic reliance on the competence and ability of the Associates, and attempts to seize completely the reins of the programme at times when it faltered.[17]

If the Associates had been older, no doubt the mutual exasperation would have been less vivid. But if the projects were to plan with the people they served, then they could not ignore the young people with whom their crucial programmes were concerned. And even with a more mature group, it is hard to see how a professional staff could divide responsibility with them: one or other must be content with an advisory role. The projects were not only committed to institutional alliances which constricted their freedom of action: they were also committed to an intellectual rationale. They could not unequivocally sacrifice their professional judgement to the inexperienced demands of their public.

In retrospect, it seems evident that the projects could never wholeheartedly share responsibility for their programmes with the people they served: they had too many other commitments to both theory and practice. They recognized that their manner of reform needed democratic safeguards, but in trying to build these safeguards into their own organization, they assumed an impossible harmony between different means to the same fundamental end. The competence of each citizen to uphold his liberty depends upon political, legal, economic and psychological resources which no one organization can secure. The means to each require a different emphasis, a different alignment of interests, a different perception of the problem.

The poor can be seen, firstly, as an interest group which like any other must compete for attention against rival lobbies. The neglect of their interests arises from their failure to organize and assert their potential influence. Their economic power is collectively considerable, despite their poverty, as bus boycotts, consumer boycotts and rent strikes demonstrate. And their political power is greater than their voting strength, because they can appeal both to an uneasy middle class conscience and a general fear of open conflict. But to be poor is not itself a status which defines a common political interest. It is, rather, a humiliat-

[17] 'Youth in the Ghetto', (HARYOU, 1964), pp. 91-2, 576-7.

ing condition which most people are ashamed to acknowledge, and from which anyone with the ability to lead has also the ability to escape. Hence the organization of the poor has to centre upon more specific interests which concern them especially, but not them alone—rack-renting, racial discrimination, education. As tenants, members of a racial minority, parents, beneficiaries of social services, the poor can act in their own defence without the stigma of inferiority, and their case has a universal relevance.

But in a highly structured democracy, where every interest tends to institutionalize its representation, these characteristic concerns of the poor need to recruit comparable resources of organization and leadership. Spontaneous protest is too sporadic: soon discouraged by frustration, it lacks the power of sustained bargaining. If the poor are to attract the able organizers they need, the defence of their interests must offer a career which rewards the ambitious with growing prestige and power. Community organization falters because it cannot offer any future to the neighbourhood leaders it promotes but a lifetime of parochial effort. The real leaders are the professional community organizers, who alone have the incentive of a career with widening opportunities. No one can fairly be expected to put the best of his energies, year after year, into the affairs of his neighbourhood without recognition or reward. Political parties understand this: they distribute patronage, curry local favour, and above all, hold out to every ward leader the opportunity of promotion.

Nor does the neighbourhood provide a natural focus of organization, except for those concerns which arise from the immediate environment—garbage collection, police protection, redevelopment plans. Community organization seems to assume that those who live near each other share a community of interest, which ought to find expression in a generalized social cohesion. But unemployment, discrimination, punitive welfare regulations, even the denial of educational opportunity are not neighbourhood issues, and only accidently unite the residents of the same block. Community organization, since it provides no hierarchy of affiliation from local to national levels, trivializes major interests by its parochial bias. The pressure for reform becomes fragmented, unsure of itself, and easily patronized.

Only the Civil Rights Movement seems to command the

present resources to act as the lobby of the poor.[18] It has a
hierarchy of organization from national to local groups, and
professional leadership. As it broadens its concern from overt
discrimination to the subtler economic and social barriers, it
champions the cause of all victims of injustice, whatever their
colour. And it acts from a principle of equal rights which does
not stigmatize its following.

Community action projects will not find the Civil Rights
Movement a comfortable ally. Vulnerable by their commitments
to public agencies and political accommodation, they will be
amongst the first targets of attack. But the power of the Civil
Rights Movement will determine how radical are the reforms
which the projects can press upon their institutional colleagues.
The projects cannot themselves redistribute power since—
dependent upon the consensus of established leadership which
created them—the power is not theirs to give away. But they are
commandingly placed to exploit the practical opportunities for
change which open with every shift in the balance of forces. So
long as they do not manoeuvre to weaken militant leadership,
even when it attacks them, they can use it as a powerful incentive
to authentic reform.

But to mobilize the sanctions which lie within the grasp of the
poor, and redistribute power through political action, may not
immediately help the individual to secure his rights. The poor are
at a disadvantage, not only because their interests are collectively
unprotected, but because they are individually less equipped to
protect them. They lack money and knowledge to seek redress.
The projects tried to meet this need through programmes of legal
aid, and despite the New Haven experience, were certainly less
vulnerable than in their attempts at community organization.

[18] Or, from a rather different standpoint, organized labour. Moynihan, in his
Berkeley address, (*op. cit.*), remarked: 'Our social insurance system is unfinished. Our
wage system is unbalanced and incomplete. Our employment nexus is frighteningly
inadequate. These are fundamental political issues, and there does not yet exist a
consensus that they should be resolved. Trying to cure poverty without attending
to these matters is treating symptoms. The only force in American society—or any
other industrial democratic society that I know of—that is capable of providing
the mass citizen support for solving these fundamental problems, and for sustaining such efforts over long periods of time, is the trade union movement. The
trade union movement was the original anti-poverty movement in this nation, and
it remains incomparably the most significant one . . .' (Though some of its practices—
such as restricting apprenticeships—seem now to contribute to the frustrations of the
poor.)

Once a system of legal aid can be established, respect for the impartiality of justice, and the lawyer's duty to his client, make political pressure illegitimate. The crisis in New Haven arose because, in deference to the County Bar Association, the programme restricted its legal staff to an advisory role, whose interpretation was bound to be controversial. Yet the Cahns, in their paper, doubt whether the resources of legal protection can be fully exploited under the sponsorship of an agency like CPI.[19] They advocate a neighbourhood law firm which, besides traditional legal services, would help to secure rights under social welfare provisions, and protest against abuse of natural justice, where legislation or administrative regulation seem unwarrantably overbearing. 'Thus there are at least four areas in which legal advocacy and legal analysis may prove useful in implementing the civilian perspective: traditional legal assistance in establishing or asserting clearly defined rights; legal analysis and representation directed toward reform where the law appears contrary to the interests of the slum community; and legal representation in contexts which appear to be non-legal and where no judicially cognizable right can be asserted.' Such a guardian of the citizen against the state could only function independently of any political or institutional ties. Thus, though community action projects can promote legal aid, they probably cannot themselves run such a programme without constricting the scope of its challenge.

But legal service—as the Cahns themselves recognize—could perpetuate the dependence of the poor upon their professional advocates. The more ably it champions their rights, the more it risks inheriting, in radical disguise, a tradition of middle-class paternalism. This dilemma leads to the third aspect of the community organization which the projects attempted.

The theory of a poverty cycle emphasized the oppression of spirit, the apathy and social disintegration which robbed the poor of any power of initiative in their own interest. The programmes had not only to provide opportunities, but regenerate a will to respond to them. In part, then, community organization was a form of treatment for collective depression. Discussion, participation, the devolution of responsibility, the self-analysis

---

[19] CPI, in fact, recognized this, and later promoted a legal aid programme organized as a directly funded corporation independent of both CPI and the City, authorized to handle civil and criminal cases without restriction.

of community problems imitated the techniques of group therapy. This conception grew out of a fundamental faith in individual autonomy. But its expression in terms of social health was partly misleading.

The therapeutic analogy breaks down, because the projects approached the community with a preconceived diagnosis, while a doctor waits for a patient to present his symptoms, and can be dismissed at will. A community cannot, like an individual patient, ask for treatment and describe its symptoms. Hence it cannot initiate and ultimately control the relationship with its helper. Social therapy, therefore, tends towards a paternalism which undermines the very qualities it is seeking to promote: self-confidence and self-respect. A concept such as Leonard Cottrell's 'doctor of community deficiencies' risks being self-defeating, unless the deficiencies are first in some way acknowledged and presented by the community itself. The dilemma arises whenever the restoration of individual dignity is taken as a psychological problem, inherent in those who are demoralized, rather than as a moral problem, inherent in the society which humiliates them. We derive our sense of worth from the whole context of relationships which define a social being. To restore dignity, you must above all treat people as deserving of respect. The poor cannot respect themselves until the employers, social workers, teachers, doctors, policemen, politicians, and public officials who relate them to the values of society at large respect them. And this means not only politeness and humility, but an honesty of purpose which does not seek to disguise the shortcomings of the services offered. Though community self-help can be useful and satisfying, the projects could probably best meet the psychological need of reassurance and acceptance by their influence on institutional attitudes, and especially by the integrity with which they presented their own programmes of service.

The organization of interests, the defence of individual rights, and the rehabilitation of self confidence is each a means to the redistribution of power. But each is a distinct purpose, which leads towards, but cannot contain the others. And none can be effectively pursued within an organization primarily concerned to foster enlightened co-operation within the power structure.

In its reply to the Cahn's paper, CPI did not refute their analysis of the pressures to which it bowed. Nor, conversely, did the investigation of Mobilization for Youth challenge the right of protest. From their very different standpoints, both attacks exposed the conflict of loyalties to which the projects were vulnerable, and forced them to accept their limitations. But, as the projects realized, the self-assertion of the poor and the uncompromising defence of their rights were as much a part of the strategy of reform as institutional co-operation and professional understanding. They were only wrong to think they could hold them all together under one command.

VIII

RESEARCH

THE projects did not ask the city's leaders, or the people of its neighbourhoods to endorse without reserve any specific programme of reform. The means, and even the exact ends were open to revision. The projects asked only the right to demonstrate the worth of their ideas, to experiment with innovative techniques, and to evaluate the experience impartially.

This pragmatic approach was, in part, a rationalization of the concentration of resources. The President's Committee had only a slender appropriation to promote a national policy. If it were not to dissipate its funds, it had to be highly selective. But no system of allocation could have convincingly justified the choice of any dozen Communities as most deserving. An experimental rationale freed the committee to concentrate its grants more or less arbitrarily. It could choose its experimental priorities, and seek out receptive communities where its plans would have a fair test. Conversely, the six rather fortuitously evolved grey area projects became nationally significant, if they were presented as pathfinding demonstrations. So long as the programmes were widely relevant, the necessarily arbitrary selection of communities to test them was finally unimportant. By the same argument, the projects themselves could justify the concentration of these programmes in a few neighbourhoods.

The demonstration strategy gave the projects some discretion in working out their plans and procedures. It disarmed the scepticism of cautious institutions, though it sometimes irritated agencies or Civil Rights leaders impatient for wholesale action. The programmes were tentative, funded for only a few years, and on trial. No one was finally committed. Even if the reformers had not been genuinely uncertain of their methods, and concerned to submit policy to objective analysis, they might still have chosen to present their programmes as demonstrations, since no other approach could have secured them so much room to manoeuvre.

For these reasons, the projects claimed to be experimenting, even when their actions were hardly consistent with the logic of scientific method. Unproved ideas were borrowed and adapted from one project to the next, without controlling the variations in the interests of comparative analysis. Programmes were introduced before the resources to evaluate them had been assured. The innovations to be tested were sometimes no more than the extension of well-tried practices. Eager to take advantage of new appropriations voted by Congress, the projects evolved their plans opportunistically, leaving research to hasten after money with as coherent an evaluative design as could be put together. Cities could not be treated as laboratories, ignoring their urgent need of all the resources they could attract. The projects expanded according to the grants they could obtain, rather than the logic of an experimental progression. But they never lost sight of the obligation to evaluate their efforts: and this commitment involved them in a research methodology whose implications they had barely foreseen.

The projects could not disown their experimental character without breaking their understanding with the funding agencies and the cities' institutions. As the research directors began to specify their needs, it became clear that the integrity of an objective evaluation could only be defended by the ruthless subordination of all other claims. However tentative the premises of an experiment, their testing imposes meanwhile a more explicit and rigorous definition of means and ends than an administrator can comfortably work to. The projects postponed any final commitment to their reforms, at the cost of an intellectual commitment which they could not easily sustain. Just as the intrusion of an academic and professional elite into policy-making put in question the political legitimacy of the projects, so the projects' political involvement contaminated the rationality of the experimental design.

The dilemma was fundamental to the strategy. However confident of their solutions the project directors were, so long as they undertook to demonstrate them impartially, they were committed to the same logic as the most sceptical experimenter. They needed to gather evidence that would answer a set of complex questions, in a setting where laboratory controls and exactitude of procedure were impossible to secure, and where the criteria which defined success or failure were often elusive.

To show that the programmes were effective some objective measures of achievement had first to be put forward. This, in itself, was difficult enough. Even if the ultimate criteria—the reduction of poverty and juvenile crime—were in principle measurable, the intermediate criteria were either unquantifiable or doubtfully relevant. Whether a young man was less alienated, more mature, more employable for the experience of a work crew; whether a neighbourhood was more integrated and assertive of its rights for the experience of community organization; whether home-school co-ordinators reconciled the socal values of parents and teachers were largely questions for intuitive personal judgement. The more reliable interim measures by which the educational programmes could be tested—reading ability, or the verbal skills of nursery school children—were only speculatively valid. No one yet knows whether these skills do, in fact, save a child from a future of poverty and unemployment.

If some kind of criteria could be established, the projects had then to show that any improvement followed from their innovations, rather than from a general betterment of social chances, or the intervention of fortuitous circumstances. And they needed to guard against the possibility that the excitement and stimulus of any experimental programme, rather than the specific technique they introduced, had been responsible for the appearance of success. But even if their evaluation could secure this measure of control, it left several crucial questions open. Which of the innovations, all directed at the same target, had made the difference? Or if no improvement took place, had good and bad ideas cancelled each other out? Did the successful innovations merely replace the work of previous agencies, re-directing job seekers to the projects from employment bureaux, or down-grading remedial reading elsewhere in the school system to the advantage of experimental classes? And was the success achieved with those whom the projects were primarily designed to help?

A programme which satisfied all these points had still to be shown to be replicable and practicable. Did its success depend upon a concentration of talent, which could not generally be recruited? How much did it cost? Were the communities in which the programmes were tested exceptionally responsive? What did the success of the projects owe to the prestige of national attention? The projects had to demonstrate, at least, that their successes were achieved by resources which many other communities ought to be able to command.

Finally, the evaluation would have to examine the relationship of each programme to the others, since the projects sought to show, not only that each innovation was successful, but that success depended upon a coherent plan of complementary reforms. If they were to be truly successful, the projects needed to show that they had stimulated in institutions a willingness to innovate and revise that went beyond the project's own proposals. As experiments, then, the projects needed to prove, by objective criteria, the validity of three interrelated claims: that each of their programmes would contribute, directly or indirectly, to the reduction of poverty or juvenile crime; that these programmes were widely applicable to other communities; and that their impact was greater when concerted in a campaign of simultaneous reform.

Such an analysis would be a formidable task, even if the projects had been designed only with research in mind. To complete it in the face of all the other demands upon them was a heroic undertaking. Only one project set itself to meet, in full, the logic of an objective demonstration. In its proposal to the President's Committee, Action for Boston Community Development elaborated a sophisticated research design, which illustrates the theoretical feasibility, but also the daunting practical problems, of a strict methodology.

The proposal has, first, to define the ultimate aim by which all its programmes are to be judged. The document—which runs to three hundred odd pages—therefore begins with a meticulous analysis of the rationale and objectives of the proposal, which it states as 'the reduction of the volume and seriousness of criminal-type behaviour on the part of male youth from 12 through 16 years of age'. But when, after a hundred pages of prefatory discussion, the programmes are introduced, the twelve- to sixteen-years-olds receive scant attention. Apart from some of the proposals for remedial reading and guidance in school, most of the experiments—multi-service centres, legal aid, pre-kindergarten, work-study, youth employment and vocational education —deal with older or younger, or no particular age group. In the

face of such apparent inconsistency, the document retrieves the
logic of its argument by appeal to the influence of the programmes
on 'improved role performance, particularly in family and work
roles, of individuals in the immediate social environment of the
members of the target population'. In other words, if your elder
brother has a better chance of a job, your younger sister a better
chance in kindergarten, and your mother can get better advice on
how to deal with the landlord, rheumatism, and father, then you
will be less inclined to vex your years from twelve to sixteen with
illegitimate protest. This is certainly plausible, but it saddles the
research design with an ultimate criterion of success—the
reduction of lawlessness in twelve- to sixteen-year-old boys—
remote from the immediate aim of each programme.

Every component of the proposal is, then, to be evaluated
according to its influence on delinquency, through some related
aspect of behaviour. So, for instance, reading programmes
should, by overcoming classroom frustrations, lessen the need to
work off hostility in lawlessness; and by a more tortuous but
consistent logic—better employment opportunities for older
brothers or fathers will help to reconcile young people to the
social order. The evaluation has therefore two stages. First it
must determine whether each programme did, in fact, achieve
its intermediate purpose. Did reading skills improve, were more
people employed, as a result of the programme? To answer these
questions, each experimental group is to be paired with a matching
control group, and any differences in their experience measured.
But this model of experimental method is rejected for the second
step—the discrimination of the programmes' influence upon
juvenile crime.

The proposal argues that a stable control group, matched for age
and criminal liability, would be impossible to identify. It suggests
instead that the crime rate of young people within the scope of the
project be compared with the rate to be expected, if the programmes
had not been open to them. All the boys aged twelve to sixteen
living in the areas chosen for the project's programmes are to
be individually recorded on a set of cards and their progress
followed to their seventeenth birthday. As a boy outgrows the
age range, he is dropped from the group, while the rising twelve-
year-olds are added. This 'moving cohort' is the object of analysis.
Each boy's card will note personal characteristics, gathered from

his school record; information of the project programmes in which he takes part; and his contacts with the police. At the same time, the expected rate of law-breaking in this population is to be worked out, at first from a retrospective analysis of the available information on delinquency, and later refined in use. This forecast is designed to establish what the rate would have been, if the project's programmes had not intervened. The predicted rate, for both the population as a whole, and groups within it of like characteristics, can then be compared with the actual rate, as measured at specified intervals. Some of the boys in the cohort will take part in several programmes, some in one, others in none at all. Those who take no part should—if the demonstration is successful—break the law about as often as predicted, while the crime rate of the others should fall increasingly below the forecast, the more programmes they experienced. The data is open also to more refined analysis: which combinations of programme experience seem most effective? and was the experience more influential upon some groups of boys than others?

The research design meets most of the logical requirements of an objective evaluation—contriving measures of each programme's intermediate effectiveness, its relevance to the ultimate purpose, and the extent to which concerted programmes reinforce each other. It fails only to allow for the 'Hawthorne' effect— the improvement to be expected from the stimulus and novelty of any experiment, irrespective of its specific nature. Given the complexity of the design, it is probably as well that the project did not commit itself to the further set of controls needed to allow for this.

The prediction of delinquency rates runs into more serious difficulties. No established and validated method of prediction is available. If the rate to be expected is worked out largely from the current rate, at the time of the programmes' inception, then the final comparison is just between the amount of delinquency in an age group of the project area, before and after the demonstration, weighted to allow for obvious changes in the population. The research proposal has already rejected this basis of comparison, as open to misinterpretation and the intrusion of too many unknown factors. Instead, a more sensitive method of prediction is to be devised, which takes fuller account of individual characteristics. But, for lack of time and opportunity, the method cannot be fully tested, independently of the experimental analysis. Whatever the differences between the forecast and the actual rate, it may be difficult to say with confidence whether the result shows the influence of the project, or the unreliability of the predictive method. This will be so especially where the results are puzzling or inconsistent.

The logical rigour of the research also depends upon a rather narrow definition of the project's aims. It does not take account of the institutional changes which the project hoped to stimulate, nor its general influence upon the poorer neighbourhoods of Boston.

But these methodological difficulties seem far more manageable than the practical problem of implementing so ambitious a design. Each component—the testing of a specific programme, the devising of a method to predict delinquency rates, the analysis of the association between each programme's purpose and delinquency—is alone enough to occupy a research team for several years. A vast amount of data is to be gathered, coded, and kept up-to-date in an elaborate tracking system. Without the faithful co-operation of schools, agencies and police departments, the method will collapse—and from the first, the willingness of the police to release confidential information was in doubt. If records were carelessly kept, if information were refused, if a programme were not consistently carried out, or independently extended to a control group, the interlocking logic of the demonstration would be jeopardized. If the police were to change their policy—making fewer arrests, giving more warnings, taking more or less cases to court—the consistency of the rates on which the whole evaluation rested would be undermined. As programmes were delayed or revised, research funds held up, as the school superintendent began to spread reforms throughout his system, the integrity of the design became increasingly threatened.

Such a research programme was also, of course, expensive. The proposed budget ran to half a million dollars a year, and called for a staff of about 40, apart from consultants and interviewers. To spend a fifth of the total cost of the demonstration on research seems proportionately reasonable, but it was a great deal of money and talent to risk on a plan that could so easily be upset by circumstances beyond its control.

The Boston proposal represents the most thorough and

uncompromising attempt to submit an experiment in social reform
to the discipline of controlled measurement. No other project
took the implications of a demonstration so literally, or invested
so heavily in research. New Haven and the North Carolina fund,
for instance, spent about 10% of their budget on evaluation,
Oakland—in practice—not quite 5%. But all the projects proposed
to submit at least some of their programmes to systematic measurement, using experimental and control groups. And they generally
discovered that, even on a less elaborate scale than Boston, the
requirements of research were hard to sustain in the setting of
an action programme. The purposes of a programme were not
clearly articulated, or changed, procedures modified, records
neglected. A report on the youth training project in East Los
Angeles, for example, notes that 'the service orientation of the
staff was a predominant factor in the way in which this programme
has been conducted. While, short term, this tends to produce
results and undoubtedly benefits the clients served, it makes for
long term difficulty in adhering to or controlling research and
design study. This became clear almost from the outset. As soon
as the staff, through experimentation or "trial and error", discovered a better way of serving trainees they adapted their
procedures, methods and techniques accordingly. It was impossible to be inventive, flexible and expedient on the one hand and
at the same time do careful, scientific, controlled research on the
other.'[1]

To escape these frustrations, research was attracted towards
more independent studies, less easily upset by the vagaries of
action. By drawing a sample of the population to be served by the
project, and tracing how attitudes or circumstances changed over
the years, the project's influence could be at least indirectly
measured, irrespective of the specific programmes introduced.
CPI's research director, for instance, interviewed a sample of
1,600 teenagers in New Haven, and—for comparison—400 in
Bridgeport. The questionnaire was designed to find out 'occupational aspirations and expectations, attitudes towards work and
work experience, relationship towards parents, attitudes towards
neighbourhood, attitudes towards school, reference groups,

[1] Joseph L. Weinberg, 'Evaluation Study of Youth Training and Employment
Project, East Los Angeles', (U.S. Department of Labor, Office of Manpower,
Automation and Training, August 1964, mimeographed).

participation in cpi programmes and other organizations in the community, self-reported misconduct, attitudes towards basic rights and attitudes towards minority groups, and social class orientation. A number of scales measuring personality variables, social-psychological variables, and other factors have also been included. These scales measure socialization, aggression, self-image, delinquency proneness, emotional immaturity, alienation and others'. Such a study not only avoids the delay and confusion involved in research based on participation in the programmes, but it defines for itself the relevant changes to observe, and so by implication makes its own interpretation of the project's purpose. Similarly, the North Carolina Fund undertook a survey of low-income families in the State. These studies could be justified, firstly, by their contribution to an understanding of needs. The findings would guide the development of new programmes. And eventually, when the sample had been reinterviewed, changes in attitudes, aspirations, or well-being could be correlated with participation in the project's programmes. At the same time, the research director was free to conceive the enquiry in terms which interested him as a sociologist, and derive from it theoretical as well as practical conclusions.

But the more research sought an autonomous frame of organization, the less immediately useful it was likely to be to the programme directors. As guides to new proposals, general surveys seldom yield information pointed enough to define the nature of a specific innovation. Even if they can, the collection and analysis of survey data on this scale usually takes several years and cannot be closely integrated with programme development. When the original sample is reinterviewed, too few may have taken part in the demonstration programmes even to guess at their influence. To discriminate changes, and relate them to any specific cause was bound to be questionable. The evaluation could therefore only be general, speculative, and slow. Meanwhile, it could tell nothing about the programmes' progress. And preoccupied by theoretical interests, research often neglected the straightforward analysis of whom the projects were serving, and with what result. Melvin Herman, who directed the work programmes at Mobilization for Youth, remarks:

> All the work programmes that I have observed report serious problems in the collection of reliable data . . . On occasion, the

researchers are not sufficiently familiar with the actual programmes themselves and are, therefore, unable to establish categories in which data should be collected. Or the researchers state that they are not primarily interested in programme evaluation but rather in basic research which requires different kinds of data from those of evaluative research. (One researcher told me, to my dismay, 'There are no significant researchable questions in the work programme.') Sometimes, senior researchers have shown distinct lack of interest in the accumulation of basic descriptive statistics, leaving this task to junior staff who often exhibit more interest than competence . . .

Often the action programmes begin before their research teams have time to tool up . . . Youngsters came into the MFY work programme at a rapid rate and were slotted into a variety of services as quickly as these could be provided. Unfortunately, the research department was unable to devise a way to record the concrete services to each youth, by whom, and with what results. Consequently much data was hopelessly lost.

After some months, the operators of the work programmes, in order to meet their own needs for information, did devise a card file . . . the data actually recorded were supplied by harried operating personnel untrained in securing or recording research data. The problem of recording was further complicated by the inability of either research or action personnel to maintain a complete follow-up of the status of trainees after they completed the programme.[2]

If the research directors chafed at the inconsistency and incoherence of much that was done, the programme directors were equally impatient of pretentious methodology and theoretical preoccupations which failed to answer their needs. In practice, if not in theory, the claims of research and action were hard to reconcile. As this became apparent, a subdued but fundamental controversy arose amongst the research directors of the grey area projects, between those who insisted on the methodological rigour implicit in the commitment to experimental demonstration, and those who were prepared to improvise a more speculative evaluation with whatever resources lay to hand. Clarence Sherwood of Boston argued: 'Unless the social science researcher

[2] Melvin Herman, 'Problems and Evaluation', *The American Child*, Vol. 47, No. 2, (March 1965).

participates, indeed leads the dialogue and bargaining required
for the development of an impact model—including the identification of goals, the description of input-output variables, and
the elaboration of a rationale that specifies the relationship
between input variables and goals—these tasks are likely to remain
undone. Once the impact model is formulated, the researcher must
continue to remain within the environment, like a snarling watchdog ready to oppose alterations in programme and procedures
that would render his evaluation efforts useless.' The researchers,
in effect, must exercise a controlling authority over the whole
endeavour if it was to make any demonstrable contribution to
reform. 'At no other point in time have we had so great an
opportunity to have an impact on the social order; if we are to
realize our potential within our current stance as social scientists,
however, we need more than additional technical innovations.
An outlook, an ideology, almost a morality if you will, must be
developed in order to function appropriately as agents of social
change.'[3]

But Michael Brooks, the research director of the North Carolina
Fund, countered this fiercely logical idealism with another moral
principle—'the ethical necessity for continuous feedback of
research findings into community action programmes, thereby
producing adjustments and improvements in their operation.
While this is the correct procedure from the action—and indeed,
the ethical—point of view, it has the unfortunate effect of tossing
a monkey wrench into the research design constructed at the
programme's outset. The person interested solely in the research
implications of a programme might prefer that it be carried
through to completion without alteration, whether successful or
not, so as to yield unsullied findings of maximal generalizability
(and perhaps publishability as well). Given the social ethic
which underlies the community action programme, however, it
is necessary to devise an evaluation procedure which not only
accommodates, but in fact facilitates the feedback process'.[4]
And he quotes the remark of one of us: 'in social research you
are usually either disreputable or unhelpful'. The researcher is

[3] Howard E. Freeman and Clarence C. Sherwood, 'Research in Large Scale
Intervention Programmes', *Journal of Social Issues*, Vol. XXI, No. 1, (January 1965).
[4] Michael P. Brooks, 'The Community Action Programme as a Setting for
Applied Research', *Journal of Social Issues*, Vol. XXI, No. 1, (January 1965).

less a snarling watchdog than an amiable retriever, uncovering whatever achievements fall to the project's aim.

If the research director accommodated to the flexibility of an evolving strategy of innovation, he could still, by an imaginative exploitation of resources to hand, improvise a well-informed evaluation—as Oakland shows. The Oakland project, at a cost of about forty thousand dollars, was the first to produce an evaluative report on its programmes. The objectivity and degree of controlled measurement varies, but by using the staff of the operating agencies to gather records of performance, the project was able to provide, at the close of its first phase, a working guide to its achievements.[5] The evaluation only extends to the immediate purposes of the programmes, and offers the most concrete information about the school programmes, where changes are easiest to measure. But if it leaves the fundamental questions of the project's effectiveness open, it shows at least where experimental action most obviously brings change. The research director also devised an ingenious plan to discover the influence of the project as a whole upon the established leadership. The project proposed to use its Citizen's Advisory Committee to interview the Mayor, the project's Executive Committee, minority leaders, businessmen and union representatives about the influence of the project upon them. How did these leaders perceive their organization's relationship to the project? Had they changed their procedures, staff or objectives as a result of the project? Did they intend to pursue the experiment? Had inter-agency co-operation improved? Such questions would both bring to light whatever had been the project's influence on Oakland's leadership, and involve the Advisory Committee in the evaluative process.

But the controversy was not merely concerned with the reasonableness of compromise in scientific procedures. It turned on the relationship between research and action. Both Clarence Sherwood and Michael Brooks acknowledged that the two operations were often at odds in practice, but Sherwood vehemently denied that they conflicted in principle. He maintained that research and action shared identical interests. It was futile to promote techniques or strategies of reform whose worth was unknown. Wherever, in its eagerness to exploit opportunities,

[5] See Chapter III, p. 63, for its findings on the education programmes.

action outran knowledge, it merely squandered its energies. The integration of research and action brought a rare objectivity to social reform, and this in itself was perhaps the most radical and productive of all the project's innovations. By this argument, any apparent conflict between the demands of research procedures and political or operational pressures would be spurious. If the project compromised its disciplined objectivity, it forfeited its essential contribution to the evolution and implementation of policy. Intelligent social action should define its purpose, and choose—on the basis of the fullest information it could muster—the means most likely to achieve it. .Wherever the consequences of action are inadequately known, the extent of ignorance must be carefully described, and then methodically eliminated. Research becomes an integral part of any rational progress.

This model of systematic problem solving pre-supposes that the ultimate purpose is fixed at the outset, and remains constant. The sequence of steps from the statement of aim to its final realization can then be perceived as a whole, and ignorance defined in relation to it. The logic of this approach is irrefutable, so long as the elimination of ignorance is a manageable task. But in the setting of social behaviour, where our knowledge is so crude and sporadic, the procedure threatens to postpone indefinitely the determination of policy. The Boston research design committed itself to answer, within three or four years, several fundamental and intractable questions: how is delinquency related to personal characteristics, and social environment? How is it related to the specific abilities demanded in school, or work? And how are these abilities themselves to be developed where present techniques are unsuccessful? At the same time, it sought to test the application of theory in a practicable plan of action. The undertaking seems impossibly ambitious: it is as if one were to set out to prove in three years a marketable design of automobile, before the principles of the internal combustion engine had even been worked out. Yet, viewed in relation to the ultimate purpose, no other procedure is valid. So long as social action is understood in terms of problem solving, the only alternative to the patient accumulation of knowledge is more or less random behaviour.

This conception of the relationship between research and action rests upon an orthodox—if idealized—understanding of scientific method. But it holds only for those situations where an ultimate purpose defines the nature of the problem to be solved. If—as we discussed in an earlier chapter—social action more characteristically avoids any precise, unwavering statement of aim, then such a conception of research is continually frustrated. Boston's research director complained that one of his greatest difficulties was the failure of programmes to clarify their aims. But should the project have disciplined its thinking to conform to his demands? If the model of problem solving behaviour is abandoned, much that seemed logically inconsequential and self-defeating in the project's practice begins to appear more rational.

Since we are often very uncertain of the consequences of social action, we need to reduce as far as we can the unknown factors relevant to a decision. The shorter the span of action under review, the less we do not know, and the quicker we shall discover the wisdom of our decisions. Hence it is much easier to make rational choices if a plan of action is broken down into a series of proximate steps, and the plan is open to revision as each step is completed. The ultimate purpose can then be only vaguely, or even inconsistently stated, since it is no more than an indication of the general direction of the initial effort, a justification of the appropriateness of the first steps. As it will be continually re-interpreted in the light of experience, a precise and inflexible definition of the ultimate goal would only be an encumbrance. Clarity of aim grows dimmer, as the steps proceed into the future. Today's decisions are articulate and circumstantial, but we can say with decreasing confidence what they should lead to in a month, a year, three years. To describe an ultimate purpose is, in both public and private life, an exercise in the analysis of un-formed and competing motives, intrinsically tentative and unstable. Social action is thus more an endless exploration than the search for solutions to specific problems. We know where we start from, and in which direction we are heading, but we cannot know where we will end up.

In the face of ignorance, then, the most rational decisions are those which leave open the greatest range of future choice. And this freedom depends upon a refusal to commit oneself irrevocably to ends as well as means, since they react upon each other in a continual redefinition of the nature of the situation. In the field of social action, no other procedure may be practicable, since ignorance can never, even in principle, be overcome. Even if the complexity of factors which enter into a social situation could all be grasped and submitted to analysis, that situation will not recur. The future will always be different. Problems return or remain, but transmuted by the circumstances of the day into a new challenge, which we have never altogether foreseen, and for which we are unprepared. Thus it is more rational to accept ignorance as a condition of action, than to postpone decision in the unrealizable hope of certainty.

Viewed in this light, the interests of action and experimental research, as Boston conceived it, are not at all the same. Research requires a clear and constant purpose, which both defines and precedes the choice of means; that the means be exactly and consistently followed; and that no revision takes place until the sequence of steps is completed. Action is tentative, non-committal and adaptive. It concentrates upon the next step, breaking the sequence into discrete, manageable decisions. It casts events in a fundamentally different perspective, evolving the future out of present opportunities, where research perceives the present in the context of a final outcome. Research cannot interpret the present until it knows the answers to its ultimate questions. Action cannot foresee what questions to ask until it has interpreted the present. Action attempts to comprehend all the factors relevant to an immediate problem, whose nature continually changes as events proceed, where research abstracts one or two factors for attention, and holds to a constant definition of the problem until the experiment is concluded. Each seeks to limit the ignorance of which it must take account, the one by shortening its time span, the other by arbitrarily excluding factors and purposes which may also be relevant.

This is not to say that systematic experiment is irrelevant to social action, but only that both cannot be carried out by the same operation. Each tends to frustrate what, for the other, is the most rational procedure. Since in human affairs events are so complex as to be infinitely variable, an experiment can only establish a predictable association between elements abstracted from the living situation. To do this, it has to create a more or less artificial environment, from which extraneous factors can be excluded. It depends upon the possibility of repeating the sequence of events under study. The more rigorously the environment can be controlled, the more certainly can a universal association be established. But, at the same time, its relevance to natural life becomes more speculative. It can never be sure that these associations will hold outside the social laboratory, in the unique complexity of an historical event. Hence fundamental research into laws of human behaviour has to proceed in detachment from the interpretation of these laws in practice.

In contrasting the exploratory nature of action with the systematic solution of predetermined problems, we do not mean to imply that actions never set themselves to solve problems, or that research never explores. A sequence of experiments, like a sequence of actions, is open to revision. Unexpected results suggests a change of direction, new hypotheses, even a radical reinterpretation of the problems to which the line of research is relevant. But here, too, the combination of research and action is frustrating, since each inhibits the other from following its bent. The conception of the Boston project required that its research and operational divisions concert their aims in a manner which not only saddled its actions with an impracticable rigidity of purpose, but committed the research programme to an experimental sequence that was far too long. To insist continually upon a specific application of research findings only constricts its freedom to exploit promising discoveries.

In practice, then, the projects could not realize their claim to be experiments without abandoning their determination to benefit the communities in which they worked. They were not demonstrations but explorations of the possibilities of reform. And exploration makes use of information at levels of analysis which differ radically from an experimental design. Most immediately, progress depends upon a continual feedback of information from the field of operation. As each step is taken, its consequences become part of the situation from which the next step must evolve. The projects needed to know, from week to week, how each of their programmes was going, how agencies were reacting to their intervention, how the neighbourhoods in which they worked responded to the initiative. The discrimination of these clues to action calls for an imaginative serial analysis which can be rapidly communicated.

But because it is pragmatic and flexible, an exploration also needs to be retrospectively interpreted, in a different manner from an experiment. The final outcome cannot simply be related to the initial aim and method, since these have undergone continual revision. The whole process—the false starts, frustrations, adaptations, the successive recasting of intentions, the detours and conflicts—needs to be comprehended. Only then can we understand what has been achieved, and learn from the experience. Research in this sense is contemporary history. Even though no one ever again will make exactly the same journey, to follow the adventures of the projects offers a general guide to the dangers and discoveries of their field of action. From such a guide, anyone may evaluate the experience according to his purposes.

The projects' relationship to research depended, then, upon whether they were experiments or explorations. If they were, essentially, experiments in social action, they could only respect the logic of experimental method, and lay aside their concern with practical achievements. But, though they claimed to be experiments, their whole manner of operation seems more consistent with an exploration. Thus, while they could hope to draw on experimental findings, they were not themselves designed as social laboratories. They needed to use their own resources for research to make the day-to-day analyses from which each succeeding step could take its departure, and to interpret retrospectively the process of discovery.

In practice, the function of research within the projects was confused by extraneous pressures to undertake an intellectual commitment which they could not sustain. The President's Committee imposed a blue-print of planned intervention, in the hope that articulate theory, rigorous method, and objective measurement would protect the projects from political corruption, and compel assent to reform by the unassailable logic of the findings. But in seeking to display the power of scientific knowledge, the projects attempted to exploit, all at once, strategies of change which cannot be comprehended within a single operation.

IX

THE POVERTY PROGRAMME

B Y the spring of 1965, the original sponsors of community action were preparing to hand on their responsibilities to the poverty programme, at once proud that their movement had graduated into a major instrument of national policy, and nervous of its continuing integrity on so large a scale. Under the second title of the Economic Opportunity Act, $340 million were appropriated until June 1965 'to provide stimulation and incentive for urban and rural communities to mobilize their resources to combat poverty through community action programmes'. For the second year, the sum was doubled. After four years of doubtful achievement, many frustrations, and a few precarious triumphs, the endeavour was rewarded by a fifty-fold increase in its funds.

With such Federal backing, the Ford Foundation began to withdraw. During 1965, it gave terminal grants to Boston, New Haven and Oakland. But these graduation presents were a dwindling proportion of the projects' total resources: in 1962 the Foundation had met over half CPI's cost, three years later only a quarter. Nor was it planning any more grey area projects. The Public Affairs staff cast about uncertainly for a new direction, at a loss to find their frontiers overwhelmed by an already established orthodoxy of reform.

At the same time, twelve of the sixteen projects funded under the juvenile delinquency programme were to be transferred to the Office of Economic Opportunity, which had already absorbed most of the President's Committee's professional staff. Four were to remain for a while under their original auspices: Washington, because it had just been launched under the special appropriation of the 1961 delinquency act; and Boston, New Haven, and Mobilization for Youth, to complete their evaluation as demonstrations. Now that delinquency no longer needed to cover a broader concern with social deprivation, the 1961 Act was to be continued for a further three years as a programme of professional training, and short-term experiments in the treatment of young people who had broken, or were likely to break the law. Released from preoccupation with the frustrations of poverty, delinquency legislation returned towards the longstanding interests of the Children's Bureau—and could even acknowledge that some young offenders were middle-class.

So, at the close of its first four years, the staff and essential purposes of the President's Committee were assimilated to the poverty programme. But, as before when community action acquired a new sponsor, it also acquired a new bias.

The Ford Foundation had conceived the grey area projects at a time when, from the Capitol to city halls, a legislative stalemate seemed to frustrate all hope of reform. 'Our "won't power",' as Paul Ylvisaker put it later, 'is growing more rapidly than our will power. Those responsible for public policy are finding it increasingly difficult to have legislative proposals exacted.' To the Foundation, therefore, community action had originally been a means of achieving, through the voluntary co-ordination of public and private agencies, a constructive policy which could not be expressed through legislation. But the President's Committee was born in the exhilaration of Kennedy's hundred days, when intellectual clarity, unencumbered by bureaucratic tradition, promised to fashion a new order. The 'vacuum of constructive leadership' was filled at the centre: the problem now was to diffuse the logic of rational problem solving throughout America. Community action became an instrument of planning, through which the expertise of social science would coerce local administration into intelligent reform. As the Ford Foundation had stressed institutional coherence, and sought to promote a new coalition of community leadership, so the President's Committee stressed intellectual coherence, and sought a proven theory of social rehabilitation.

The poverty programme took these ideals for granted, and changed the emphasis again. Power to enact reform was no longer so much at issue. After twenty years of stultification, a President committed to social justice could at last command a majority in Congress; and the Federal example was spreading. State government had promoted the North Carolina Fund, and—

influenced by CPI—Connecticut was proposing the first state educational opportunity bill to aid its city schools. Once government began to direct substantial resources to the purposes of community action, the movement also outgrew its experimental terms of reference. The Office of Economic Opportunity could not wait to learn whether the programmes introduced by the earlier projects would prove demonstrably effective, charged as it was with the generalship of a national campaign. Community action projects could be funded quickly, and suggested the kind of bold new initiative which the President's declaration of a war on poverty seemed to promise. They appealed to the Bureau of the Budget as a means of bringing Federal agencies into line. And they enabled the Federal government to deploy the new resources directly to cities, without involving state governments more sympathetic to other interests. So, proved or not, community action was a politically attractive instrument of policy.

OEO worried less about the institutional or intellectual organization of reform, than about the influence of community action on the distribution of power. Sensitive to the insistent urging of civil rights, it was determined that the poor themselves should share control of the new resources at least equally with government and the professional agents of social service. So each of the successive sponsors of community action, reflecting the changing circumstances of their charge, emphasized in turn one amongst the three strategies of reform we have discussed. Yet they did so, not as a choice between incompatibles, but as the assertion of a complementary, and previously understressed ideal.

The Economic Opportunity Act defines community action as a programme which combines the resources of an urban or rural area in actions which promise to reduce poverty or its causes—'through developing employment opportunities, improving human performance, motivation and productivity, or bettering the conditions under which people live, learn and work'. It is to be organized by a public or private non-profit agency, and to be 'developed, conducted, and administered with the maximum feasible participation of the residents of the areas and members of the groups served'. The definition is consistent with the conceptions of the Foundation and the President's Committee, but its interpretation begins to diverge. The Act passes lightly over experimentation, research and planning. The allotment of resources is to be governed by need, not by the knowledge a proposal promises to add to our understanding of social problems. The Director of community action programmes may distribute a fifth of his funds at his discretion, but for the rest, a third is to be allotted to states in proportion to their numbers receiving public assistance, a third according to their unemployed, and a third according to the number of children in families with incomes under a thousand dollars. Such a pattern of distribution implies that the programmes are to relieve poverty wherever it prevails, and not merely show how it might be relieved. Research, training and demonstrations are not to absorb more than fifteen per cent of the annual appropriation. And since the community action programmes are expected to recruit funds from other Federal and local resources, the proportion will be less again of their total expenditure. Experimental innovation gives place to the disseminating of a new convention of social service.

Even if the whole research, training and demonstration allocation were to be spent on the systematic evaluation of action, it would still be proportionately less than the research budget of ABCD. To protect the original experimental design, the Office of Juvenile Delinquency therefore proposed to continue their responsibility for Boston, New Haven, and Mobilization, as its director explained to a Senate Sub-Committee: 'This will enable us to milk these projects of the hard data which would tell us which programmes were useful, which were not useful, and why . . . We feel that the other projects being transferred to the Office of Economic Opportunity may well have the demonstration and evaluation aspects muddied up by the inclusion of large sums of money and projects all over the city'.[1]

In a sense, the promoters of community action had succeeded too well. Their ideas had become fashionable before they were proved. In spreading the philosophy which underlay the grey area projects and the President's Committee, the Foundation tended to overwhelm its own demand for experimental objectivity. In a society without a recognized forum of intellectual life, a national philanthropy becomes a prestigeful and uniquely well-

[1] Hearings before the Sub-committee on Employment and Manpower of the . . . United States Senate . . . on S.1566 to Extend the Juvenile Delinquency and Youth Offences Control Act of 1961, April 7 and 8, 1965, p. 38.

placed broker of new ideas. It receives unsolicited a host of ideas for its support, and goes in search of others, tirelessly elaborating a network of academic, administrative and political contacts. Less spontaneous and accessible than the salons or coffee houses of other civilizations, the discreetly luxurious offices on Madison Avenue are still a market place of intellectual exchange. The Public Affairs department, besides, recruited to its staff imaginative schoolteachers, social workers, writers, and lawyers, gave their ideas the backing of its money and sometimes passed them on to government: it also received them back when out of favour. So it created a constituency for its conception of reform. The more successful this intellectual brokerage is, the more policy is shaped by a set of common assumptions. Reform becomes at once more coherent, and more subject to fashion. Ideas gain currency, and passed from hand to hand, acquire an authority which soon outruns their proved effectiveness. It is hard to encourage a consensus, while remaining ruthlessly sceptical of the grounds on which that consensus rests. The methodical exploration of means was overtaken by impatience to put them to use—and as an excuse for the arbitary distribution of scarce resources, it could now be forgotten.

The poverty programme also abandoned the President's Committee's preoccupation with planning procedures. The criteria of an acceptable plan were greatly simplified, and very generally stated:

The plan itself need not be complex. It must answer only five basic questions:

1. Does it demonstrate a basic knowledge of the facts of poverty in the area?
2. Does it promise to attack the real causes of poverty?
3. Does it promise effective solutions of the problems which it identifies?
4. Are there community organizations which will work together to carry out the plan responsibly, speedily and efficiently?
5. Is the community itself dedicated to the achievement of the goals, contributing its own human and financial resources towards that objective?

Above all this must be a programme in which projects are carried out not *for* the community, but rather *by* the community—with external financial assistance—to attack community problems.[2]

Neither the Act itself, nor official interpretations of its intent, suggest that plans need be guided by any articulate conceptual framework, nor that they need by fully worked out before any action is undertaken. The Act is only concerned to establish the incidence of need, and kind of programmes which qualify a proposal for support, indifferent to the planning methodology by which it was devised. Any community with many poor is entitled to support, if it is genuinely prepared to undertake programmes of employment, training, health, housing, social welfare and remedial education likely to put people on their feet. It need not offer a sophisticated justification of these innovations.

The poverty programme could afford to neglect theory, since the relevance of employment, training, health and education to economic opportunity scarcely needed to be argued. A delinquency programme which virtually ignored delinquents called for a more elaborate justification than the same programme presented as a means to end poverty. But in retreating from the President's Committee's prescription for rational planning, the Office of Economic Opportunity could also point to the Committee's own experience. For already, in 1963, it had to be recognized that the theoretical model was unworkable. Within their communities, projects came under mounting pressure to show what they could do. They could not postpone action indefinitely, while they struggled to bend institutional interests to a comprehensive rational design. 'There will be a tendency to determine programmes based on the availability of co-operating organizations', the Committee reluctantly admitted, 'At some point, such a reversal of the planning process will make the overview meaningless . . .'[3] The whole programme was also under attack in Congress. The Chairman of the House Special Education Sub-Committee initiated hearings which threatened to cripple its administration. She argued that the President's Committee's policy was absurdly pretentious: 'in the original authorization of $30 million for three years . . . we certainly did not expect to

[2] 'The War on Poverty, The Economic Opportunity Act of 1964.' A compilation of materials relevant to S.2642 prepared for the select sub-committee on poverty, pp. 53–4.
[3] 'Policy Guide to the Presentation of Proposals for Funding under Public Law, 87–274', (September 1963), p. 10.

bring about any social reforms either city-wide or nation-wide. It would be ridiculous . . . we hoped by this legislation that we would learn some new techniques and some new ways to prevent and control juvenile delinquency'.[4] Comprehensive planning dissipated funds which should have been spent either to finance small-scale, practical demonstrations, or to enable what was known already to be put to effective use. To head off these criticisms, the projects were hustled into action before their plans were ready.

The line between planning and action was not only politically untenable, but implied resources for comprehensive projects which the President's Committee did not command. The Committee had hoped that the plans it promoted would gather funds from other appropriations, but failed to persuade Federal departments to concert their grants within the framework of community action. It was embarrassed to find that it had encouraged more comprehensive projects than it could support. But it could hardly tell cities which had been planning for two years that there was no money to be had for any programme. Smaller grants for specific undertakings were offered by way of compensation. Instead of launching a comprehensive project all at once, the Committee began to think in terms of building it up, programme by programme. So, under the stress of criticism and lack of funds, the principles of planning were gradually compromised. The theoretical framework relaxed into a general overview; action could be phased in while plans were still developing; and their content was left entirely to the communities' discretion. The logic of scientific problem solving collapsed in piecemeal pragmatism.

The poverty programme therefore set out knowing how politically and administratively embarrassing a strict methodology of planned experimentation could be. But for all that, there was still little firm evidence that the innovations achieved—often and cheaply enough—their ends. The Office of Economic Opportunity compromised by treating research and demonstration as a separate interest, no longer integrated with every programme; and the evaluation of community action projects was undertaken more selectively, by organizations independent of the

---

[4] *Congressional Record,* Proceedings and Debates of the 88th Congress, 2nd Session, House of Representatives, June 16, 1964, p. 13494.

projects themselves. Twelve intensive studies by outsiders were planned in the first year. Thus the poverty programme relaxed its scientific criteria, not because it now knew what would work, but because it saw that systematic experimentation within an explicit, dominating theoretical framework was not the most practical way of striving for an immediate effect.

If in this the Office of Economic Opportunity recognized that research and action implied different orders of priority, and so different forms of organization, it plunged headlong at the dilemmas of citizen participation. Undaunted by the early projects' experience, it stood uncomprisingly by the ideal of grass-roots democracy. The programmes were to be 'developed, conducted and administered with the maximum feasible participation' of the poor themselves.

This principle had evolved in part from a belief in self-help, which President Kennedy shared with several members of the informal task force he had set up to explore a poverty programme. Richard Boone, for instance—who had gone from the Public Affairs department of the Ford Foundation to work for the President's Committee—had been impressed by the use of non-professionals in social work with street gangs. The poor might sometimes help each other more effectively than a social worker from a different culture. And by their involvement in both programmes and community decisions, their sense of dignity would be restored to them. At the same time, the Civil Rights Movement was beginning to challenge the legitimacy of community action, unless the poor were represented. Participation was thus to restore dignity, redistribute power, and ensure that, wherever possible, the poor themselves were recruited for the jobs that the projects would create.

But the poverty programme was also convinced from the experience of the President's Committee, that only the Cabinet, nationally, and the mayors locally, were powerful enough to co-ordinate the resources it needed. Hence it still faced the inherent conflict of a simultaneous commitment to two different conceptions of democratic accountability. From whom were the projects to take their lead, elected government or those they served? As a guideline for the delinquency programme put it, 'When specific goals are predetermined, the project must face the actual danger or the charge of manipulation of people. When goals are not predetermined, the project must face the problem of lack of control and unanticipated directions, with which the project may have difficulty living.'[5]

In the face of this dilemma, the new policy favoured those projects which had risked their fortune in support of popular protest. Community Progress, for all its achievements, was criticized in the Office of Economic Opportunity for pre-empting local leadership by its own administratively subordinate neighbourhood staff. But Mobilization for Youth, in spite of all the vilification it has suffered, was urged to try again. Radical democracy was in fashion. At hearings before a Senate sub-committee in April 1965, the Senators went out of their way to record their support. Senator Javits, questioning the Director of the Office of Juvenile Delinquency about 'social action programmes like rent strikes, civil rights protests, marches on Washington', and the operations of HARYOU-ACT, assured him, 'I repeat I am most sympathetic on all these things.' 'Let me encourage you to be bold,' concluded the Chairman, Senator Clark, after he had heard the Director of Mobilization describe his commitment to militant community action.[6] But it was one thing to assert the principle, and another to secure its implementation.

What *was* the maximum feasible participation of the poor in an endeavour that was also to include 'the political, business, labour and religious leaders, the schoolboard, the employment service, the public welfare department, private social agencies

[5] 'Suggested Guidelines for Federal Support of Neighbourhood Organization...' prepared by the Demonstration Technical Review Panel of the Office of Juvenile Delinquency for the Commissioner of Welfare, reprinted in the record of the Senate sub-committee hearings already cited, p. 129.

[6] 'MR. EECK: ... "I think one of my problems is to keep Mobilization from becoming too cautious. ... A most important dimension of our programme is to help people who are apathetic, who do not speak for themselves, who had very little knowledge of legal channels whereby assistance, in our democracy, can redress wrongs. We have been very successful at that, but as we get successful we do encounter criticism, because when people start talking to redress their problems, there sometimes occurs a shift of power. That ... programme I hope to keep up at full steam and it may well be that we will have criticism of it again. It seems to me unavoidable. But to give that up would be to me to give up the soul of the project."

SENATOR CLARK: "Let me encourage you to be bold".'

(Hearings before the Sub-committee on Employment and Manpower of the ... United States Senate ... on S.1566 to Extend the Juvenile Delinquency and Youth Offences Control Act of 1961, (April 7 and 8, 1965, p. 183.)

and neighbourhood houses',[7] and to which preference was to be given in the local allocation of all Federal grants? The Office of Economic Opportunity—under pressure from Negro communities—began to insist that it meant effective representation, and encouraged the idea that the residents of poor neighbourhoods should themselves elect a majority of the project's board.[8] And this was more than the mayors of most American cities could willingly accept.

In San Francisco, for instance, a group of Civil Rights leaders refused to endorse the City's poverty programme until the Negro, Chinese and Spanish-speaking communities were properly represented on its Council. The Mayor replied that he could never be persuaded to surrender control. His Economic Opportunity Council—a corporation created to receive poverty funds— had by May 1965 prepared a four and a half million dollar programme. But the neighbourhood groups would not approve it, so long as the Council was dominated by whites. The Mayor compromised: eight representatives of the poor neighbourhoods were to be elected to the executive committee, to seven of his own nominees. But at the same time, control was transferred from the executive to the full committee, on which the Mayor's men were still a comfortable majority. The neighbourhood leaders treated the proposal as an evasion. Throughout the conflict, the Office of Economic Opportunity maintained that it would not accept any programme without the approval of the neighbourhoods to be served. The City had therefore either to negotiate an agreement, or forego Federal support. At the end of July, only two minor programmes had been started. In August, the five Negro members of the Economic Opportunity Council walked out in protest. A month later, the Mayor gave way. Sixteen new neighbourhood representatives were to be elected to the full committee of the Council, giving them a majority of one, and the Office of

[7] 'The War on Poverty, The Economic Opportunity Act of 1964', *op. cit.*, p. 52.
[8] In the congressional debates on the Economic Opportunity Act, the interpretation of 'maximum feasible participation' was never discussed. OEO took it to mean that, amongst others, at least one representative of each neighbourhood served by the project should be included on its governing body—selected, wherever possible, by democratic procedures; that residents should also be encouraged to advise in programmes and carry some of them out through their neighbourhood organizations; and that either individually or in groups they should be given opportunities to protest against programmes or propose changes.

Economic Opportunity released the first two millions of its grant. Thus with much greater resources, and confidence in its Federal mandate, the poverty programme could sometimes impose its principles where the President's Committee and the Foundation had settled for noncommital gestures of good faith.

But to capture formal control does not itself resolve the underlying dilemma. If the programmes of community action projects are still to be carried out for the most part by established public and private agencies, then these agencies will now face the conflict of loyalties which before troubled the projects. The civil service is to implement the wishes of the neighbourhood representatives who control the poverty programme, while it remains responsible to conventional government for its established functions. Community action has still to be contained within bureaucracies which answer to the community at large, through city hall, the committees of voluntary agencies, the state legislature. Unless the representatives of the poor are satisfied with gradual change—peripheral innovations, modified regulations, a redistribution of a few per cent of the budget—their demands seem likely to be more than social agencies can assimilate, without antagonizing those who pay for most of their functions. Unable to serve two masters with incompatible claims upon them, bureaucracies will surely seek to evade unwelcome commitments. By delay and obstruction, by the authority of their professional knowledge, by reinterpreting intentions, they will outmanoeuvre the radicalism of the poor, as they outmanoeuvred the President's Committee and the Ford Foundation. And in this they will probably meet, as a democratic administration must, the wishes of the majority.

The growing insistence on the participation of the poor itself acknowledged how vulnerable the programme was to the pressure of established power. As soon as community action became national policy, it was bound to provoke local government to defend its jurisdiction. And a policy dependent upon public funds and public institutions, which called on communities to commit wholeheartedly their own resources, could not lightly disregard the duly elected representatives of democracy. Though Mayor Shelley gave way in San Francisco, elsewhere the intransigence of city halls found powerful allies in Washington. The

Office of Economic Opportunity had to accept that it could not always keep the projects out of the Mayor's hands.

The Budget Bureau, fiscal arm of the White House, has told the Office of Economic Opportunity that it would prefer less emphasis on policy-making by the poor in planning community projects [reported the *New York Times* on November 5, 1965].

'Maximum feasible participation' by the poor in the anti-poverty programme is called for by the law. In the Bureau's view, this means primarily using the poor to carry out the programme, not to design it. . . .

Individuals who read the law differently from the Budget Bureau had heard that the bureau was withholding $35 million to remind the anti-poverty agency that encouraging the poor to organize and raise their voice was unsettling politics.

Those individuals believe that pressure for this policy was coming from the Mayors of big cities, most of whom are Democrats.

The Mayors have openly protested demands of the poor for policy planning positions. The Mayors see a threat to their patterns of governing and to their political security if the poor develop into articulate, militant lobbies at city hall.

A high Government source said that the reduction in working capital was routine ['to provide a contingency fund and more flexibility']. However, he said it was true that the role of the poor, in the Budget Bureau's view, should be primarily, though not necessarily exclusively, in operating the programme.

This has been the view of Mayor Richard J. Daley of Chicago, who led the Mayors' protest to Vice-President Humphrey last spring. In Chicago, poor people are hired as neighbourhood workers. A few have been admitted to policy levels, but they were selected by the political establishment and then only after the city-wide programme had been shaped by the Mayor's deputies . . .

Many cities have received large anti-poverty sums, accompanied by praise for their work, although involvement of the poor in policy-making has been minimal, sometimes nil.

Confronted by political interests it could not dominate, the

Office of Economic Opportunity countered with a new tactic. Already, in the spring, it had met Mayor Daley's protest by announcing that where a community poverty project did not offer the poor enough control, the Office would reserve the right to fund an independent programme which more authentically represented them. In November, it discretely reasserted its intention:

> This week, the Federal Agency issued to community action projects a memorandum setting forth the terms under which local programmes could obtain approval and money from Washington without going through the local community action agency. . . .
>
> The terms for by-passing the local agencies are difficult and the route is tortuous. However, the official recognition of a by-pass threatens the monopoly the city agencies have in community action and poses a new threat to the Mayors.[9]

It was for this, perhaps, that $35 million had been so ambiguously withdrawn from the working budget. Though the tactic was partly bluff, it recognized a radically new principle. A strategy of community-wide co-operation might well be incompatible with the uncompromising assertion of minority interests; in these circumstances, the Federal Government should be prepared to support, in the same community, both official and countervailing conceptions of a viable programme.

The Public Affairs department of the Ford Foundation was beginning to think in the same terms. Government sponsored community action ran the risk of becoming conventional, and corrupted by political patronage. Philanthropy could challenge it to maintain the integrity of its performance, by encouraging independent interpretations of the same ideal. 'I'm becoming a great believer in competition in the public interest,' Paul Ylvisaker remarked.[10] These unofficial poverty programmes—sponsored, for instance, by a council of churches—could set standards of imaginative innovation and authentic service by which to judge the national endeavour. And so the original concern to co-ordinate all the resources of a community give way to a renewed trust in diversity.

[9] *New York Times*, November 5, 1965.
[10] Quoted in 'The American Way of Giving', *Newsweek*, (March 14, 1966).

The Poverty Programme

But community action did not simply return to its starting place in the American tradition of divided authority and competitive effort. The reformers reviewed their approach on the ground of five years experience. Like climbers spiralling up a mountain, as they came back to a familiar point of view, they stood higher and could see further. As the movement gained ground, it disseminated its philosophy, its techniques and its strategies. The theory of the poverty cycle, and the paradoxical principle of individual rehabilitation through institutional change settled into a new orthodoxy, setting new criteria of performance for government and social agencies at every level. Any school system, welfare administration, housing authority, settlement house, police or probation department, employment office or vocational training school that claimed to serve the poor, had now to prove itself under an insistent cross-examination: was it innovative? Did its service reach the most disadvantaged? Did it co-ordinate its policy with other agencies? Did it involve the poor and respect their views? Did it understand the nature of poverty? By asking such questions, the sponsors of community action had helped to invest imaginative service to the poor with prestige, so that it became rewarding—not merely for the grants it attracted, but because influential opinion increasingly acclaimed it.

These new standards of judgement provoked a slow but cumulative redistribution of resources. The funding of community action by national agencies also created a precedent for extending direct Federal support to impoverished urban areas, for services which had always been jealously guarded as local responsibilities. A movement of reform which had originally been directed at community leadership, paradoxically made most impression upon national government, and prepared the way for growing Federal intervention in community affairs. The projects were both closely identified with their communities, and local agents of national policy. The bridge which arched from these foundations did not always meet too well in the middle, but once open, it was bound to attract an increasing traffic.

So although the attempt to synthesize all legitimate means to reform in a single organizational framework was breaking down, the rediffusion of activity took its departure from the principles established in those first five years. The exploitation of research, democratic pressure, and institutional resources might go their separate ways in mutual suspicion. Agencies might once again be encouraged to compete in service. But the old divisions between one kind of service or specialism and another, between national and local, public and private, academic and political concerns had been breached. Everyone now accepted that unemployment, ill-health, bad housing, educational disadvantage, reacted upon each other to perpetuate poverty. Any intervention in so complex a problem would have to take its bearings from a wide range of complementary actions.

The researcher who sought to inform the issues of social policy must be prepared to venture outside the conventions of his academic guild. He would have to work out his own synthesis of insights from history, political science, sociology, psychology, adapting the logic of objective inference to trace the interplay of many-sided patterns of individual and corporate behaviour. The Civil Rights leader would have to look beyond discrimination to the injustices embedded in the social structure, organizing not merely against the forms of inequality, but against their underlying causes. Above all, within the administration of social policy, a new kind of public servant had become crucially important, at once more independent of established authority and more responsive to the people. Responsible towards government, but free to work out his own policy by negotiation and expert analysis; holding no elected office, but in continual consultation with the people whose needs he served; with influence to guide the course of any social institution, but unencumbered by routine duties, he held an ambiguous but potentially commanding position at the heart of the community power structure. Of all the innovations of community action, this may prove the most important: it created the professional reformer, and invented an organizational framework appropriate to his function.

After five years of effort, the reforms had not evolved any reliable solutions to the intractable problems with which they struggled. They had not discovered how in general to override the intransigent autonomy of public and private agencies, at any level of government; nor how to use the social sciences practically to formulate and evaluate policy; nor how, under the sponsorship of government, to raise the power of the poor. Given the talent and money they had brought to bear, they had not even reopened very many opportunities. The search for coherence, knowledge, and a viable organization of the poor was still perplexed by inherent contradictions. As each was pulled towards a different kind of sponsorship, independent of the others, the integration of a rational programme of democratic reform seemed as remote as ever. But even if the ideal is ultimately unrealizable, at least in these five years community action developed a range of skills, concepts, organizations, models of action, which equipped the search with much more sophisticated means. And by this it had already stimulated a realignment of resources and ideas which powerfully influenced the variety of initiatives that now competed for priority in the exploration of reform.

X

CONCLUSION

'I is pleasant to be transferred from an office where one is afraid of a sergeant-major into an office where one can intimidate generals, and perhaps this is why History is so attractive to the more timid amongst us,' wrote E. M. Forster. 'We can recover self-confidence by snubbing the dead . . . The schoolmaster in each of us awakes, examines the facts of History, and marks them on the results of the examination.'[1] An historian of contemporary events lacks this consoling assurance. The living answer back, and as actors in the drama, they can reasonably claim to know more about what happened than their critic. They can protest, too, when they have been marked unfairly. They know what it costs, in personal courage and political skill, to change a bad decision into a passable one: the critic notices only the shortcomings of the result. They know how the historian's retrospective interpretation of their decisions may have ignored the fortuitous circumstances, the constraints and personal conflicts which shaped them, tidying the complexity of events into a few neatly-labelled chapters. The relevance of any pattern the contemporary historian reads into the immediate past —his abstraction from the inconsequence of everyday life—is very insecure. He forgoes the historian's final authority—the wisdom of hindsight. 'Why was it right of Drake to play bowls when he heard that the Armada was approaching, but wrong of Charles II to catch moths when he heard that the Dutch Fleet had entered the Medway? The answer is, "Because Drake won" . . . We must take a larger view of the past than of the present, because when examining the present we can never be sure what is going to pay.'[2]

[1] E. M. Forster, 'The Consolations of History' in *Abinger Harvest* (London: Edward Arnold, pocket edition, 1953), p. 191.
[2] *Ibid.*, p. 193.

Conclusion

Reflecting after eighteen months on the events we have described, we can only guess whether Community Action will pay—how much, and in what coin. If we were to examine the success or failure of each project now, as we write, the marks we might have awarded eighteen months ago would already need revision. Mobilization for Youth guarded more of its radical spirit than then seemed possible; PCCA revived in Philadelphia, while the Boston project ran into serious trouble; Oakland, which had done so little to encourage the self-assertion of the poor, discovered a new militancy.

In an earlier draft of our conclusions, we treated the projects as an experimental test of the philosophy which seemed to underlie them. The President's Committee especially—by its emphasis on theory, rational planning and evaluative research—invited this kind of analysis. In these terms, as we tried to show in the discussion of the experience of action, the fragmentary evidence of the first three years does not seem to validate the theory. The poverty cycle assumed an inherited disability to respond to opportunity. But the projects had little difficulty in evoking a response from the people they tried to serve: their most urgent and intractable problem was to satisfy the demand they raised. But it was a mistake, perhaps, to take the arguments of the project prospectuses so literally, apart from the context of political action they sought to promote. They were not really meant as more than provisional, if sincere, public justifications of the need to make a new start somewhere. If, as we suggest, the projects were explorations rather than experiments, whose final destination was open to continual revision, it only distorts their nature to overwhelm them with their own tentative claims to a rationalistic method. So, lacking the larger view, we have tried to draw some conclusions about the process of reform, rather than its outcome.

The struggle of community action to reconcile contending ideals, its uneasy turning round upon its own arguments, are perhaps characteristic of any movement of reform in the face of fundamental dilemmas of social choice. American society recognizes more frankly than most the inevitability of this conflict, and its political arrangements reflect a faith in its vitality. At the same time, community action reacted against the stultifying irrationality and paralysis of leadership in which such a system can collapse. From our enquiry into the evolution of community action, two general questions seem to arise. Firstly, can such a movement of reform subordinate this conflict of ideals and interests to some new procedure of political accommodation, or only try to guide it towards a more constructive outcome by its selective advocacy of the most poorly represented needs? And secondly, if only the latter is practicable, how do the strengths and weaknesses of the American political process affect the possibilities of reform?

I

We have tried to show how, as community action evolved, it continually shifted its emphasis. Policy tended to move in a circle, turning from one alternative to another, as the drawbacks of each became apparent. At the outset, for instance, the reformers saw the involvement of the mayor as crucial to their plans. A few years later, the Office of Economic Opportunity was trying to prise the initiative from city hall and hand it to the poor themselves. Faith in the integration of community effort gave way to a renewed trust in competition. Yet, though the tactics changed, the underlying issues remained the same. The involvement of city government in imaginative social planning, the subordination of bureaucratic infighting, the reconstruction of the school curriculum were as important in 1966 as they had been seven years before. The apparent inconsistency of policy arose, not from inconsistency of purpose, but from the intrinsic difficulty of reconciling ideals which led naturally towards very divergent solutions.

Community action was trying to promote both a new freedom of initiative and the mutual reinforcement of disciplined co-operation; to rationalize the planning of policy through the insights of social science, and yet make it more immediately responsive to the demands of those the policy was to serve; to assimilate the poor into the opportunity structure of American education, yet to emancipate schools from the middle class prejudices which often reflected honestly enough the structure's demands. 'Comprehensiveness' and 'Competition in the public interest', 'the poverty cycle' and 'maximum feasible participation' of the poor, the 'integrity of planning' and 'planning with the people, not for them'—each slogan points towards one aspect of an interlocking complex of needs, where each can be fully satisfied only at the expense of its complementary opposite.

As a movement of reform, then, community action is very different from, say, the campaign for civil rights or medical care. These are concerned with particular improvements in society. But the projects were more concerned with the processes of society at large—with the way institutions adapted to each other and to changing needs, with the strands of leadership which had to be drawn together and bound to the urgent problems of city life. From the nature of the complex issues with which they wrestled, no final resolution is ever likely. But it seems that they were torn between two conceptions of their task—one productive, and the other perhaps inevitably stultifying and frustrating. One conception interpreted community action as a stimulus to invention, a means to break out of patterns of service and administrative structures which seemed unable to recover their relevance without outside intervention. It was more concerned to liberate ideas than to foresee their outcome The other conception sought to create a new structure of social planning that would not merely innovate, but determine how these innovations were to be integrated in a new balance of community leadership and institutional responsibilities. Essentially, the first accepted the pluralistic bias of American political life, and tried to exploit its potential vitality, while the second saw this pluralism as itself a crucial obstacle, and tried to subordinate it to a master plan. The first corresponds more closely with the Ford Foundation's interpretation of the part they sought to play, and the second with the President's Committee. But in the event, the two became confused within the projects themselves. Even where they sought, in principle, to act as facilitators, rather than directors of social change, they were led by the need to give form to their purposes, and establish their credentials, into a situation where they accepted irreconcilable claims upon their own organization, and so became involuntary arbitrators of the communities' best interest. But this was a role they could not sustain, because there is no place for such an arbitrator in the American system.

The openness of American society to competing interests and new ideas goes with a refusal to allow any preconceived reconstitution of a balanced order to forestall further change and adaptation. Any interested party has the right to propose reform—the mayor, a social welfare agency, a redevelopment administrator, the poor themselves. None of these is obliged to concern himself primarily with the needs of society as a whole: he is partisan. Disinterested reformers, whose concern is not constricted by any jurisdiction, can only influence this 'partisan mutual adjustment'[3] if they too become, in some sense, partisan—even though their' stake in the outcome is different. Since their right to ally their resources to any interested party is questionable, they may represent their purpose rather as seeking a new form of fairer accommodation. But there is a crucial distinction between innovations which try to give a particular issue more constructive expression, and those which try to create a means to arbitrate between all manner of needs. It is one thing to create a framework within which social agencies can plan co-ordinated policies: this is a legitimate and neglected need. But to prescribe how agency policy is to be reconciled with, say, the demands of Civil Rights leaders, or how it is to use the insight of social research presupposes the right and wisdom to determine the nature of society as a whole. A disinterested reformer, just because he is disinterested, is easily misled into searching for such a non-partisan framework within which all conflicts can be resolved. But the attempt to create a non-partisan framework collapses for lack of any secure and truly representative basis within the community power structure from which to promote it.

Here the evolution of community action went most seriously astray. Because the projects were trying to give form to so many new approaches at once, they overreached the limits of the role they could play. They tried to establish means, not only to give expression to a variety of needs, but to determine the way in which these needs should be reconciled. And this, we suggest, no one in American society has the power to do. The range of functions which accrued to community action tended to cast it in the role of arbitrator, and so rob it of the chance to advocate any of its functions effectively.

This is certainly not what the reformers themselves intended. But the needs to which they were trying to give more effective expression lacked any institutional form they could willingly reinforce. No instrument of social planning which co-ordinated both public and voluntary agencies existed in the cities. Univer-

---

[3] In Charles Lindblom's phrase. See *The Intelligence of Democracy: Decision Making through Mutual Adjustment* (New York: Free Press, 1965).

sities had neither the resources nor the interest to undertake experimental social action. The poor had no organization through which to protest their rights. A new agency had then to be created, and once it had been formed for one purpose, it seemed appropriate to use it also for others—especially as these purposes seemed a natural extension of each other. The reintegration of services and search for new approaches implied planning and experiment, and these in turn presupposed a framework of ideas and research to test them; the conception of a representative agency was obviously incomplete without the participation of those the agency was to serve. But as we tried to show, though each complemented the others, they were very different kinds of intervention whose legitimacy rested on a different interpretation of their mandate.

Either you do something primarily because its usefulness is worth testing, or because the community's leaders want it, or because the poor want it. Once there is conflict, you must choose. The rival justifications cannot inform impartially the same organization, because each works with a different order of priorities. Politically, the agency was preoccupied with the shaping of a more liberal and progressive consensus of community leadership. But the research directors were primarily concerned with the validation of testable theories, while community organizers were groping for a more direct expression of democratic rights. In taking up together these divergent functions, the agency was, in effect, trying to impose its own resolution of the rival claims of expert knowledge, political manoeuvre and the self-assertion of the poor to determine the direction of social policy. But since it had usually little power to enforce any solution, it brought the conflict within its own organization, and often stultified in indecision, unworkable compromises and endless disputes. It lacked authority to integrate jurisdictions, and by pressing them to innovate and co-operate, only made each more anxiously self-protective. It could not appeal to any community of interest compelling enough to override more immediate loyalties to agencies or personal advantage. And therefore it could not be accredited both as a spokesman for the poor and the agent of established power. In the political struggle to determine whose interests should dominate, the detached pursuit of knowledge and the validation of techniques became confused and confusing, irrelevant to the immediate conflict. As we saw in the development of several projects, communities could be led into 'neurotic' solutions, where the balance of power came to rest in an organization that could not function, but served to disguise the unresolved issues. Only as an agency became partisan, and chose between its possible roles, could it recover its coherence.

This is perhaps the most important general conclusion of our study: that no movement of reform in American society can hope to supplant the conflicts of interest from which policy evolves. It can only act as advocate, not as judge. If it is to be persuasive, it must be single-minded about the interest it represents, and so willing to surrender any claim to universal authority. Once this is recognized, community action can be seen as the starting point of a variety of innovations, each of which, if it is to influence the progress of reform, must be disentangled from the constraint of its rivals. Perhaps the most far-reaching was the development of a new political structure. CPI, for instance, evolved as a particular interpretation of a kind of executive planning which everywhere in the world is becoming more detached from the immediate control of government. The planner is 'an increasingly common hybrid type in Western society, the professional administrator cum political operator. He often has a particular field of expertise in which he has achieved some eminence, but he is not content merely to tender expert advice. He is a lobbyist, an intriguer—in short, a fixer who is also a technician. Indeed, precisely because he does possess technical mastery over his subject, he knows better than any ordinary politician just how far he can go in making a compromise with the interest groups involved in any question, without losing the substance of his cause.'[4] The quotation, as it happens, refers to the Commissioner of the European Economic community; but it describes as well the role which the director of CPI so skilfully played. James Reston, writing of community action programmes in the Middle West, called attention to 'the new breed of public servants coming into American political life today . . . A new political structure is being created in America'.[5]

The viability of this conception of executive planning depends

[4] Andrew Shonfield, *Modern Capitalism* (London: Oxford University Press, 1965), p. 408.
[5] *New York Times,* June 24, 1966.

upon detachment from any one political jurisdiction. If it were simply the agent of the Federal departments from which it draws its funds, it would rebuff local initiative, affronting the traditions of American democracy, and adapt very clumsily to local circumstances. If it were controlled by city or county, it could not defend the minority interests uncertainly protected by elected government, nor act across jurisdictional boundaries. But its effectiveness also depends, as we have tried to show, upon the extent of the political coalition already established in the community, from which it derives its authority; and upon a realization of the limits of this mandate. Mitchell Sviridoff accepted that CPI rested on the Mayor's backing, and was ultimately constrained by it. He was sceptical of undirected neighbourhood organization as a political asset, and never tried to integrate research and social theory with the development of his plans. But he knew exactly how to exploit Federal grants and adapt them to New Haven's needs, steering proposals with a practiced hand from desk to desk, disentangling red tape, getting regulations rewritten. As the local agent of a Federal redirection of resources to the poor, CPI was highly successful, given what funds there were. As it was, it achieved more than most projects by astutely capturing more than its share.

But community action also contained the seeds of other lines of development. The militancy of Mobilization for Youth led it to emphasize the legal protection of the poor, and challenge the discretionary powers of public welfare. It helped to generate a new concern with legal aid, citizen's advice bureaux, the employment of people from the neighbourhood in the services which they used. And the 'maximum feasible participation' of the poor, in the few cities where it was given a radical interpretation, created a form of community action which owed little to established agencies or conventional politics. Only the concern with experimental research seems as yet to have created no new form of organization likely to survive as an independent function. But the experience of the projects at least discovered more exactly what was needed, whether to ensure a viable experimental design, or to evaluate a course of social action.

The progress of this movement of reform seems, then, to depend first upon sustaining, as an independent initiative, each of the purposes to which it gave a new expression—executive social planning; the marshalling of protest against exploitation and neglect; advocacy and advice; applied research into the techniques of service and the structure of social welfare; the creation of new kinds of jobs and new forms of training; the reinterpretation of the language of schooling, so that it makes sense to the children of the ghettoes; the rebuilding of the ghettoes themselves . . . But it seems essential not to confuse these separate functions, nor to try too insistently to rationalize their relationship with each other. The organizations which embody them will disagree over tactics and priorities, if not over fundamental ends, and any master scheme which tries to preclude their conflict can only be an exercise in notional planning. Yet in itself, none of these innovations, however imaginative, can achieve much without funds which only a national reallocation of resources could provide. Their progress depends on the amount of money which the nation as a whole is willing to devote to them. If America is inhibited by its political philosophy from drawing up a master plan for the Great Society, it needs all the more an over-mastering commitment to the ideals community action represents.

At the same time, such a redeployment of independent interventions raises once again the questions which led the Ford Foundation and the President's Committee to turn at the outset to the creation of community action agencies. How are all these innovations to be financed? If the Federal government must provide for each separately, will it be forced to channel its funds directly to more conservative, established bureaucracies, and lose the great advantage of the President's Committee—that it could, for a while, support bold initiatives under the cover of fairly conventional legislation? If evaluative research is divorced from the agency it evaluates, can it any longer exploit access to files and documents? The answer lies, perhaps, in using community action agencies as sensitive mediators of innovation, whose funds are not narrowly pre-empted for specific programmes, but which surrender control of many of the more controversial innovations which they help to create. Without CPI, there would probably not now be a service of legal aid in New Haven; but CPI would itself have had great difficulty in protecting its integrity under its own auspices. By constituting an independent service, it escaped the dilemma. Community action has helped to explore the point at which an innovative agency can no longer itself contain the diversity of needs it takes up, and how the complexities of Federal support can be adapted to the evolution of new services. If there is no final solution to the dilemma, we have tried at least to clarify the nature of the risks that lie in overburdening a single agency with manifold social purposes, in the hope that it may enable community action to extricate these purposes more skilfully from the inhibitions we have discussed.

2

We have tried to interpret the evolution of community action as a particular illustration of the strength and weakness of the American process of reform. This process rests on a faith that the continual interaction of competing interests and principles will sustain a progressive enlargement of the possibilities of their fulfilment. So, confronted by the dilemmas of social choice, reform does not seem most characteristically to search for a balance. Instead, it takes up each of the incompatible principles by turn, and campaigns for it as if no sacrifice of its alternate were entailed. And this seemingly irrational refusal to come to terms with the fundamental dilemma may, after all, be more productive than accommodation. By repudiating whatever balance has been struck, it continually challenges society to explore new ways of meeting the problem. It raises the dilemma to a higher level of sophistication, where there is both more variety of endeavour, and more coherence, though each still inhibits the other. The debate goes round and round, raising the same perennial issues, but the context of argument changes.

This cyclical evolution of social policy has analogies with processes of development in other fields. Development research in industry sometimes gains by ignoring, for a while, the integration of performance requirements to be met. Suppose an aircraft of a certain speed and range is specified. Each component of the specification can only be maximized at the expense of the other—the faster the plane, the shorter its range. But instead of taking this into account from the first, it pays to develop both speed and range without regard for the consequences to the other. The final outcome will still be a compromise, but the plane is likely to be faster, and to go further, than would have been thought possible if a balanced development had been sought throughout. Similarly, an imbalanced economic development may have advantages, within limits, since it stimulates a greater use of latent resources to correct imbalance.[6]

This conception of reform presupposes that by giving expression to all the contending purposes of human society, they will stimulate a progressive enlargement of the possibilities of their mutual accommodation. The gravest danger is therefore deadlock and stultification. What began as a response to challenge hardens into complacent temporizing with all manner of urgent and unresolved problems. The task of the reformer is therefore to upset the balance in the best way he can, to set the process moving again, and keep it from once more coming to rest. The vitality of progress depends upon imaginative intervention, and to ensure this the right to innovate is diffused throughout society, and new ideas meet with a ready response and are alertly spread.

Once Paul Ylvisaker and his colleagues had persuaded the cautious Foundation to endorse their conception of the grey area projects, their initiative created a stir out of all proportion to its contribution to city budgets; the Rev. Leon Sullivan's experiment in Philadelphia attracted national interest almost before it was launched; the Cloward and Ohlin theory of delinquency caught the imagination of the President's Committee; when the North Carolina Fund invited proposals for support, it was overwhelmed with applications from almost every county of the State. Even criticism hostile to the whole endeavour, like the Cahns' analysis of CPI, was readily discussed and sifted for its new ideas by those it attacked. The network of informal discussion between Washington, New York and the cities buzzed with the excitement of a continual re-creation of the impetus of reform.

The innovators within the Ford Foundation, the President's Committee, the Office of Economic Opportunity thus had an influence which enabled them to initiate policies, but not to control their execution. They had, therefore, to shift the emphasis of their intervention as the thrust of any one idea began to lose its momentum. The success of their prescriptions could itself become an obstacle, threatening to petrify the challenge of the moment as a new orthodoxy. This manner of intervention depends

[6] These examples are taken from a paper by Albert O. Hirschman and Charles E. Lindblom, where they are developed into a general argument for 'disjointed incrementalism'. See 'Economic Development, Research and Development, Policy Making: Some Converging Views', *Behavioral Science*, Vol. 7, No. 2, (April 1962).

on a sense of timing—on a sensitivity to the inarticulate frustrations which can be crystallized as a force for change; and on an imagination which, as the will to seek new solutions droops under the weariness of hackneyed slogans, can find fresh concepts to liberate ideas. It exploits the enthusiasm of fashion to disrupt whatever equilibrium seems to menace the vitality of imbalance. It is deliberately one-sided and inconsistent, because it is consistently manipulating a complex and subtle process to the same end. No one reformer, perhaps, ever manages quite such ruthless disloyalty to his own ideas. But as one or another finds the crucial phrase, and commands the centre of attention, the movement of reform as a whole swings with him. And as it takes up each new slogan, it still contains within it all those that went before, never repudiated but only laid aside.

But even if this faith in a creative imbalance is ultimately justified, it can only make progress by exploring new forms of accommodation. Unless a movement of reform can institutionalize its latest purpose, and bargain for the kind of readjustment it believes necessary, it adds nothing to the stock of insight and experience. The process only works so long as the revolutions of fashion leave behind a growing resourcefulness. Ideas of reform, like Buddhist souls, are chained to a wheel of reincarnation, striving at each rebirth to grow towards beatitude. The reformers in the Ford Foundation and the President's Committee did not simply generate an idea one year, and, perceiving its shortcomings, generate another the next. As they took up each aspect of the problem, they tried to establish their innovations within the structure of community life, as a permanent expression of a need. Here they ran into much greater difficulties. For while they had the resources to propagate new lines of action, they lacked the power to ensure that a viable form of organization would result.

The more widely the freedom to initiate change is spread, the more difficult it becomes to control the outcome. In this lies the complementary weakness of reform in America. All the money, energy, talent and manoeuvre that goes into a movement of reform may achieve little more than a glossy prospectus and a distinguished committee. So the inventiveness of community action tended inevitably to dwindle progressively towards its realization. The prospectuses were mostly less than the imagination which inspired them, the organizations less than their prospectuses, the programmes less than the organization intended. A vision of opening opportunities for millions of maltreated youngsters might end with a dozen children in a makeshift nursery school, or a class of seamstresses learning a poorly-paid trade for which they were already in demand. The weakness of the movement lay in the impossibility of supervening in the competition of interests amongst which its innovations had to win their place.

The dilemmas of community action illustrate, not only the problems of reform in America, but also, perhaps, a universal aspect of the process of deliberate change. Since every society is informed by a great variety of ideals and interests competing for expression, it compromises them all and can fully satisfy none. And since the means to resolve any social issue cannot be divorced from the ends they serve, this fundamental incompatibility re-appears at every level of discussion. Any policy implies the reasons by which it could be refuted. In appealing to the values which justify it, it must disparage others which are also valid, and whatever balance it strikes enjoys only a grudging and provisional acquiescence. To overcome inertia, and dramatize its own necessity, reform seems to proceed most characteristically by polarizing the issue, and insisting upon the side of the debate least honoured in the prevailing order. It disrupts the equilibrium between ideals which, at their extremes, are mutually irreconcilable. Because of this, the movement of reform tends to be circular, continually redressing the balance by returning to preoccupations against which the last reform was itself a reaction. But although its insight is deliberately partial, its purpose is not simply disruptive, but to provoke a new accommodation. Only revolutions aim to disallow finally the interests and values which oppose them— and even then, since they cannot abolish the complexity of human society, the change is usually less absolute than they proclaim.

Where it is successful, each reform institutionalizes new interpretations of a need, enlarging the possibilities of reconciling social purposes in an upward spiral. And the whole process can also regress—as in a grossly unjust society, where a privileged minority initiates a cycle of repression and counteraction, by which the chances of any reconciliation are more and more narrowly confined. We do not mean to suggest that no issues are every finally resolved. Changes in technology or advances of knowledge can revise the context of argument so radically that an issue becomes irrelevant. The claims of some interests or values dwindle into insignificance, or are finally repudiated. But the process we have tried to distinguish seems to characterize reform in every society, wherever the possibility of change is accepted.

Societies differ, not in the need to revise progressively their social arrangement, but in their emphasis upon the complementary aspects of the process—disruption and reintegration. Totalitarian societies tend to guard jealously the power to enforce their periodic reconstructions of a workable compromise, and persecute between whiles any criticisms of their arrangements. When they stultify, it is for lack of courage or means to challenge the existing order. The heretics, driven underground, only recover their influence when frustration and gross inefficiency become so obvious that orthodoxy is no longer tenable, and government startles its citizens by a sudden change of direction. American society, so liberal in its tolerance of criticism and innovation, suffers from a corresponding impotence to enforce any reintegration. It tends to stultify in stalemate, which can be as frustrating and grossly inefficient as communist orthodoxy. The hundred flowers flourish, but they do not make a garden. Each ideology represents an extreme choice between competing principles. One ensures the power to determine how the aims of society are to be reconciled, at the cost of pre-empting all initiative of reform, and so inhibiting the creative energy of its people. The other gives this energy full play at the cost of leaving it to expend itself in muddled, abortive effort. As de Tocqueville observed 'Democratic liberty is far from accomplishing all its projects with the skill of an adroit despotism . . . but it produces what the ablest governments are frequently unable to create: namely an all-pervading and restless activity, a superabundant force, and an energy which is inseparable from it and which may, however unfavourable circumstances may be, produce wonders.'

The most difficult task of an American reformer is somehow to make the circumstances more favourable, without inhibiting this diffuse and restless energy. He is misled when he mistakes the show of activity for the progress it should stimulate; or when, impatient with his frustrations, he attempts to capture the process itself, and confine it within his own rationalization. When Saul Alinsky accused community action of 'political pornography'—a

Conclusion

spurious pretence of intervention—or the Cahns' accused CPI of seeking to monopolize all initiative, they pointed at the failings to which American reform is most vulnerable, even if they were in too much of a hurry to suppose the worst.

Can the process of reform we studied, however skilfully it is manipulated, ever radically improve the chances of the poor? And if it cannot, will Americans prefer to hold to their conception of the way issues must be resolved, even at the cost of ineradicable injustice? Is there a better way? It seems at times that equally liberal but more centralized societies like Britain achieve a less frustrating compromise between diffuseness of innovation, and the power to make it effective. And yet there are long years when Britain seems to possess neither the adroitness of a despotic regime nor the abundant energy of America: the government cannot master events, yet it pre-empts too much of the initiative to leave any independent reform much scope to innovate. Is the necessity of continual adaptation drawing all societies towards a similar conception of authoritative but self-critical planning?

But these questions lead beyond the scope of our analysis. Here we have tried only to illustrate, by a particular movement, something of the nature of reform in America, in the hope that it may help those who seek a more humane society to discriminate their strategies.

XI

EPILOGUE

1. RECAPITULATION: 1965–70

THE history of community action between 1960 and 1970 can be played over as a set of themes, stated and restated now in concert, now in counterpoint, sometimes with the full brass of presidential rhetoric, sometimes in discord, but always returning to the same key notes—co-ordination, innovation, participation; slums, poverty, power. The Ford Foundation began, in reaction to the crudity of urban renewal, by offering to city government a means of integrated social reform. The President's Committee on Juvenile Delinquency stressed the rational techniques of innovative planning—diagnostic theory and experimental evaluation. The Office of Economic Opportunity (OEO) stressed the voice of the people. A year or two later, the Model Cities legislation recapitulated the Ford Foundation's first theme, returning to the ideal of broadly based social problem solving integrated with city government, just as OEO was retreating from local planning towards programmes with a national emphasis, and losing its co-ordinative function. At the close of the decade President Nixon was reasserting the experimental, innovative role of OEO, as the model cities programme turned, after all, into a tussle over citizen's control. Meanwhile, the voice of the people—all kinds of people—grew in protest against the claims of authority, as the issue of democratic right broadened from urban renewal and local planning to constitutional rights in welfare, the protection of consumers, the legitimacy of university government and the conduct of the Viet Nam war.

At times the themes converged in concerted policies, at times drew apart, but they wove in and out continually to compose the history of the decade. Each represented an insight which could

239

neither be ignored, nor reconciled with the others. The solution lay in national economic policy, and the reform of social welfare; it lay in the renewal of the cities' institutions; it lay in redressing the powerlessness of the poor, or overcoming the complex of handicaps which disabled them; it lay in a systematic analysis of cause and effect. Each insight competed for priority, and became entangled in the competition of rival claims.

Between 1960 and 1965, the Ford Foundation, the President's Committee on Juvenile Delinquency and the OEO had evolved three principles of intervention, each of which seemed necessary to reform. Firstly, the resources of local governments must be redirected and co-ordinated, to concentrate efficiently on the most urgent social needs. Secondly, new ways of meeting these needs must be explored and their usefulness systematically evaluated. Thirdly, the needs must be determined by the people to be helped, without whose endorsement no plan was legitimate. Ideally, the first of these principles would draw upon the others in mutual reinforcement: as people defined their needs and experiment showed how best to meet them, a comprehensive plan of action would evolve. But each raised problems which the reformers could not solve. How could co-ordinated planning over-ride the self-protective interests of governmental jurisdictions, without imposing a higher order of authority for which there was no mandate? And if it could not, what prevented the co-ordinating agency from becoming yet another competitive jurisdiction, confusing still further the division of responsibility? How could the logic of scientific experiment be applied in political situations, where the experimenter could not rely on the stability of the context in which the experiment took place? How could people be allowed to assert their own definition of their needs, without undermining the authority of the government elected to represent them? And when conflict arose, how could public money gathered and appropriated by these authorities be used for their own harassment? In the five years which followed, these unresolved dilemmas set the poverty programme rebounding erratically on its course. As government returned again and again to the same principles, it encountered familiar difficulties and was driven to retreat. Faith in the ability of democratic institutions to redress inequity; in the power of expertise to solve any problem, when the will was there; in the constructive energy of ordinary citizens,

Epilogue

when they banded together to help themselves—all suffered under
these repeated frustrations.

This disillusionment was mirrored in the larger tragedy of
Viet Nam, as the credibility of government, confidence in its
sophisticated techniques of war, and the morale of its recruits
gradually wore down in another battle in the name of freedom
and self-determination. But while the build-up of men and arms
in Viet Nam proceeded stealthily, behind a screen of cautious
public announcements, the war on poverty was declared in the
most uncompromising terms, and never received the funds to
honour them. The faltering progress of the anti-poverty programme must be set against the background of military expenditures which increasingly strained the economy. But its history is
also a recapitulation of the dilemmas we have tried to interpret in
the preceding pages, and its frustrations arose out of them, as
much or more than from the consequences of the war in Asia.

This restless interplay of incompatible principles suggested the
closing reflections of the last chapter. American society fosters a
diffuse initiative for change, which repeatedly loses its momentum
in the search for a coalition of interests broad enough to support
it, only to be succeeded by another optimistic beginning. As
Daniel P. Moynihan remarks:

It is an American fault to insist on extravagant goals—as if to set
out to achieve anything less than everything suggests a lack of
sincerity, manliness or both—and to be exceedingly busy with other
matters when it subsequently develops that little or nothing happens.
The social history of the 1960's is already littered with the wreckage
of crash programmes that were going to change everything and in
fact changed nothing, save possibly to diminish ever so slightly the
credibility of those who claimed credit in advance for achievements
that never, somehow, came to pass.[1]

Yet was there really an alternative, either in less presumptuous or
more revolutionary changes? Even wrecks alter the landscape,
marking a path of leadership that perhaps had to be explored.
The first part of this postscript looks back over the rise
and decline of the anti-poverty programme, trying to determine
what choices were open, and how far political circumstances

[1] Daniel P. Moynihan, 'The Crisis in Welfare', *Public Interest*, No. 10 (Winter
1968).

241

constrained them. From this, and the more fundamental analysis which follows in the second part, we may be able to see more clearly the choices which seem open in the next decade.

Was Community Action Misconceived?

If the second half of the decade repeated the confusion of cross-purposes which beset the first, was community action a mistake—a set of interventions which could never achieve what they set out to achieve in America as it is, and only distracted attention from more practicable reforms? This implies that the anti-poverty programme need not have become embroiled in such contradictions, and botched an opportunity for more worthwhile action through misjudgment. Or should we rather treat community action as an expression of the pressures on American society, whose significance lies in the nature of the dilemmas it tried to contain? From this point of view, success or failure do not mean very much, except in relation to the expectations of this or that participant: it is the dilemmas themselves we need to understand. The two approaches are not mutually exclusive: of course people made mistakes, and of course their choices were constrained. But if we can discriminate how large was the element of political or social misjudgment in this troubled history, and how much was more or less inescapable, we may see more clearly where the choices lie.

Community action certainly disappointed the hopes of those who sought a new instrument of co-ordination, a stimulus to widespread innovation or popular control of planning; and it confirmed the cynicism of critics who never expected from it any great benefit to the poor. Nor, by the time the Economic Opportunity Act was passed, were the inherent contradictions in its strategies still unnoticed. The controversies which had already arisen and the stultification of so many city demonstration programmes made them obvious enough. The pioneering stage of community action can be seen as an experiment, whose implications only gradually became apparent. But after five years of frustration and tenuous achievements, the risks were known, at least to some who promoted community action as a national policy. Were they then at fault, misleading the political leaders they advised, and rashly pursuing an ideal they could not hope to realize?

This is essentially the answer Daniel P. Moynihan gives in his critique of the anti-poverty programme, *Maximum Feasible Misunderstanding*. Community action was an aberration from the pragmatic leadership of responsible politicians, and did much unnecessary harm to the true interests of the poor. Moynihan argues that the controversies which debilitated the anti-poverty programme were not inevitable, but arose from an irresponsible misinterpretation of the legislative mandate. He asserts that the clause in the Economic Opportunity Act, which required the 'maximum feasible participation' of the poor in community action, was 'intended to do no more than ensure that persons excluded from the political process in the South and elsewhere would nonetheless participate in the *benefits* of the community action programmes'.[2] It may not have occurred to the drafters of the legislation that the clause could be interpreted otherwise. But in the absence of any direction, reformers on the OEO staff took it as a mandate to promote the organization of poor people as a counterweight to the prerogatives of established power. 'The Conway group gave to the community action programme of the poverty programme a structure that neither those who drafted it, those who sponsored it, nor those who enacted it ever in any way intended.'[3] A tentative theory about the alienation of the poor became a dogma about the evils of powerlessness, and a cautious attempt to open opportunities to poor people became a strategy of stirring up trouble.

Moynihan implies that, but for these disruptive tactics, Congress would have committed its support to a far more ambitious and expanding attack on poverty: 'an immense opportunity to institute more or less permanent social changes—a fixed full employment programme, a measure of income maintenance—was lost while energies were expended in ways that very probably hastened the end of the brief period when such options were open.'[4] A few impetuous radicals, oversold on some half-baked sociological theories, seized the day while wiser men were

[2] Daniel P. Moynihan, *Maximum Feasible Misunderstanding* (New York: Free Press, 1969), p. 87.
[3] *Ibid.*, p. 98.
[4] *Ibid.*, p. 193.

occupied elsewhere. Robert Levine, another historian of the anti-poverty programme, who joined the staff of OEO in 1965, also describes some of his influential colleagues as impractical ideologues, whose rashness at least caused the programme avoidable grief. President Johnson himself, perhaps, came to share the same sense of what had gone wrong. He is reported to have accused OEO of being run by 'kooks and sociologists'—and probably did not intend any distinction between them.[5]

Sociologists do not have a political constituency, and this is the essence of Moynihan's case. 'The role of social science lies not in the formulation of social policy, but in the measurement of its results'—and should never presume, from a plausible theory, to decide the very different questions of political action. At very least they must make their meaning clear to the politicians on whom they will have to depend. When intellectuals take over policy, they lack the professional politicians' sense of the constituency for reform, and are likely to attempt the impossible. They then not only spoil the opportunity for practicable interventions, but raise expectations which cannot be met, aggravating tensions which undermine the basis of constructive action. As an interpretation of the anti-poverty programme's fate, the argument can point to the controversies which some of the more radical programme's provoked. But it presupposes an extraordinary naïvety amongst the political actors who allowed their judgment to be pre-empted.

Moynihan does not explain how the intellectual reformers—OEO officials, foundation executives, social scientists—came to have the influence he claims for them. Politicians do not usually surrender the initiative to their officials and advisers, nor take on trust proposals without examining their political implications. It is surely more likely that if, at the outset, the OEO tried to make the most of the clause about participation, it believed it had political backing. And if this backing was withdrawn when controversy arose, the setback only repeated, in the context of federal politics, the same disintegration of support from which so many local programmes suffered, as soon as they tried to implement their plans. The consensus behind the community action title of

[5] Robert A. Levine, *The Poor Ye Need not Have with You: Lessons from the War on Poverty* (Cambridge, Mass.: M.I.T. Press, 1970), p. 86.

the Economic Opportunity Act was probably even more fragile, from the circumstances in which the Act was passed. Indeed, the problem of defining the constituency for a campaign against poverty continuously underlay the programme's development, from its inception to its decline.

The Attrition of the Anti-Poverty Programme

'The War on Poverty did not arise, as have many great national programmes, from the pressure of overwhelming public demand; the poor had no lobby. Nor was it proposed by the staff thinkers in government agencies who are paid to conceive ideas. It began when President Kennedy said to his principal economic adviser, Walter Heller, . . . in December 1962: "Now, look! I want to go beyond the things that have already been accomplished. Give me facts and figures on the things we still have to do. For example, what about the poverty problem in the United States?" That comment set in motion the staff work that, more than a year later, took concrete form as the War on Poverty.'[6] According to another account, Kennedy did not commit himself to proposing legislation specifically directed against poverty until a few weeks before his assassination nearly a year later. Some of his advisers doubted whether the issue would have any appeal in the election campaign of 1964. But it seems clear that the anti-poverty programme was a presidential initiative, which Kennedy had freely chosen, and his successor eagerly endorsed.

Both men could find in the issue of poverty an expression of their political self-image—Kennedy as the innovator, pushing the frontiers of American society towards new fields of social endeavour; Johnson as the heir to the New Deal. Kennedy had been shocked by reports of near starvation, and worried by evidence of persisting gross inequalities. He foresaw too that the legal enforcement of civil rights could not carry racial justice much further, without a complementary policy of social and economic redress. And he needed a programme to give his slogan of a new frontier a more forceful interpretation. Johnson identified these purposes with his own homelier style, and stamped them with his name. But while both presidents believed that the

[6] James L. Sundquist and C. S. Schelling (eds), *On Fighting Poverty: Perspectives from Experience* (New York: Basic Books, 1969), p. 7.

country would respond to a campaign against poverty, neither seems to have calculated in any detail the political constituency for reform, nor to have had any specific programmes in mind.[7] In a sense, the design of the Economic Opportunity Act was remarkably open: the advisers put forward their various proposals, the departments of the federal government looked to their interests, but the only demands the legislation had initially to satisfy were those of the President himself.

Unlike the Ford Foundation's grey area projects, which had been presented to cities partly as a means of relieving their financial difficulties, the anti-poverty programme was not conceived in terms of institutional needs. It was a response to the President's desire for an issue that would define the direction of his leadership, and catch the nation's imagination. Once poverty emerged as the issue, his advisers faced the difficulty of formulating a strategy to match the complexity and size of the problem, within a politically acceptable budget. Both Kennedy and Johnson seem to have assumed that they could not prudently put forward proposals costing more than about a billion dollars. Yet the new legislation was to represent a comprehensive, co-ordinated attack on poverty, and a dramatic departure from conventional approaches. As soon as the President's advisers became aware of the experiments pioneered by the Ford Foundation and the Committee on Juvenile Delinquency, they began to explore their potential for the war on poverty. A modest proposal from the

---

[7] Frances Piven, however, argues that there was an underlying political calculation. Both Kennedy and Johnson, she suggests, were concerned about the black vote in northern cities, which might be crucial in a closely fought election. The cities were mostly governed by Democratic mayors more sensitive to the interests of whites than to their growing black minority. If black voters were alienated, and denied their share in the patronage of city government, support for a Democratic presidential candidate might suffer. A national anti-poverty programme, clearly identified with a Democratic administration, could channel jobs and services to the ghetto, even if city hall was reluctant to extend its patronage. 'Through both neighbourhood and citywide structures, in other words, the national administration revived the traditional processes of urban politics: offering jobs and services to build party loyalty. But for the federal government to revivify the processes of urban politics, it had to initiate a unique administrative arrangement: *the hallmark of the Great Society programmes was the direct relationship between the national government and the ghettoes, a relationship in which both state and local governments were undercut*'. Frances Fox Piven and Richard A. Cloward, *Regulating the Poor: The Functions of Public Welfare* (New York: Pantheon, 1971), p. 261. But though this implication can be drawn from the programmes, Piven and Cloward do not provide evidence that either President, or their advisers, ever actually spelled out such a strategy.

Committee, to include a budget for experimental community organization in the Act, was expanded by William Cannon of the Budget Bureau into a plan for ten demonstration areas, each with a development corporation. In this way resources would be concentrated, and co-ordinated through the corporations, rather than the Federal Government—where the Budget Bureau despaired of making much headway. Renamed Community Action Programmes, the notion of selective, comprehensive demonstrations became for a while the dominant proposal. The plans were modified later, on the insistent advice of the Secretary of Labour, to include programmes with a more immediate influence on unemployment. But community action—diffused from ten demonstrations to as many as need and imagination could justify —remained the distinctive feature of the Act. It promised an innovative attack on the roots of poverty and a new approach to the problems of co-ordination, without committing very large funds. Yet it would not seem a trivial response to the needs, since the commitment was indeterminate: as it evolved, creating in communities a broadly-based constituency for the programme, more and more resources could be channelled through it. Thus community action satisfied, as perhaps nothing else could, the President's demand for a strategy that was neither exorbitantly expensive, nor uninspiringly incremental.

No one involved in planning the anti-poverty programme seems, therefore, to have looked closely at the troubled history of the models it was proposed to copy, nor to have seen their conflicting implications.[8] In the long run, community action could only be sustained if the administrations, congress, city halls, and at least a section of the poor understood it, and were prepared to back it through all the controversies it was bound to generate. But little attempt was made to establish such a consensus of support. President Johnson launched the war on poverty as his

[8] Daniel P. Moynihan was a rare exception. He tried in vain to convince the Budget Bureau that their conception of community action as a co-ordinating structure was controversial. Laden with Mobilization for Youth documents, he pleaded with them to understand that 'they had one view of community action, Shriver another, and its advocates yet a third. *I had no view* ... But I did want the various parties to be aware of the divergent interpretations so they would not get a nasty shock when the first signs of "trouble" appeared. In particular I wanted the White House to expect a certain amount of trouble and be ready for it when it comes' (personal communication).

own initiative, without inviting Congress, even within his own party, to share the credit.[9]

> 'This administration,' he told a joint session of Congress on January 8, 1964, 'today here and now declares unconditional war on poverty in America. . . .' He did not say, 'this country' or 'this government' but specifically 'this administration', and he distinctly did not ask 'this Congress' to declare the war. . . . Mr Johnson was intent on making this programme uniquely his—the cornerstone of his Great Society. . . . Yet, when the involvement was so personal and so exclusive, it could only arouse resentment amongst others who sought to share the credit for the nation's 'unconditional war on poverty'.[10]

The Republicans, especially, were given short shrift. In the House of Representatives committee on the bill, they were scarcely allowed a hearing. 'We were subjected to procedures that eliminated almost any meaningful questioning of any witnesses and prevented any normal bi-partisan consideration in executive session,' complained one of its members. 'In every case amendments offered in good faith by members of the minority were summarily rejected by the majority of our committee.'[11]

Not only Congress, but state and local government were subordinated to the administration's initiative. A Senate amendment giving state governors limited powers of veto was reluctantly accepted—and rescinded a year later. Nor did the legislation give city government any mandatory part in community action programmes: private agencies were eligible for direct Federal funds.

---

[9] The reasons may have been partly technical. 'Normally, when a bill is drawn by the Executive Branch, senior members of committees and/or their staffs are consulted about their general provisions and may also help in the drafting process. However, the poverty bill was generated and drawn up by the Executive Branch without Congressional participation. It was not even clear which Committee in each house would consider the bill. Because the measure cut across jurisdictional lines—at least four committees in each house had jurisdiction over some part of the bill—the designers of the legislation did not know whom in Congress to consult.' Sar A. Levitan, *The Design of Federal Anti-Poverty Strategy* (Institute of Labour and Industrial Relations, University of Michigan and Wayne State University, March 1967), p. 40.

[10] William C. Selover, 'The View from Capitol Hill' in *On Fighting Poverty: Perspectives from Experience, op. cit.,* p. 159.

[11] Peter Frelinghaysen at a Senate hearing, quoted in 'The View from Capitol Hill', *op. cit.,* p. 161.

Thus both the design of the anti-poverty programme, and the way it was to be carried out remained in the hands of the President, his advisers and the director of the newly-created OEO. This exclusiveness reflected the President's desire to assert his leadership, and a fear that the programme would lose its momentum, if the established power structure was allowed to control it. In effect, the President appealed over the heads of Congress, state and local government to the people, inviting them to interpret his challenge to their idealism. In this way he could dramatize the issue, without committing himself very far before the response had been tested. Although articulate, liberal opinion had become increasingly concerned about poverty, no one could be sure that most people cared. Even if the persistence of poverty represented, most comprehensively, the underlying weaknesses in the structure of American society, it was not at all clear what important political constituency reform would appeal to. The reforms would have to create their own constituency, as they evolved out of the process of community action.

The OEO was therefore caught between risks it could not escape. Unless it set out boldly, it would betray its promise of 'unconditional war', and lose the initiative to established departments of federal government with better friends in Congress. But to achieve anything substantial in its first year meant hurried improvisation, where the inevitable muddles and misjudgments would hand the opposition their chance of revenge. Sargent Shriver, OEO's director, chose to plunge forward, extemporizing plans and guidelines, and backing the confident idealism of his staff with his personal judgment. By the summer of 1965, ten thousand young people had been recruited to vocational training centres in disused army bases, managed under contract by private business; half a million children were gathered into 'Head Start' pre-school programmes for the summer; and the first of what became over a thousand community action agencies were funded. These results were impressively energetic, but dangerously vulnerable. There was no time to work out a policy for the training centres: 'Job Corps in the first year was thus a chaotic nightmare eventuating not only in a programme of lower quality than it should have been for kids whose needs were not as carefully matched with programmes as they should have been but also in the violence, sex and other scandals that hurt Job Corps so badly

in its first two years'.[12] Several of the community action programmes turned out to be bitterly controversial. Head Start was
safer, but in the haste to set it going, it was initiated as a summer
programme using vacant facilities, which did not match the plans
for sustained, structured training in conceptual skills.

These weaknesses enabled partisan critics to attack the programme without seeming callous towards the poor. Republican
rhetoric swelled with indignation. 'This programme has been in
operation for a year,' declaimed Senator Strom Thurmond in
August 1965, 'and its history provides a catalog of futility, abuses,
political partisanship, wastefulness, slipshod administration and
scandal.'[13] A few months later, Senator Scott, who had voted for
the programme, stated 'The war on poverty, as administered from
Washington by the Office of Economic Opportunity, is distinguished today not for its accomplishments, but for its failures.
The war on poverty has degenerated into a nightmare of bureaucratic bungling, overly paid administrators, poorly organized
fieldworkers, and partisan politics.'[14] These attacks were predictable, and Sargent Shriver was ready to make a virtue of them:
'At the beginning Head Start was criticized—Job Corps was
criticized—use of non-professionals was criticized. And I'm sure
that we are by no means out of the woods with regard to controversy,' he told a Chicago audience in December 1965. He
continued:

> If we were, that would be cause for real concern. Listening to the
> poor can be unpleasant. Trying out new approaches can threaten
> those who prefer to stick to present methods. Controversy is always
> inconvenient. Always comes at the worst time. Recognizing prob-
> lems before we are fully ready to deal with them on our own terms
> can generate heat. But ignoring those problems, tuning out the
> voice of the poor, clinging to our past methods and approaches—
> can produce even more heat. It can produce a holocaust as it did
> last summer in Watts. We can no longer play it safe—for soon there
> will be no safe place, no place to hide.[15]

Shriver could take Republican opposition in his stride, putting

[12] *The Poor Ye Need Not Have with You: Lessons from the War on Poverty, op. cit.,*
p. 58.
[13] *Congressional Digest,* March 1966, p. 67.
[14] *Ibid.,* p. 81.
[15] *Ibid.,* pp. 82, 84.

Epilogue

scandalous anecdotes in perspective, appealing to the challenge
of innovation and the menace of riot if the challenge was not met.
But OEO depended on narrow, if powerful, political support—the
President's personal backing. In the Summer of 1965, Johnson had
been urging his cabinet to cut back their spending for the benefit
of OEO: by the Fall, he began to withdraw. If he had ever endorsed
the philosophy of community action as a counterweight to the
power of city hall, he was not prepared to stand by it, once the
big city mayors of his own party began to protest. More probably,
he conceived the participation of the poor in terms of jobs and
responsiveness to their views, rather than a formal share of
power. The OEO, however, set guidelines that at least a third of
the controlling board of a community action agency should be
representatives of the neighbourhoods served, preferably chosen
by election; and it tried to withhold funds from cities which
refused to give way.[16] At the same time, it had funded independent projects in some cities, of which the most notorious was
the Syracuse Community Development Association, whose
demonstration marches against a Republican city government
understandably enraged the mayor. By the summer of 1965, the
United States Conference of Mayors had become a determined
lobby against any conception of community action which
threatened their authority. It accused Shriver of 'fostering class
struggle', and denounced his attempt to fund projects apart from
the agencies approved by city hall.

The administration bowed to these pressures. The Vice-
President assured the mayors that he had been hired as their
'built-in special agent to make sure that you are represented in
this programme twenty-four hours a day, 365 days a year.'[17]
The OEO administrators were told through the Budget Bureau to
concentrate on jobs for the poor, not representation. The director
of the solidly conservative General Service Administration was
appointed Sargent Shriver's deputy. Less ideologically committed executives began to replace the leading advocates of
neighbourhood control on OEO's staff. But most damaging of all,
the President himself, disillusioned with the poverty programme

[16] The principle was later endorsed by Congress, and embodied in amendments
to the Act.
[17] In an address to the National League of Cities, August 1965, quoted in 'The
View from Capitol Hill', *op. cit.*, p. 181.

as a political asset and increasingly preoccupied with the Viet Nam war, withdrew his personal involvement.[18] The OEO had called for $3.4 billion to carry the programme through 1966 to 1967 and had been led to expect as much: but when the administration's budget was sent to Congress in January 1966, only $1.75 billion was proposed—and the final appropriation was $138 million less. Deserted by their general, the battalions of the war on poverty could only retreat from their more exposed positions, and try to consolidate some of the ground they had won.

The OEO was thus left without any wholehearted supporters. Its controversies had soured the President, the mayors were angry, Congressional backers were cautious while opponents gleefully exploited rumours of scandal and subversion. And as it tried to pacify these resentments, OEO alienated its more radical friends, who saw their ideals betrayed. When, for instance, it withdrew from a project it had funded in Mississippi—The Child Development Group—whose organization of the black poor had aroused the State's senator, it laid itself open to the charge of deserting the poorest and most deprived Americans in response to the most reactionary of established interests, however valid its reasons may have been in practice. At a convention of representatives of the poor in Washington, Sargent Shriver was personally vilified and repudiated.[19] Attacked from all sides, denied the funds to match the bold promises of its inception, and weakened by evidence of careless management, the OEO could never do enough to satisfy the militant advocates of the poor: yet it had already attempted more than either local or national government was prepared to tolerate.

By 1967, it seemed doubtful whether the programme would

[18] The programme was administered from the White House, and its staff represented the largest concentration of Presidential staff. The prestige of the White House was to facilitate Shriver's task of co-ordinating the work of cabinet officers. As presidential support dwindled, so too did the prospects for co-ordination and a budget proportionate to the aims.

[19] The convention was organized by the Citizens Crusade Against Poverty in April 1966. The *New York Times* reported, 'Mr Shriver plunged on with his speech despite the uproar and shouts of "you're lying" and "stop listening to him" from a rebel group that moved up near the stage. The director of O.E.O. looking strained and upset was hustled from the International Inn immediately after his speech despite pleas to remain for questioning. "I will not participate in a riot" he declared'. Quoted in John C. Donovan, *The Politics of Poverty* (New York: Pegasus, 1967), p. 69.

continue at all. It had barely survived Congressional opposition in 1966, and the elections of that year had now returned a Congress where conservative Republicans had ousted many liberal Democrats. The new House of Representatives pointedly voted to exclude OEO's staff from a general pay increase for Federal employees, an ominous and vindictive gesture. The White House seemed coldly indifferent. Summer riots hardened opinion against the supposedly disruptive influence of community action. Yet OEO and the programmes it represented did survive—with a slightly larger annual appropriation, voted for each of the next two years. This unexpectedly generous endorsement owed much to Sargent Shriver's tireless advocacy. He stumped the country, organizing backing from influential businessmen, mayors, the League of Women Voters, emphasizing the less controversial of his programmes, and pointing to the evidence that community action agencies, so far from provoking riot, had more probably restrained it. The fears of city governments were met by a formal concession: Congress passed an amendment granting them the right, if they wished, to take over the private non-profit-making community action agencies which typically ran the programmes in their cities.[20] But above all, the OEO survived because no convincing alternative to its programmes existed for tackling problems which could not be ignored. No government, local or national, could afford to throw aside its most publicized means of relieving poverty and quieting urban unrest, ineffectual or abrasive as they might seem, without risking a more damaging outcry. And by this time, the most controversial of OEO's policies had been tamed.

1967 inaugurated the middle-age of the OEO. The maverick newcomer had settled down, modestly trimming its ambitions to a stable budget and constraining tolerance, and trading autonomy for respectability. In the event, the right of city government to take over community action agencies was scarcely used; so unassuming had they become. Even the new administration, for all its Republican prejudices, has not yet, after two years in office, found a way to retire the OEO.

The political history we have sketched here represents a progressive attrition of the philosophy evolved in the preceding five

---

[20] The amendment was proposed by Congresswoman Edith Green, and popularly known as the 'bosses and boll weevils' amendment.

years. Local planning and co-ordination, the organization of poor neighbourhoods to assert their interests all became residual concerns of OEO.[21] Community action agencies together provided thousands of jobs for poor people and some useful services. But as policy evolved, its emphasis shifted more and more from local initiative towards national programmes, for which community action agencies were merely the instrument, if they were involved at all. Such were Head Start, the Concentrated Employment Programme (a group of vocational training and job placement schemes administered nationally by the Department of Labour, but implemented through community action agencies), legal services and neighbourhood health centres. These— together with the Job Corps, other vocational and educational programmes, economic development schemes, and social benefits not administered through local community action agencies— accounted for much the greater part of the anti-poverty budget. The predominance of these nationally conceived programmes tended to undermine the principle of participation, since the local agencies initiated so little of the whole endeavour. Programmes planned and operated locally by the thousand odd community action agencies absorbed barely half even of their own expenditure. 'These locally planned and operated programmes plus Research and Demonstration thus form less than one-half of the CAP budget, less than one-fourth of the OEO budget, and less than two per cent of the total War on Poverty.'[22] Probably no more than one per cent of OEO's funds were devoted in any way to the organization of the poor: and OEO's funds themselves were only a tenth of all federal expenditure directed against poverty.

The OEO had set out, in a clamour of publicity and partisan politics, to confront the dilemmas which neither the Ford Foundation nor the President's Committee on Juvenile Delinquency had successfully resolved. It failed where they had failed, in reconciling political accountability with experiment and the redistribution of power. The controversies in which it became embroiled reacted upon all its endeavours. The Child Development Group in Mississippi; the protest marches in Syracuse and

[21] These ideals survived, however, in other programmes influenced by OEO—in education, health, and the Model Cities programme we discuss below.
[22] *The Poor Ye Need Not Have with You: Lessons from the War on Poverty, op. cit.,* p. 158.

Newark; voter registration drives amongst poor people in Durham, North Carolina, Houston and Palm Beach County, Florida; support for the Blackstone Rangers youth gang in Chicago were a very small part of community action. Even OEO's policy that representatives of poor neighbourhoods should sit on boards of community action agencies bent to the obduracy of powerful mayors. But the resentment these few challenges aroused were enough to cool the President's enthusiasm, and robbed OEO of its crucial political support. Even without the Viet Nam war, it might never have regained the political credit to secure funds comparable to its commitments. To survive at all, it withdrew the autonomy of community action agencies, turning them essentially into the local administrators of national programmes—over some of which OEO itself had been forced to surrender control. Thus it abandoned the strategies of intervention it had inherited from its predecessors, and at first enthusiastically endorsed—turning from innovative, locally-inspired projects, planned and controlled largely by poor people themselves to more conventional services conceived in Washington, and increasingly controlled by the old-established departments of federal government.

In the course of this retreat, it lost goodwill, its claim to priority in resources and much of its purpose. For if OEO and its local community action agencies merely ran a routine of educational, vocational and social services, the administration might perhaps be done more logically by the agencies which had always been responsible for such services. In his first message to Congress, in February 1969, President Nixon had indeed proposed that OEO should give up responsibility for its established programmes, and concentrate all its energies on its innovative role, 'devising programmes to help the poor, and serving as an "incubator" for these programmes during their initial, experimental phases.' It would then retrieve one of its original ideals. But if experiments, as they matured, were then to be incorporated in the programmes of other agencies, OEO would neither be able to co-ordinate their impact, nor secure community control of them.

By mid-1971, the intentions of President Nixon's administration seemed to repudiate the war on poverty's essential strategy. The OEO was to be dismantled—research and experiment apart— its functions re-distributed amongst the departments of federal

government. A national system of welfare benefits was to guarantee
to every family at least a minimum of support, while State and
local government received block grants, to use as they thought
best, without federal direction. Thus resources would be channelled to established agencies of government, without any of the
former insistence on co-ordination, institutional reform, or
citizens' participation: and the poor were to receive money as
needy individuals, not power as deprived communities denied a
voice in their destiny.

This synoptic outline of the anti-poverty programme's political
history, as it affected community action, raises some puzzling
questions. Why did President Johnson launch the Economic
Opportunity Act with such uncompromising rhetoric, when the
commitment of resources was so cautious? Why was community
action adopted as a leading strategy with so little regard for the
conflicts it had already aroused? Why did the President withdraw
his active support so entirely, once he was confronted with the
controversies inherent in carrying the strategy out? And why,
for all that, did the programme survive, despite congressional
hostility and the President's indifference? The answers begin to
fall into place, if we look at the constituency for reform. In many
ways, poverty was a very attractive issue for a President seeking
a theme to announce his leadership. ' "War on Poverty" is a
terrific slogan,' as a Republican congressman ruefully conceded,
'particularly in an election year. It puts doubters under suspicion
of being in favour of poverty.'[23] Not only was it politically unchallengeable, it drew together a number of contemporary preoccupations—with structural unemployment, the progress of
civil rights, hunger in depressed rural areas, unrest in urban
ghettoes. But at the same time, it promised benefits directly only
to the least articulate and influential of the electorate: the
majority might well repudiate the programme, however they
sympathized with its ideals, if they were threatened with higher
taxes. So the war was to be fought by making savings elsewhere,
without raising the national budget by a single dollar, as its
director boasted. Only such a strategy as community action, we
suggest, could match the ideal of a boldly imaginative thrust at
the roots of poverty within these fiscal constraints. A highly

[23] Representative Charles B. Hoeven of Iowa, quoted in *On Fighting Poverty:
Perspectives from Experience, op. cit.,* p. 28.

selective, experimental approach, dependent on broadly-based community support, left future political and financial commitments open, at least partly rationalizing the meagreness of the initial funds. It blurred the disparity between means and ends, balancing idealism and political caution so adroitly that scarcely anyone, understandably, looked searchingly at the problems of interpreting it.

Yet community action was not mere political casuistry. The anti-poverty programme had to create a constituency influential enough to sustain its momentum. If communities prepared their own plans, and initiated their own projects, an articulate local leadership should emerge which understood the needs, and would press for resources to meet them. And this indeed happened: when the anti-poverty programme seemed to have no friends in Congress or the administration, when militant reformers were crying betrayal, Sargent Shriver appealed to grass-roots support, and won enough backing to turn a hostile Congress towards sympathetic compromise.

If this interpretation is right, community action arose from the ambivalence of the presidential initiative— the desire to assert an idealistic leadership, which did not risk any great commitment before reactions in the country had been tested, but offered means if the response was favorable. Despite Moynihan's argument 'a fixed full-employment programme, a measure of income maintenance' could never have been viable proposals: either presupposed a national constituency for social reforms which neither Kennedy nor Johnson nor their principal advisers believed had yet been created. But given this political setting, need community action have provoked so much controversy? Was there within the OEO, as Moynihan seems to imply, an intellectual conspiracy to subvert community action into radical confrontation?

Conflict and Participation

In the first place, rumour must be distinguished from fact. From the outcry amongst Republican Congressmen and aggrieved mayors, it would have seemed that across the United States radical —perhaps even communist—employees of community action agencies were inciting riot and subverting the authority of city government. In practice, the programmes of these agencies were all too blandly conventional. The manoeuvres we described in earlier chapters, by which the school system and the established institutions evaded the innovative intentions of the Ford Foundation and the President's Committee, worked as well to contain the anti-poverty programme. Despite OEO's insistence on the representation of the poor, they were scarcely involved in the initiation of community action agencies, and though they were brought onto their controlling boards in time, the programmes continued to reflect the interests of the original promoters—the mayor, the voluntary agencies, the school system, welfare departments, universities. A study of community action in twenty medium-sized cities remarks: 'Given the involvement of the existing institutional systems in the design of the local anti-poverty agency, its structure, its future programme development practices, and its initial operating programmes, it is difficult to comprehend the logic of Moynihan in his charge that emphasis on citizen participation led to the death of the poverty programme. ... To repeat, there were *no* poor people, *no* residents of poverty neighbourhoods, *no* members of the groups to be served involved in the initiation of the local community action agencies or in the initial programme development in the twenty cities in this sample.'[24] Nor did the essential pattern change as time went by. The community action agencies ran barely a fifth of the programmes themselves, contracting out the rest mostly to the school system and voluntary welfare agencies: and very few of any programmes were directed towards institutional change. Over 90% were concerned with individual change, designed to counteract the debilitating influence of the culture of poverty, and a few with economic changes. Kenneth Clark and Jeannette Hopkins draw a similar conclusion from a review of community action in fifty-one cities—85% of the programmes were concerned with services, 10% with income support, and scarcely more than 5% with institutional changes.[25] To those who under-

[24] S. M. Rose, 'Community Action Programs: The Relationship between initial conception of the Poverty Program, Derived Intervention Strategy and Program Implementation'. Brandeis Thesis, 1970 (Ann Arbor, University Microfilms, 1970), pp. 181–2. See also Stephen M. Rose, *The Betrayal of the Poor: The Transformation of Community Action* (Cambridge: Schenkman, 1972), especially chapter seven.

[25] Kenneth B. Clark and Jeanette Hopkins, *A Relevant War Against Poverty. A Study of Community Action Programs and observable Social Change* (New York: Harper & Row, 1969). These proportions would not be accepted by some other analysts.

stood poverty, not as the consequence of personal disabilities, but as a failure of the social structure, such a distribution of effort exposed the insincerity of the whole endeavour. So far from challenging established power, community action turned out to be merely another instrument of social service, essentially patronizing and conservative.

In a sense though, this evidence could be taken to support Moynihan's argument. For if, in practice, community action was bound to accommodate to the realities of power, and OEO was promoting nothing more threatening than variations on conventional welfare and educational services, it was doubly foolish to proceed as if much more radical changes were in hand. Such rhetoric could only raise false hopes in the ghetto, and alienate government, leaving OEO caught between its radical and conservative critics. This indeed happened: the few attempts to carry through the conception of community action as confrontation did arouse controversy which damaged its future. Even if the Viet Nam war pre-empted its chances of greatly expanding resources, it might still have been less abruptly disowned. The OEO's insistence on the representation of the poor alarmed mayors, without their waiting to see whether it posed any real threat to them, and their protests influenced the President to back away. The experiments in support for independent community groups were a tiny proportion of its programmes, but gave OEO a sadly inflated reputation as the champion of militant protest. Just as Mobilization for Youth, on which the OEO staff modelled their ideal, had been nearly destroyed by a few bold gestures untypical of its work, so the anti-poverty programme was brought down by its least representative projects. Could it then, as Moynihan implies, have gained more by straining less against the limits of its political scope?

In reality, OEO could hardly have avoided the issue of citizen participation, whatever the legislative mandate and the risks of controversy. Wherever civil rights groups or neighbourhood organizations could claim to speak for the ghetto, they were bound to demand control. Planning and demonstration programmes meant to them the white definition of black needs, and they had learned to expect little worthwhile from them. Their own claims to leadership would be threatened, too, by hopeful initiatives in which they had no part. No such leadership had emerged in many cities: but where it had, and wherever it might appear, a community action agency which did not represent it would be angrily repudiated. The Ford Foundation had not set out, through its grey area projects, to institutionalize the power of the poor. Its first interest was the co-ordination and re-direction of established services, and the control of the community action agencies it fostered reflected this. Yet it came to stress participation more and more, as—in Philadelphia, for instance—militant spokesmen of poor neighbourhoods challenged the legitimacy of its intervention. Unless community action responded to these pressures, it would be rejected by its con-stituency—and there was no telling where the next crisis might come. Newhaven's CPI which seemed so firmly under the control of an enlightened establishment, eventually had to face a challenge from its poor neighbourhoods. Oakland, where in 1960 the Ford Foundation had found no grass-roots leadership on which to build, became a national symbol of aggressive black autonomy. The anger of black people deprived of their opportunities was everywhere becoming more strident and more ready to strike.

Thus OEO could not have escaped conflict: it could only choose which battle to fight—against city hall or ghetto leadership. If community action surrendered to the control of established institutions, it risked a demoralizing struggle to assert itself against the very people it was trying to help. It would then have been discredited in the eyes of most of its supporters, its pro-grammes unworkable, and city government left with an under-taking that only made things worse. In their own interests, there-fore, city governments would seem wise to compromise: they could not easily reject the offer of federal funds to relieve their problems, and if they were to have community action at all, it could only succeed if poor neighbourhoods accepted it. The OEO was surely right to believe that the days when poor people would passively accept what they were given were numbered every-where. The blandness of most community action programmes, even when neighbourhood representatives partly governed them, does not contradict this. It merely shows that the poor, like the rich, cannot be very imaginative or challenging with a small budget, mostly pre-empted for designated services, and dis-pensed through agencies they do not control. It shows, too, how little city government had to fear. Thus OEO's policy of forcing reluctant mayors to share control was not a gratuitous indulgence of ideological prejudice, but a fair assessment of the balance of risks and its own political options. The staff of local community action agencies sometimes encouraged militancy, but the rumours that they ever provoked riot are insubstantial. There is more solid evidence that the agencies cooled violent conflict, channelling frustration into more constructive protest. In retrospect, we see only the controversies OEO did provoke, not the conflicts it avoided, whose bitterness and repressive implications would have been more profoundly disruptive. If it miscalculated, it underestimated the fickleness of the President's support, and shortness of the perspective in which politicians weigh their chances.

The Model Cities Programme

This interpretation is confirmed by the experience of another initiative of the Johnson administration, seemingly intended as an alternative to community action more securely under local government control. In January 1966, the President called on Congress to enact 'a massive demonstration cities programme' to rebuild or revitalise slum areas. The Demonstration Cities and Metropolitan Development Act was passed in October, and its first title authorized the Department of Housing and Urban Development to 'provide grants and technical assistance to help communities of all sizes to plan, develop and carry out comprehensive city demonstration programmes. These are locally prepared programmes for rebuilding or restoring entire sections and neighbourhoods of slum and blighted areas by the concentrated and co-ordinated use of all available federal aids together with local, private and governmental resources.'[26] The grants were to be in two stages—firstly, to meet up to four-fifths of the cost of planning, and secondly to carry out the plans. Twelve million dollars were allocated for planning in 1967 and 1968, and five hundred million by 1969 for implementation—about as much as OEO's budget for community action. Not only the budget, but the purposes and organization were very similar. As well as improving the supply of decent housing for the poor, the plans were to 'make marked progress in reducing social and educational

[26] From a summary of the Act prepared by the Department of Housing and Urban Development, see *Congressional Digest*, February 1967, p. 40.

disadvantages, ill health, under-employment and enforced idleness,'[27] and they were to be directed by a city demonstration agency, to which the grants would be paid. (Sensitive to the ambiguous meaning of 'demonstration', the name was soon changed to model city agency).

The Model Cities programme was a retreat towards the Ford Foundation's earliest formulations of community action. It related to urban renewal and blighted neighbourhoods, rather than poverty at large, emphasizing the comprehensive co-ordination of physical and social plans: and it recognized the final authority of city hall. The model city agency might be 'a city, county or any local public agency established or designated by the local governing body ... Applications for assistance to plan demonstration programmes ... must have the approval of the local governing body of the city.'[28] Grants to agencies independent of city hall's consent were thus ruled out. On the other hand, instead of maximum feasible participation of neighbourhood residents, the new legislation called only for 'widespread citizen participation'—without specifying which citizens, or how widely spread. The Department of Housing and Urban Development interpreted this phrase more stringently: residents in the neighbourhoods to be replanned must be able to express their views through an organized process, with enough information and technical assistance to make their participation effective.[29] But there was no question of neighbourhood control. The Model Cities programme seemed deliberately designed to restore the initiative in reform to established authority, in reaction against the radical tendencies of community action.

In the event, conflicts as bitter as any in the history of community action arose between city and neighbourhood over the

[27] *Congressional Digest*, February 1967, p. 40.

[28] *Ibid.*, p. 40.

[29] 'The neighbourhood citizen participation structure must have clear and direct *access* to the decision making process of the City Demonstration Agency so that neighbourhood views can influence policy, planning and programme decisions. That structure must have sufficient information about any matter to be decided for a sufficient period of time so that it can initiate proposals and react knowledgeably to proposals from others. In order to react intelligently in programme matters, the structure must have the technical capacity for making knowledgeable decisions. This will mean that some form of professional technical assistance, in a manner agreed by the neighbourhood residents, shall be provided.' Dept. of Housing and Urban Development, cda letter No. 3, October 30, 1967.

demonstration plan. In Philadelphia, for instance, a neighbour-hood council bargained obstinately for funds and staff to develop its own plans in conjunction with city hall, for six out of the fifteen seats on the policy committee of the model cities pro-gramme and representation on all the task forces. After two years of struggle, the resignation of three model cities administrators and repeated disappointment, the council, believing itself betrayed, took its case to court, charging the city and the Department of Housing with illegally restricting their right to participate.[30] In Baltimore, black leaders insisted that the six new community councils in the model cities area should be funded directly from Washington. In Oakland, a neighbourhood association fought successfully for autonomous staff and funds, delaying for two years any grant to the city. Roland Warren comments on the experience of nine cities studied by Brandeis University:

> In most of the nine cities the model cities developments during this entire period were dominated by the struggle of neighbourhood residents with city hall for various degrees of power or control over the programme ... The idea of planners finding 'creative new ways of involving residents' must have an especially hollow ring in those cities where resident involvement has developed and escalated as a result not of the innovative initiatives of planners, but rather of the active determination of neighbourhood resident organizations to fight their way into a position of greater decision-making power than city administrations wanted to give them.[31]

Thus although legislation and departmental policy intended, at the outset, to settle the issue of control in favour of city govern-ment, the community leadership in the urban ghettoes deter-minedly forced it open again.

An analysis undertaken for the Department of Housing and Urban Development by Marshall Kaplan helps to explain the circumstances which determined the course of this struggle.[32]

[30] See 'Maximum Feasible Manipulation' and the postscript by Michelle Osborne in *City*, Oct./Nov., 1970.
[31] Roland C. Warren, 'Model Cities First Round' in his *Truth, Love and Social Change* (Chicago, Ill.: Rand McNally, 1971), pp. 227–8. The cities were Oakland, Denver, San Antonio, Detroit, Columbus, Atlanta, Newark, Boston, and Manchester.
[32] *The Model Cities Program,* Dept. of Housing and Urban Development (New York: Praeger, 1970). The cities studied also included Atlanta, Denver, San Antonio and Detroit, with Cambridge, Dayton, Gary, Pittsburgh, Reading, Richmond, and Rochester.

In each of the eleven cities he studied, two factors seemed crucial: the conflicts already stirring in the city, and the strength of resident groups. One city, Atlanta, was relatively peaceful, and no cohesive, integrated groups had emerged in the model neighbourhood. Here the staff of the model city agency, backed by the mayor, were free to define unchallenged how the residents' views were to be consulted. In four cities, neighbourhood residents were better organized, but again there were no tensions serious enough to make co-operation risky. Here residents and city government shared control equally, by explicit mutual agreements. In other cities, the tensions were such that government hesitated to grasp the initiative. Where residents' groups were already well-integrated, they dominated the planning from the first: and elsewhere, after a period when the agency staff were left without direction from either side, the residents became increasingly influential.

> The programme's uncertain dimensions and cloudy future when combined with a tense local environment, made the risk of visible and sustained City Hall participation seem to many local officials to be quite high ... Most executives in cities where turbulence was a factor opted to 'play' it down the middle. Where the residents related to Model Cities were not well organized nor able to speak for a large number of residents they would elect in most instances to maintain only a peripheral interest and involvement in the programme ... Their role when juxtaposed with a relatively weak resident base would lead to the development of a staff or resident influence system. If the resident or resident-dominated Model Cities group (or groups) was strong and reflected obvious community support, the chief executive would, given the local tensions, understandably acquiesce in a major if not *dominant* role for this group during the planning period.[33]

Thus the issue of control was decided by the way city hall perceived the risks of leadership, and these in turn depended on the inherent tensions, and the coherence of organization in the ghetto. Even where no neighbourhood groups had appeared strong enough to challenge government leadership, the mayors of troubled cities were wary of initiatives that might only give new cause for contention. Looking back, we can see how in

[33] *Ibid.,* p. 22.

Philadelphia, for instance, or Oakland, a similar ambivalence of government inhibited the Ford Foundation's grey area projects: and in both cities the uncertainties of control provoked continual conflict.

In all probability, the controversies over citizen participation in community action depended far more on such local factors as these, than on the policies of the OEO. In practice, its insistence that at least one-third of community action agency board members should represent the neighbourhoods served may well have forestalled more conflict than it provoked: firstly because—as Marshall Kaplan's analysis suggests—co-operation is easier where roles are explicit, and secondly because any clarification of confused political options helps to channel diffuse tension into practical negotiation. It also relieved city government of some of the political responsibility for conceding power to the ghetto. But whatever the guidelines of policy had been, or the tensions already present, community action and model cities were bound to generate conflict, from the disparity between their aims and resources.

Both programmes set out with very ambitious aims—to eradicate poverty, to revitalise slums—but each contributed only about five hundred million dollars of new funds to the resources which neighbourhood residents might help to spend. These sums were distributed amongst over a thousand community action agencies and one hundred and fifty Model Cities agencies: thus even the more concentrated Model Cities grants were scarcely larger than the grants the Ford Foundation and the President's Committee on Juvenile Delinquency had made to each of the cities they supported. A single big city spends as much as the whole federal budget for community action on its schools alone; New York City spends three times as much on public welfare. The only justification for tackling so many great problems at such trivial expense lay in planning and experiment. But what are plans and new ideas without resources to implement them? In practice, there was little to plan but the allocation of community action or model cities grants themselves, and all these would pay for were marginal increments to present services. Here and there, a community might find a way to try an original idea; but even in this their freedom was constrained by the terms of the grant and the prejudices of the established institutions on whose staff, management and expertise they largely depended. Thus people were encouraged to plan for vast problems they had no means to solve, and found themselves wrangling over a playground, the site of a neighbourhood service centre, a slum clearance scheme —conventional projects which scarcely touched any crucial need. As Roland Warren protests:

> Never again should we ask the slum residents of 150 American cities to come out to endless rounds of frustrating meetings, to be lectured on what a splendid opportunity they have to improve their neighbourhoods if they will only participate responsibly in decision-making; never again should we expect them to jump through the same old participation hoops, with the help of the same old professional people at their elbows telling them why this or that innovation is impractical; never again should we promise them the improvement of conditions of living in 150 cities for 575 million dollars a year. It is an insult to their own intelligence and integrity as human beings, and to our own.[34]

When people are offered a token share of power, at the price of co-operation and acquiescence in a feeble response to their needs, they will be shrewd to take the power but refuse the co-operation, exploiting each concession to demand more. Even a few thousand dollars to set up an office and employ a professional staff can strengthen a neighbourhood association greatly, if the money is used to review official policy, rather than to provide marginal extra community services. It buys better knowledge of legislative rights, better access to newspaper publicity and potential political allies; it buys information, expert advice, more sophisticated presentation which can turn confused indignation into reasoned argument, exposing the weaknesses in the official case. In Oakland, where the response to the model cities initiative was most militant, the neighbourhood association fought obstinately for an autonomous planning grant, and a wider and wider jurisdiction, forcing concessions from a reluctant city hall. Any group who followed such a strategy could expect some support within federal departments. From the point of view of OEO or Housing and Urban Development Department staff, the funds they had were far less than they needed, and if they could create an articulate constituency

---

[34] Roland C. Warren, 'The Model Cities Program: Assumptions—Experience—Implications', paper presented at the Annual Forum Programme, National Conference on Social Welfare, Dallas, May 17, 1971.

for their programmes, the pressure on Congress for a larger appropriation would carry more weight. Thus the inherent frustrations
of community action were enough in themselves to generate
conflict: a war on poverty without ammunition invited mutiny.

Evaluative studies confirm these tactical implications. Of all the
new services initiated by the anti-poverty programme, the most
militant—the legal advocacy of poor people's rights—seems also
to have had more influence on institutions, and won more substantial benefits for the poor than any other. Admittedly,
evaluative studies are hard to interpret unambiguously. What
are relevant criteria of success? Or a reasonable cost? What
would have happened anyway, without new endeavours, and
did they displace rather than supplement existing services? But
by any crude measure, the performance of most of the anti-
poverty programmes seemed disappointing. The evidence for any
improvement in job opportunities attributable to the programmes
was at best tenuous, and the numbers small: the most successful
project (Job Opportunities in the Business Sector) seemed to be
helping mostly those above the poverty line—and in an economy
where unemployment was declining generally. A study of the
Jobs Corps by the General Accounting Office concluded that it
did little good, if any—though some other analyses were less
pessimistic. None of the vocational training programmes looked
at all promising. Evaluations of the educational innovations
returned equally dusty answers. Head Start did not seem to
promote any lasting improvement in children's school performance, popular as it was. Amongst the services for older children,
Upward Bound—designed to encourage high school students to
enter college—was perhaps the most hopeful: but although it
helped to sustain their educational ambitions, it failed to help their
grades. As a whole, the tentative and sometimes conflicting conclusions of these studies suggest, at best, that the measurable gains
attributable to the programmes were slight, costly and
ambiguous.[35]

The one innovation whose contribution seems, by comparison,
much less arguable was legal aid, because it gave poor people
more power to contest their rights.

[35] The conclusions of many evaluative studies are tabulated in *The Poor Ye Need
not Have with You: Lessons from the War on Poverty, op. cit.*, chapter 5, 'An Equally
Biased Evaluation of the War on Poverty'.

The change thus begun and brought about by the Legal Services Programme ... has been the legitimate function of changing legal practices so that they fit the written laws, including the Constitution of the United States. In the field of welfare law in particular, suits brought by oeo Legal Service projects have had major effect. They have been responsible for abolishing the length-of-residence requirements under the Constitutional clause requiring each of the states to give equal rights to residents of the others. Legal Services have weakened or abolished man-in-house rules, and in local cases, they have forced the welfare authorities to conform with state law ... They have achieved similar successes in landlord/tenant litigation and in other fields. The Legal Services Programme is difficult to evaluate quantitatively; not all the cases are taken up to court; not all the judgments are in money. It has been estimated that outlawing the residence rule alone was likely to bring to the poor enough money to be able to pay the annual cost of the entire Legal Services Programme, but this kind of calculation is always a bit dubious. It does seem certain, however, that both on its own terms of making available to the poor good law and good lawyers, and on the broader terms of breaking the institutional barriers to people getting out of poverty, the programme should be marked a success.[36]

It was also the only programme to induce widespread institutional changes, both in the practice of welfare departments, and legal profession itself.

The inauguration of hundreds of new neighbourhood legal services ... had a far-reaching effect on the practice of poor law. Many private legal defence organizations soon shifted some of their resources into the poor-law field ... The Law Students Civil Rights Research Council began to recruit hundreds of law-student volunteers to work with welfare rights groups and to perform legal research for attorneys representing recipients. Moreover, oeo created a new kind of legal personnel—non-professionals trained in special facets of the law who were able to extend the reach of the neighbourhood legal services programme. Hundreds of poor people were recruited and trained to perform various kinds of 'lay advocacy' tasks.[37]

[36] *The Poor Ye Need not Have with You: Lessons from the War on Poverty, op. cit.*, pp. 168–9.
[37] *Regulating the Poor: The Functions of Public Welfare, op. cit.*, p. 315.

University Law schools, too, responded to these changes, founding research and advisory centres on legal aspects of social welfare and housing policy. 'The ferment also affected law school curricula —new courses in poverty law were introduced in dozens of universities, and some two thousand law students registered for them in the 1965–7 academic years.'[38]

The law is a double-edged weapon. If radical interpretations gain too much ground, they may provoke illiberal changes in the regulations, as militant welfare lawyers discovered to their cost. The Supreme Court may reverse its stand as new judges are appointed by a new administration. The law, too, reflects the consensus of society. But the vitality of the legal programme, despite its disappointments, suggests that where scarce resources are used as a purchase, to lever greater concessions from the power structure, they are more productive than investments in supplementary vocational training or education. So, too, the militancy of local groups was likely in the end to win them more than compliance, even at the cost of delays in grants, the ill-will of city hall and resentment in Congress.

For all these reasons, then—the anger in the ghettoes, the hesitancy of civic leadership, the lack of resources and feeble influence of most of the services—community action would surely have had to confront the issue of citizens' control in it, whatever federal policy had been, or the wording of legislation. And the most abiding achievement of the war on poverty may prove to be, that it helped to articulate this issue. Community action did provide a structure through which black leaders could emerge and learn to argue with the political establishment. It gave them jobs, access to professional advice, a platform; it created a career for brokers between the ghetto and the society which enclosed it, drawing them into a network of political contacts which ramified from the neighbourhood to city hall and the Washington bureaucracy. It offered a way into conventional political careers. Much of this might have happened anyway: but community action facilitated it, and here and there, at least, helped to redress the balance of power in American cities. Urban black communities still lack the resources to overcome their handicaps, but they represent an increasingly articulate, coherent and self-confident constituency for reform. Almost in spite of itself, community

[38] *Ibid.*, p. 320.

action implanted at least one of its ideals. Once made, the promise of participation proved hard to withdraw, however established government tried to tame its awkward implications.

We have tried to interpret the anti-poverty programme as a movement of reform in search of its constituency. From this standpoint, its controversies were not rashly provoked, but a necessary consequence of its political equivocation. To draw the threads together, let us recapitulate the main points in the argument.

1. By 1963, President Kennedy's attention had been drawn to the accumulating evidence that hunger, unemployment, slums, racial and regional deprivation were persistent evils, which economic growth itself did not cure, and might even aggravate. This implied a disjointedness in the structure of American society which could in time threaten its stability. It also implied that the problem could not be solved merely by stimulating economic activity, or superficial measures of relief. Any lasting solution would have to tackle the underlying failures. Poverty described these complex issues in a simple word.

2. Kennedy still hesitated to campaign on the issue of poverty. What would it mean to most Americans, who were not poor, and might neither understand nor sympathize with the plight of those who were? Both he and his successor were attracted by a theme which expressed their sense of leadership, and whose idealism was unchallengeable. But they did not risk rebuff on such an untried issue by asking for a proportionate commitment of funds.

3. Presidential strategy therefore required a programme that was neither alarmingly costly nor patently trivial, which could be given dramatic emphasis as a priority of domestic policy. But convincing ways of relieving poverty on a national scale were hard to devise, without equally dramatic expenditures for which the country was not prepared. In these circumstances, only a catalytic programme designed to provoke a broad community support, open-ended in its ultimate commitment of resources, and innovative in its approach could plausibly match the much-publicized ideals. The grey area and juvenile delinquency programmes had

already pioneered a model of exploratory, self-sustaining community action. Nothing else in view so nearly fitted the specification. Thus the anti-poverty programme was a subtly guarded gesture of leadership: it pointed the direction, but left the response to be determined by a diffuse process of local planning. If the initiative succeeded, the President would have widespread backing for much larger appropriations; if it failed, he could write off the experiment, and turn to other issues.

4. The oeo thus faced the task of creating, across the country, a constituency for action against poverty articulate and coherent enough to sustain the programme. oeo was caught between opposite dangers. If the community action agencies were dominated by the established power structure, they would most likely be used to reinforce the conventional approach of existing institutions, and the war on poverty would dwindle into a means of subsidizing local government. In many cities, feeling in the ghettoes was already militant enough to repudiate such an outcome. An anti-poverty programme rejected by the poor would be a futile provocation. On the other hand, a programme supported only by the poor would have too narrow a constituency. In these circumstances, oeo asserted the principle that poor people must be strongly represented in community action, and it brought as much pressure as it dared on city hall to share control. It sometimes overplayed its hand, especially where it funded directly independent projects in competition with government. But it could scarcely have avoided the confrontation. Had oeo conceded the power of city hall without a struggle, the anti-poverty programme would have lost its momentum and purpose just as surely, and perhaps have aroused as much bitterness. The evolution of the Model Cities programme seems to confirm that the issue of participation could not have been evaded by redrafting the law or administrative guidelines. It depended, rather, on the balance of local pressures.

5. Community action did not lack a constituency, it had too many, whose interests would not be reconciled. So it tended to alienate them all; and unable to recruit the concerted support for the resources it needed, generated a growing

frustration. Yet it did help to create, here and there, an articulate pressure group in the ghetto; and it did establish, especially with its legal programme, new services which substantially benefited poor people. It demonstrated principles of participation, of social planning and systematic evaluation which cannot now be ignored. In some ways, then, it did implant its ideals. But the response did not converge in coherent, broadly-based backing for community action itself. So, in the event, the anti-poverty programme never succeeded in recruiting a constituency to defend it.

Thus the frustration was circular. The war on poverty was planned with very inadequate resources, for fear of overcommitting the President on a politically doubtful issue: and this led to a strategy of community action whose conflicting interpretations then alienated support, confirming the initial doubts. But community action was more than an expedient formula for reconciling idealism with political caution. It was an attempt to reform the underlying weaknesses in the structure of representative democracy, which made it so unresponsive to the evident deprivation of millions of Americans. In this sense, it was concerned with an issue more profound even than poverty—the viability of democracy itself. In conclusion, let us try to bring out what community action implied were the crucial failings of the political structure, and show where its conception of reform went wrong.

2. THE DEMOCRACY OF INFORMATION

In the preceding chapter, we discussed why community action was written so prominently into the Economic Opportunity Act, and what it achieved as a step towards the relief of poverty. It certainly invites assessment in these terms, for this was the brief its advocates spoke to. The disparity between opportunity and socially approved ambitions, by which Cloward and Ohlin explained delinquency; theories of a poverty cycle or the impotence of the poor—all argued for community action as a wide-ranging intervention to enhance the life chances of the most downtrodden or least competent. A strategy which relied so much on planning, research and local responsiveness was not, of course, the most direct approach to eradicating poverty. While unemployment was so high in ghettos and depressed regions, while welfare benefits were so low and so punitively administered, while schools were so over-crowded, slums so squalid, and even pockets of near starvation remained, the most obvious priority was to redistribute resources to meet these evident needs. But the cost of creating jobs, guaranteeing a decent level of family assistance, subsidizing housing, education, health and subsistence seemed politically unmanageable in a society traditionally mistrustful of federal intervention, and still complacent that economic competition would in time bring prosperity to all who deserved it. Community action was designed to disturb these conservative prejudices without openly challenging them, in the hope that a clearer understanding of poverty, and local initiatives to attack its underlying causes, would create a constituency for larger expenditures. In practice, community action means so many different things to different interests, the response was incoherent, angry and self-stultifying. As an anti-poverty programme, therefore, it became trapped into defending the need for planning and innovation, without any commitment of resources comparable to the plan, and so compounded the frustrations—a seemingly hypocritical evasion of bold promises.

But community action was not originally conceived in these terms. It was less an answer to poverty, than to a sense of breakdown in the open, democratic structure of society. Each of its successive formulations—in the grey area projects, the delinquency programme, in the Economic Opportunity Act and Model Cities legislation—implied a need to reform the process of government itself. This was its consistent purpose. The strategies of intervention changed very little with changes in the programmes' stated objectives, and set against these objectives, the interventions often seemed oblique. But as an attempt to reform the political and administrative structure, they were both coherent and pointed, even if they rarely succeeded. The whole endeavour seems, in this sense, to contain a wider and more enduring meaning than as an experiment in the relief of poverty. In conclusion, then, let us try to set out explicitly the theory underlying these attempted reforms, and show where they went wrong.

The Breakdown of Democracy

Looking back to the discussions in the Ford Foundation from which the grey area projects arose, the dominant issue was the inability of government, at every level, to make a coherent or effective response to evident social problems. The decay of social and political processes of assimilation; the misconceptions of social agencies and the ineffectuality of their planning; the fiscal crisis of cities and stultification of decision in Congress—all implied a breakdown of effective democratic government, to which present policy offered no remedy. Successive administrations had struggled with the problem of co-ordinating federal departments, civic groups had made repeated attempts at comprehensive planning, all to no purpose. These abortive endeavours exposed the obstacles to exchanging and integrating information between social agencies. At the same time, as the traditional city machine politics had declined, ordinary citizens were less identified with the government of their city, as a patron who rewarded loyalty with personal benefits. A professional bureaucracy might be more impartial and less corrupt, but it also seemed less responsive. Nor was its professionalism grounded in any theory of social intervention able to predict results. To Lloyd Ohlin and other advisers of the President's Committee on Juvenile Delinquency especially, this was a crucial weakness: government lacked any true understanding of the nature of the problems it was failing to solve. Thus policy was at once fragmentary and uninformed, either by popular criticism or systematic research.

In the Ford Foundation Paul Ylvisaker had therefore advocated community action in the context of a broad argument about the American political process. How was the energy generated in an individualistic society to be gathered for any common purpose, without inhibiting the vitality of its diffuse power structure? 'What is needed to co-ordinate and exploit the inherent power of these complicated, egalitarian societies is the development in balance of far more sophisticated nervous, circulatory and other systems than have yet been evolved either by our nation or any other. To detect and anticipate; correlate and differentiate; to probe and carry through; to collect energy and allocate it; to reflect and reformulate; to mobilize and individualize; to gather power and liberate it.'[39] Thus community action was to be a node of collective intelligence, drawing together strands of purpose and knowledge to direct the powerful muscles of the social body. The underlying problem was the self-stultification of representative government, which so divided and balanced authority that the power of veto outweighed the power to act. Yet community action would be self-defeating, if it interposed yet another institution with its own jurisdictional claims. Thus it was neither to be an authority, nor a social service; and it could be turned towards any issue—the assimilation of newcomers, delinquency, poverty, slums—where present policy seemed ineffectual. Essentially, it was designed to reorganize the system of communication through which resources were allocated.

This kind of intervention appeals, obviously enough, to reformers with relatively slight resources. For if they can change the flow of information, they can hope for an influence out of all proportion to the power they control. In part, community action made a virtue of necessity, rationalizing political weakness, and so—as we shall see—put too much faith in structures of communication. Yet, for all that, the emphasis on communication did point to crucial problems of American government, and was neither trivial nor evasive. It implied a coherent analysis of structural failures. The analysis was never, so far as we know, fully articulated in any document of community action, but it can be derived from the nature of the strategies and the assumptions which justified them. In the next section we have tried to abstract its essential arguments and present them in our own terms.

The Weaknesses in the Structure of Representative Democracy

For the purposes of argument, let us begin with a very simplified model of government. The system controls a vast energy, of which it uses a small fraction to guide the rest—in analysis, research, debate, legislative processes. Whatever the intention, this energy will flow to waste, unless the system of guidance responds continually to information about the effect of the power it has deployed. If this information is not known; if its relationship to the effort is not understood; if it is not received by the

[39] See p. 44 of this book.

relevant point of guidance, nor acted upon in time, then the energy of society is not under human control. The more this is so, and the greater the power a society generates, the more alarming this situation becomes. In these terms every highly industrialized nation, and the United States most of all, perhaps, seems to be running out of control. Its traditional principles of political guidance cannot cope with the energy it puts out.

The structure of political communication which democratic societies have evolved over the past century is founded on principles of hierarchy and segregation: it tries to master the flow of information by discriminating different sorts of data, and directing them into discrete channels, ordered by their priority of governance. The heart of this structure is its administrative bureaucracy which, in very simplified terms, is to receive information about purposes from the political system, translate them into instrumental signals, and report back the outcome. The political system, correspondingly, interprets the diffuse messages from the electorate as policy to guide its administration. Both systems are divided, functionally and geographically, into semi-autonomous sub-systems, so as to diffuse control and limit the amount of information which any part must master. Thus no part is overloaded, and each has only to deal with messages it is designed to understand—each receiver is tuned to a narrow band of signals, each transmitter beamed to its receivers, without interference. The structure is, in principle, logically coherent: the choice of purposes, determined by the political system, precedes their administrative implementation, and provides the context in which results are interpreted. It is also formally democratic: the citizen, to whom administrative action is finally directed, is also the prime mover of the political process—the ultimate source of its authority. He completes the cycle, experiencing the outcome of policy, and endorsing the next round of endeavour.

This idealized model suggests at once some of the fundamental flaws in such a system. Firstly, it does not provide for communication between the branches of the administration. Each is vertically integrated with the political authority which sanctions its work, and only at the highest level is its policy co-ordinated, if at all, with other departments. So long as its purpose can be fulfilled without major influence on purposes outside its jurisdiction, this lack of more direct channels of lateral communication may not matter, and reduces the information it need attend to. But the more interdependent the organization of society becomes, the less viable this segregation. Secondly, since the administration represents a hierarchy of authority, the higher ranks, and finally its political leadership, determine what information is to be fed back. The lower ranks can only report the answers to the questions their superiors ask. If they volunteer more than that, they risk reproof for impertinence or excess of zeal, and at all events, the information is likely to be ignored because the system is not geared to assimilate it. Since the administration is not properly a policy-making organization, but an instrument of policy, it tends to ask of itself only whether it has carried out its instructions. It will not even ask whether these instructions produced the intended results, unless its political masters require it to do so, for that too is a political question. The range of information fed back through the administrative hierarchy is therefore remarkably narrow, and does not, as a matter of course, tell whether policy is effective.

This leads to the third and most obviously frustrating flaw in the whole structure. As a client of the administration, the citizen stands at the bottom of this hierarchy. The only information he can pass back concerns his treatment according to instructions. He can protest his rights, but not the effectiveness of those rights. However poorly he is served, the bureaucracy must reply: we regret you are not entitled, departmental policy does not permit, regulations require . . . Nor is it designed to bring to the notice of its leadership that here is a man they failed to help. The citizen can only transmit his dissatisfaction through the political system, in which his particular complaint is drowned by numbers, and lost in the disparate bundle of issues he must decide by a single vote.

The more sophisticated the industrial economy, the graver these flaws become. As resources and people are released from earlier constraints, and move more readily; as the economy becomes more complexly interdependent, the autonomy of functions and regions breaks down. And this can only promote an increasing centralization of government, since the structure provides few mechanisms of integration except at the apex of political power. The citizen becomes more than ever remote from the policy-makers he is supposed to influence, his particular interests merged in a broader constituency. At the same time, the aggregate influence of the electorate has to compete with new procedures for resolving issues of policy. To collate information at the centre, the executive has to devise methods of summation, capable of reducing the inter-relationship between millions of facts to a manageable calculation. Overloaded with data it cannot readily assimilate, it turns to technically sophisticated systems of analysis, whose simplifying assumptions tend inevitably to pre-empt questions of political choice. This expertise can only handle purposes with measurable outcomes amenable to its techniques, logically coherent but morally crude. In practice, the executive consults several more or less expert and divergent analyses, amongst which the judgment of the Budget Bureau is ultimately the most influential. Since the wishes of the people would be far too diverse, conflicting and ambiguous to feed into such an analysis, electoral issues are directed towards indeterminate images and slogans, which repre-sent but do not define goals. Thus the political debate becomes divorced from the analysis of data: and both become meaningless because they are no longer related. The citizen is overloaded with information he does not trust, and cannot respond to. His leaders appear secretive and even lying in their conduct of affairs, blandly vacuous in their appeals to his support. No style of government has ever talked so much, printed so many words, broadcast so many facts, while communicating so little of its real intentions. There seem to be two processes of government: one formal and democratic, where the people are represented, but increasingly empty; the other obscure, technical and decisive, where expertise colludes with political self-interest. The crucial problem is then to reintegrate informed analysis and democratically determined purpose, within a society where the variety of interests is as great as ever, but the parts are more interdependent.

These fundamental flaws in the structure of governance were exactly those with which community action was most concerned: over-centralization; the lack of lateral communication between administrations; their indifference to the effectiveness of their work; and their unresponsiveness to the people they served. The faults were perceived as lying within institutions rather than the structure as a whole. But the bureaucratic shortcomings derived from the constraints imposed by the larger system, and it was through changes in the system that community action sought to redeem them.

Thus, from the standpoint of this analysis, the theory of community action could be summarized as follows:

The behaviour of institutions is determined by the information on which they act. If the information they attend to is biased and faulty, their actions will be neither an impartial interpretation of the common cause nor the most rational means to achieve it. The structure of communication in a complex democracy is articulated in such a way as to inhibit the exchange of some crucial information. Administration becomes separated into functional and geographically segregated bureaucracies, co-ordinated by an increasingly centralized political authority, or not co-ordinated at all when power at the centre is stultified by its divisions. There is then little communication between bureaucracies, although the interdependence of society makes the actions of each highly relevant to many others. The central political authority is left with the task of interpreting the implications of this interdependence, and devising a coherent policy for each of its bureaucratic arms. The complexity and amount of information it must assimilate is only manageable, so long as it can be reduced to mechanical systems of analysis, and this places an unforeseen power in the hands of those who devise the framework of analysis —its assumptions of purpose, techniques of quantifying equivalents, and theories of interaction. It becomes more and more difficult to feed into this process, in any meaningful way, the needs of the ordinary citizen as he perceives them: he cannot challenge the expertise of policy analysis, nor govern the functioning of institutions. Yet the needs he expresses are ultimately the only legitimate source of political authority. Thus democracy drowns in the flood of information it is trying to master.

These structural weaknesses work against the interests of the poor above all, for they are least able to compensate for the formal barriers to democratic influence by informal contacts. They do not write the books which influence the experts, nor dine with politicians and administrators; they are not represented by any of the powerful lobbies which bring pressure to bear on the political process. This exclusion from informal networks reinforces the general inhibitions of democratic control, and creates profound inequalities of power. Correspondingly, the poor stand to gain most from reform in the formal structure.

Epilogue

The Strategy of Intervention

Community action therefore tried to create a structure of communication cutting across both hierarchical and jurisdictional boundaries. Ideally, each community action agency was to be a forum of continuous planning, where representatives of city hall, social services, civic leaders and the people met to exchange ideas, define the priority of needs and work out policy with the help of a facilitating staff. Planning provided a context for the exchange of information between administrative jurisdictions, which the formal structure of government inhibited. At the same time, by drawing professional administrators into a general discussion with both politicians and the users of services, it would break down the hierarchical barriers to the flow of communication. Those who felt their needs were poorly met could confront professionals, not merely as aggrieved clients, but as equal partners in the review of policy. Finally, research was to feed back an impartial evaluation of results. Thus by co-ordination, popular participation and research, community action was to short-circuit the devious links of formal communication. Decisions would be influenced by the greater understanding brought by face to face discussion and fuller, more reliable information. The reforms were conceived in terms of the needs of deprived groups, but the problems they implied were not restricted to the poor.

In the framework of this analysis, then, the three strategies of community action offered a coherent experimental design for reform. But an unresolved question of power remained, which the language of communication partly disguises. It is not enough simply to present better information; you must also secure attention to it. The process by which information is sorted and assimilated therefore becomes crucial: and the political penalties of ignoring information need not correspond to its intrinsic quality and relevance. The process must not only be intelligent, but reinforced by sanctions. Especially, it must have power to control the timing of decisions, for unless information can force the postponement or reconsideration of unsatisfactory decisions, it is unlikely to over-ride the immediate political pressures upon the decision takers. The weakness of community action lay in its inability to work out a structure that could at once reinforce the influence of new kinds of information and govern the timetable of decisions, yet not pre-empt the legitimate authority of established institutions.

The Weakness of the Strategy

At first sight, the exchange of information is not an exercise of power. Indeed, the intrusion of authority arguably inhibits its openness, because people reveal their minds more circumspectly in hierarchical relationships. But you have only to reflect on everyday discussions at home, at work, in committee, to perceive that most information connotes choice, and is introduced in support of an interest—so much so, that in domestic arguments, where the conflicts of interest are long familiar, the facts presented are scarcely more than pawns. Situations where ignorance alone inhibits action seem less commonplace. Suppose, for instance, a party pauses at a cross-roads, uncertain of their direction: if everyone is agreed on their destination, then any information to guide them on their route will be neutrally considered. But suppose they are on holiday, and the destination itself is a matter of choice. Some are for the beach, some for the mountains, some for the art galleries. Information now has partisan implications—rain is forecast, some museums shut on Mondays, the map marks a scenic road—and though all of it may be relevant, its weight is controversial. The voice from the back seat pointing out an ice cream shop may be tersely ignored. There is at once too much information and too little. The ultimate question—what the party as a whole will most enjoy—is unanswerable, but the range of circumstantial evidence for every possible choice is unmanageable. So these holiday-makers, as they discuss their route, will react to the advocacy implicit in the information each puts forward, and priority of attention will go to the members of the party whose interests are dominant. The same is surely true of policy-makers: information is prejudicial, competitive, inexhaustible and ultimately indeterminate.

In practice, therefore, communication and power cannot be divorced. Information implies action. If you agree to listen, you commit yourself to a response. If you do not want to act on what you have heard in the sense it suggests, you must put forward counter-arguments, other information—at the very least you are engaged in a confrontation where you have to defend your position. Weaknesses in that position may be exposed, purposes raised which it does not accommodate. The prerogatives of power therefore include the right to deny attention to bothersome informants. However open an agency wishes to be, it can only assimilate a limited number of messages. It will naturally select those messages which matter most to its survival, and can be most meaningfully interpreted. These are, most obviously, messages from sources with power over the agency, and those which relate to its preconceived purpose. So it is not likely to shift its attention without a shift in the structure of power, even though the information it disregards is, in some sense, more relevant.

In any complex situation, the amount of possibly relevant information is greater than an actor can easily assimilate. His wisdom lies in the shrewdness with which he selects the crucial messages. Unless he can exclude much information as outside his concern, he cannot define a manageable role for himself. In a political setting, especially, action or inaction has immediate consequences, where a misjudged statement or a false step can cause him lasting trouble. He needs to decide quickly, with a sharp eye for the most significant of the signals which reach him—and a blind eye for incompatible signals he can safely ignore. Suppose such an actor is provided with a planning and research organization, whose procedures are not under his control. Even if he recognizes that he needs the information generated by these new procedures, he will not readily be able to assimilate it. He acts in a short-sighted political view; planning and research spell out a longer-sighted analysis, in which the immediate political constraints stand out less than the more enduring economic and social factors. Both the timing and assumptions of the two interpretations are at odds. The chances are, then, that the conclusions of planning and research will reach him at the wrong moment, when his actions have already been decided, or he is not in a position to act: and they will be presented in unfamiliar terms. If this new information is not backed by much political authority, he will in the end disregard it—despite, perhaps, a genuine conviction that research and planning are vitally important.

Similarly with new democratic procedures. If citizens' participation so often broke down in mutual disillusionment, the fault lay partly in the overburdening of institutions. They were asked to respond to new political pressures, whose authority was vague and incidence unpredictable, without any relaxation of the established structure of power. They naturally sought to head off any further intrusion on their autonomy, manipulating participation as a means of endorsing rather than influencing their actions. If they could use their professional experience to define the relevant facts, then any body of citizens consulted would be hard put to refute their interpretation. If the citizens rejected their expertise, the alternative proposals could be made to appear naïve. Since, too, participation was part of the planning process, it suffered the frustrations of timing to which any planning is vulnerable.

The futility of new forms of planning, research or democratic participation without a corresponding adjustment of power becomes only too obvious, once the competitiveness of information is taken into account. These new voices cannot influence events simply because what they say ought to be relevant. They must shout loud enough to be heard, drowning more familiar voices. In the clamour of political argument, moments of silence—even of unprejudiced enquiry—are notoriously rare. The experienced parliamentarian cultivates a highly selective inattention to the flow of talk and papers on which he floats from office to council chamber, from interview to working breakfast, committee to television studio towards the verdict of us all. The structure of power is, in a sense, the messages people attend to. Government is determined by who listens to what: power by the ability to apply sanctions against being ignored.

The promoters of community action had great difficulty in coming to terms with these issues. The only pressure they could apply, to compel attention to new sources of information, was the sanction of withholding grants. The Ford Foundation, the President's Committee, the oeo could delay funding until a satisfactory structure of communication had been formally instituted. They could lay down rules about who was to be consulted, and the procedures to be followed. The President's Committee and the Model Cities Administration, especially, sought to ensure that an elaborate process of discussion, research and interpretation was fulfilled by dividing their grants into two stages, for planning and for implementation. But the status of the structure to be created presented a dilemma. If it was to determine what kinds of information were introduced into discussion, and the attention they were to receive, it would need to hold an authoritative position in the local power structure. But this implied a higher order of control, elaborating the hierarchy of government. Such a proposal was not only politically unrealistic, but against the spirit of the reforms. A superordinate planning authority would, if successful, undercut both formal and informal democratic processes: and in practice, experience showed that such co-ordinating agencies usually failed to assert their control.

From the first, the Ford Foundation had foreseen the risk that its grey area projects would evolve into bureaucracies as jealous of their jurisdiction and as self-protective as the institutions they sought to influence. If the purpose was to encourage agencies to talk to each other, absorb new ideas, listen to their public and evaluate their achievements more objectively, a co-ordinating structure which claimed over-riding authority would only have aroused new inhibitions. To establish its prerogative as the integrator of policy, it would have to channel information towards itself, discouraging diffuse discussion. It is the common fate of co-ordinating agencies to claim a superordinate position in the hierarchy of power, and when they are defeated, to dwindle into another administration competing for an autonomous field of responsibility. The grey area projects were designed to avoid this trap, by repudiating any claim to permanence or direct control. They therefore stood in an ambiguous relationship to the power structure, intervening without pre-empting authority. But this formulation, while it recognized the problem, did not resolve it.

None of the structural or procedural devices proposed by the Ford Foundation, the President's Committee, OEO or the Model Cities administration articulated a process able to determine which kinds of information were to receive priority of attention.[40] They could insist upon the creation of a structure with broadly defined aims, through which information and ideas were to be gathered

[40] The same problem has undermined the British commissions convened to choose a site for a third London airport. Both commissions found their recommendations rejected, because however carefully they assessed the evidence, they had no right to determine its political weight. Hence, each time they reported, the government concluded that the recommendations would be too unpopular to implement, and took another tack. The expert evidence on noise, cost, damage to wildlife or historic buildings, on the implications for regional development and airline preference could all be graded according to the bias of interest, and remained indeterminate. After several years of analysis the issue seems as controversial as ever—resolved, for the moment, by a government decision which disagrees with the majority findings of both enquiries.

and channelled. But they could not, even when they wished, pre-determine the priority of attention which various contributions should receive. They could only hope that a consensus would emerge from discussion. In practice, where the structure was taken seriously, sharp conflict arose over who should dominate the debate; researchers, professionals, politicians, neighbourhood representatives all claimed the right to define the issues. Once it became bogged down in these disputes, the process lost its chance of influence, since it was too loosely integrated with the power structure to control the timetable of decisions. Community action did offer an alternative framework within which to negotiate a new agreement on the priority of need. But the negotiations were abortive, because decisions would not wait upon the outcome. Those who had power could therefore afford to treat the whole process with indifference. This is a characteristic weakness of planning as a strategy of reform, and it tends to degenerate into the following sequence.

The Federal Government, a state legislature, or a Foundation, say, decides that something should be done about health, for instance—something bold, radical and uncontroversial. Money is voted for a year or two's planning, to which everyone concerned with health is to contribute their experience and proposals. From these wide-ranging, open-minded discussions the plan is to emerge. A few tentative meetings are held, guidelines circulated, information requested, but for six months nothing happens. Those with power hold back, wary of exposing themselves to unnecessary controversy. They recognize that the plan implies, by its initiation itself, a criticism of their position: but they will not react until they see where, and how seriously, their interests are threatened. Those without power are disunited and leaderless. Then, as the deadline approaches, a conference is called and organized in working groups to thrash out a set of proposals. It breaks up in confusion, as no one knows how to reduce the various suggestions to any kind of order. The whole task is then, perhaps, turned over to a university, which brings its intellectual sophistication to bear. In a series of seminars and position papers it debates the meaning of planning, of health and disease, refining its categories of analysis. The outcome is a conceptual map of the incidence of need and the distribution of resources, defined by a set of overlapping indicators of all the revelant conditions—social, economic and medical. Unfortunately there is neither the information to hand, nor the time to put this admirable scheme to use. And even if there were, it could only have served as a critical apparatus, since it cannot itself determine the priorities of aim. Finally, a firm of professional consultants is brought in, who know what the funding agency expects. It takes the proposal it wrote for its previous clients, changes the names and a few figures, and in six weeks has a plausible document placed on the appropriate desk in Washington. By then, perhaps, federal policy is undergoing revision, and the whole process starts again.

The futility of this exercise arises from the nature of the sanctions imposed. The funding agencies can insist on a procedure, but the procedure itself scarcely alters the political weight of the information fed into it. Had community action been conceived as the dominating planning instrument in the hierarchy of local government, its directors could have influenced the weighting. But such an authoritative co-ordinating agency was neither politically feasible, nor an imaginative response to the need, as the reformers understood it. They hoped to break down the hierarchy of power, to open policy to wider discussion, not concentrate and centralize it. In the event, they could only formalize popular representation in the governing body of the structure they created, and this made little difference.

As we have seen, the planning procedures of community action agencies initiated few of the programmes which were carried out. Task forces deliberated, background research was undertaken, theories of social intervention might be elaborated; but from the first, the funding agencies put forward most of the new ideas. Proposals were often implemented through direct negotiation between the funders, the administrator of the community action agency and the local authority, without reference to the planning groups—partly from haste to secure appropriations while they were available, partly in frustration at the indeterminacy of planning. This was a response to the realities of power: and as OEO evolved, even the pretence of local initiative was dropped. Most of the resources were directed to 'national emphasis' programmes, for which community action was merely the local agent on behalf of federal departments. There were corresponding frustrations in the Model Cities: local planning was subjected to unrealistic deadlines for submissions, followed by months of discouraging delay and then new deadlines, while the plans themselves were bent to the interests of the most powerful established interests and pressure groups.[41] Thus new kinds of information had few chances to claim serious attention.

Anyone invited to contribute to a plan might learn from this the warning signs of ineffectual participation. If the timing of decisions is independent of the progress of the plan; if the purpose of the plan is diffusely stated, without regard for available resources; if the planners control neither the resources nor the administration; if the invitation to contribute to the plan is indiscriminate; if the powerful appear benignly detached from the discussions; if the information gathered for the plan is presented in long, unselective documents—then from all such signs, the wary may guess that the plan will be abortive. For in such circumstances, it is clearly divorced from a political context. Whatever its virtues, the plan is unlikely to appear at a time, in a form or with the authority to influence decisions.

But if planning is either ineffectual or undemocratic—a preemptive authority, undercutting elected government, or no authority at all—how else can new kinds of information be brought to bear on important decisions? Especially, how can the politically deprived command attention? Community action also led to another answer to this problem.

The Right to Inform

As the frustrations of politically unintegrated planning became apparent, the more radical advocates of community action began to exploit a new sanction latent in both the Economic Opportunity Act and the Model Cities legislation. If the law required a procedure to be followed, then the procedure implied rights which ought to be enforceable in law. Instead of relying only on participation in discussions whose influence was largely dependent on the goodwill of those in power, the issues could also be raised in court. Here was an established structure of arbitration with unchallengeable authority and, above all, powers of injunction which could force political decisions to wait upon its deliberations. Any group of citizens who felt they had not been properly consulted, or who held that inadequate information had been

[41] See 'The Model Cities Program: Assumptions–Experience–Implications', *op. cit.*

uncritically accepted, could take the city to court. So, for instance, when the City of San Francisco proposed to demolish a neighbourhood of residential hotels, occupied largely by elderly people of small means, a residents' association sought an injunction from the court, on the grounds that alternative accommodation was not available, as the law required. The City claimed that similar hotels elsewhere in the city could absorb those displaced. The association presented an independent study of vacancy rates which proved the opposite. The injunction was granted and later sustained, despite a second survey by the City to establish their claim. In the face of this legal harassment, the City compromised at last, agreeing to provide accommodation for the residents within the redevelopment itself. This outcome could never have been achieved merely by inviting residents to take part in the redevelopment plans.

Similar actions were fought in San Francisco over other redevelopment proposals, and in each case, neighbourhood organizations were able to force compromises in the interests of their residents. The example represents a strategy of legal intervention which became increasingly popular, once the OEO provided the means.

In 1968 alone, more than 1,500,000 poor persons received free legal assistance, primarily from Legal Service units supported by the Office of Economic Opportunity. The cost of these services amounted to over $70,000,000. Special national law centres have been established by the OEO Legal Services Programme in the areas of welfare, housing, education, health and consumer problems to develop legal strategies for attorneys in neighbourhood Legal Service units in over 400 cities around the country. In addition, there are a variety of privately-funded legal centres. . . . At present there are over 1,600 attorneys available on a full-time basis to represent the poor in other than traditional criminal defence. Primarily at the instigation of these attorneys, courts have increasingly—since the mid-1960's when these programmes began—intervened in educational policy-making, urban renewal planning, the establishment of limits on police, and the revision of welfare policy and procedures.[42]

[42] Steven Arthur Waldhorn, 'Legal Intervention and Citizen Participation as Strategies for change in Public-Serving Bureaucracies', paper for 65th Annual Meeting of the American Political Science Association, New York, September 4, 1969.

Much of this legal aid went simply to representing poor clients individually in civil cases. But the Service directed its strategy above all to interventions with broader implications—firstly by concentrating on class actions, where the case would establish a precedent; and secondly by challenging planning decisions on behalf of interests which had not been fairly consulted. The San Francisco housing cases illustrate the second. The most celebrated of the first concerned the administration of welfare—especially the Supreme Court rulings that children could not be denied welfare on the grounds that their mother was living with a man to whom she was not married; that welfare could not be cut off before the recipient had exercised her right to a fair hearing; that states could not apply length of residence conditions in the granting of welfare. Each of these rulings defined and extended the right to welfare, just as the housing cases defined the right to resettlement. These actions, therefore, went much further than the prosecution of administrative malpractice. They uncovered rights implicit in the law and the constitution which had not previously been recognized. In the housing cases, the action appealed to the provisions of the Housing and Urban Development department itself: in the welfare cases, it argued rather that state practices, endorsed by the department of Health Education and Welfare, contradicted constitutional rights.

Such cases not only introduced new interpretations of the law, but brought new information to light.

Courts can also inject additional information into bureaucracies by making new facts known through court proceedings. The Brandeis briefs submitted by advocates in important test cases not only present persuasive arguments in court but also bring new facts to the attention of administrators which they can no longer ignore. Thus, when the city of San Francisco issued a permit to tear down the International Hotel, a major housing resource for retired Filipinos, a court action brought to prevent the issuance of the permit failed, but information thereby brought to the attention of City officials and others led to the devising of a plan to keep the hotel open. Similarly, a series of New York cases concerning school suspensions brought to light problems which had previously been ignored both by school administrators and the general public.[43]

43 *Ibid.*

It is not just that new facts were presented, but presented in a setting where they could not be dismissed. The courtroom is a public forum, attended by the press, where the presiding judge must consider the implications of all relevant evidence, and may have power to restrain administrative action. Governing institutions no longer control the context of discussion, and must answer convincingly or risk their case.

Action in law can therefore be seen as an alternative solution to at least one of the problems of communication we set out above. It cannot break down the barriers to communication between administrative jurisdictions, nor within the bureaucratic hierarchy, but it can force the interests and knowledge of citizens on the attention of administrators—not only to protect their individual rights, but to influence matters of public policy. The supreme authority of the constitution, as the ultimate source of rights, provides a means of raising, in law, profound and far-reaching social issues, and documenting them with fresh evidence. This conception of intervention resolves the structural dilemma which daunted community action agencies—how to assert their influence without usurping the authority of elected government. The court has power to apply sanctions against authority, without seeking to replace it. Thus action in law can command respect for neglected sources of information without reintroducing the hierarchical centralization reform set out to oppose.

At the same time, it avoids a corresponding dilemma in the interpretation of participation. Here, too, the introduction of formal structures seems self-defeating. If community action is conceived as self-government by the people, which people are in practice legitimate spokesmen? The boards of neighbourhood organizations are often self-appointed and self-perpetuating. They draw salaries and appoint their own staff, and so have a selfish interest in maintaining their hold. Even though they may have earned their position by force of leadership, they cannot claim to speak for their community once they are seriously challenged. Yet if boards were regularly elected, would they not become simply the lowest level in the hierarchy of representative government? Once again, the attempt to reform the pattern of communication ends merely by elaborating the principles of organization under attack. Legal action resolves the issue through the court, which can determine by the criteria of the law itself whether, irrespective of his formal status, the bringer of an action has a right to be heard.

Especially when it is applied to issues of policy, this strategy of legal intervention presupposes a democratic right to submit information and argument by any interested citizen. It implies that decisions are not necessarily legitimate, just because they have been taken by duly elected governments acting within their jurisdiction. The decisions must also have been opened to discussion with everyone they affect. If this implication were to be fully worked out, it would represent a powerful reinterpretation of both democracy and planning. If we extend the right to be heard, to submit evidence and present argument, to all manner of decisions; if this right is backed by legal redress, to frustrate proposals which ignore the evidence; if the professional skills to prepare and present evidence are available to rich and poor alike—then this new information will be listened to, and it will alter the context in which decisions are taken. If officials know that their decisions can be challenged, and they may have to defend them before a court of law, they will prepare them more carefully. The threat of legal action, with its costs, delays, publicity, is in itself a powerful sanction, even when its victims believe their case will stand.

This implies a pattern of government where co-ordination comes from the continuous arbitration of conflicting interests, rather than any institution, and where the interests represented are far wider than before. It implies that the common purpose can be better served by articulating conflict than by searching for consensus, and that a partial rationality is more meaningful than systematic analysis where purposes can only be taken for granted. It implies laws which make explicit a common right to give and receive information, resources to enforce that right, and people who know how to use it. But it also implies great faith in the autonomy of the law, and universality of access to it. In the last resort, these are subject to political control—and here legal strategists discovered the limits of their scope.

The Limitations of Rights

The San Francisco housing case we cited illustrates the drawbacks as well as the strength of legal action. The case was costly, and could not have been fought without the resources of the Housing Law Centre in the University of California at Berkeley, itself financed by Federal funds. Ultimately, the protest depended still on government tolerance for actions against political authority. Nor is a legal arbitration necessarily either rational or democratic, except in its own narrowly defined terms. The court agreed that the City had not established a right to displace the residents. It did not have to say whether, if the City had the right, the plan was sensible or what the people of San Francisco as a whole would wish. No views were formally represented except the two parties to the dispute. It remains open for society, through its government, to conclude that such interference with policy is troublesome and unwarranted, and change the law accordingly.

Some of the most hopeful welfare cases were confounded in just this way. For instance, an action was brought against New York State, demanding that it revise the standard of need by which welfare payments were assessed to take account of changes in the cost of living, as the Social Security Act required.

> In April of 1970, in *Rosado v. Wyman*, the Supreme Court agreed. New York was to be given a short amount of time to readjust its standard upward or lose its Federal subsidy. *Rosado* had all the outer attributes of a major welfare recipient victory; in fact, it was a disaster. It is one thing to force a state to raise its 'standard of need'. It is another thing to prevent a state from lowering its actual payment level.[44]

In the event, the Health Education and Welfare department concluded, and the Supreme Court agreed, that states were entitled to fix their maximum payments at whatever percentage of the 'standard of need' they wished. The standard might legally have to be readjusted, but nothing in law prevented a state from correspondingly adjusting downward the proportion of this figure it would at most pay. Similarly, a campaign to make grants for special needs less discriminatory ended simply in the repeal of these grants. From all this, welfare rights lawyers could only draw a discouraging practical lesson. 'If you struggle to get eligible applicants on the rolls, and win victories against illegal restrictive eligibility rules—the recipients may well be rewarded by a cut in grant levels. Such cuts happened in state after state, and nothing

[44] Edward V. Sparer, 'The Right to Welfare' in Norman Dorsen (ed.), *The Rights of Americans: What They Are—What They Should Be* (New York: Pantheon, 1971), p. 79.

in the Social Security Act appeared to prevent it—at least according to the Supreme Court.'[45]

Looking back on five years' litigation to secure welfare rights, Edward Sparer concludes sadly:

> The welfare recipients' lawyer started his struggle in 1965 not merely as a technician whose function was to assist the welfare system conform to what the elected representatives of the majority had decreed it should be. His mission was to utilize the legal process to help change the very nature of the welfare system and, thereby, to change the ground rules of American society. No mere legal technician, he was a grand strategist. No mere advocate of other people's yearnings, he yearned for the change with his clients. And for a brief moment in the 1960's when it appeared that a majority, or at least their elected representatives, were ready to accept some basic change, his mission appeared possible. In 1970, it does not. No more a significant participant in grand change, he appears reduced to what the revolutionist has often accused the lawyer of being—a technical aide who smooths the functioning of an inadequate system and thereby helps perpetuate it.[46]

Thus the strategy of legal intervention was vulnerable as soon as it overtried the limits of political tolerance. If it pressed the implications of the law too far beyond the consensual interpretation of rights, it might only provoke retrograde amendments more explicitly unfavourable to its clients than before. And since it acted as advocate of a particular interest, it provided no argument that such amendments were against the public interest as a whole. Even without any change in law, the strategy could be largely frustrated by withdrawing government funds from legal aid. Compared with participatory planning, legal intervention held stronger immediate sanctions against the neglect of arguments and information from outside the established network of power. But it could not, of itself, influence the consensus of interests which determined what sanctions the law should provide, nor the distribution of resources to make those sanctions effective. In this respect, it was weaker than community action, which at least had the right to contribute to the debate.

[45] *Ibid* p. 80.
[46] *Ibid* p. 84.

Epilogue

The Mutual Reinforcement of Strategies of Reform

This conclusion suggests a combination of strategies. If community planning is ineffectual, without legal sanctions to reinforce its influence, so redress in law will be self-defeating without a sustained political campaign to defend the rights to which it appeals. And the political campaign must sooner or later turn to planning to translate its principles into policy for the allocation of resources. The process of arbitration has to be worked out simultaneously in different contexts—aggressively, in the courts and in politics; more consensually in planning and evaluative research.

The force of legal intervention lies in its power of injunction: it can over-ride the timetable of political decisions, while new information is brought to bear on the argument, or issues reconsidered in a new light. And the court examines the issues on the plaintiff's terms, irrespective of the political authority of the parties: at least in principle, government and citizens are equal before the law. But this power of injunction, which enables anyone with a plausible case to threaten the political leadership with obstruction, is mainly negative. A court of law cannot itself negotiate a resolution of conflicting interests which is fair to everyone, not only the litigants, and an intelligent plan of action. Unless there is also a recognized process of planning, open and well-informed, continual legal challenges will only result in a stalemate. A neighbourhood organization may be able to frustrate city hall, but it still has to translate its veto into constructive negotiation.

From a governmental point of view, more open planning is attractive, if it will secure broader consent to official policies. But unless the promise of participation is backed by legislative rights, it will not carry conviction and legal obstruction is at least less negative and haphazard than violence. Government therefore has an interest in guaranteeing a more democratic process of reaching decisions. At the same time, it will be continually tempted to draw back from its promise, as the exploitation of new legal opportunities erodes its prerogatives. 'Should judges be dealing almost continually with heated social and economic controversies?' demanded the Solicitor General of the United States, protesting at a court injunction against a federally-approved project. He complained of the 'explosive development of class action suits,' the 'continuous whittling away' of legal doctrines which had limited challengers in court to executive and congressional decisions; and urged the Supreme Court to reverse the trend.[47] Given the ambivalence of government towards the derogation of its own authority, the legal sanctions which must underline any truly democratic process of planning can only be sustained by a political movement continually protesting and extending these rights. Participation, litigation, political protest are each weak in isolation, but together they can provide a framework of arguments and pressures sympathetic to reform. If we conceive planning as a complex process of negotiation between a multitude of interests, then legal rights can help to redress the balance of power between the strong and the weak, and force political decisions to wait upon the resolution of the conflicts. But no government will willingly extend the range of its attention, and submit to these constraints on the timing of its actions, unless it recognizes a powerful public opinion demanding that it should.

At the same time, all our evidence suggests that it is only frustrating to rationalize this alliance in a single comprehensive structure. Any practical achievement of reform depends on the pragmatic, entrepreneurial skill with which the range of strategies are brought to bear at each opportunity. If this conclusion seems indeterminate, appealing at once to aggressive advocacy and reasonable compromise, that perhaps is the nature of life. The alternative, in practice, is neither revolution nor an ideal of perfect rationality, but a combination of sporadic violence and conservative manipulation. Above all, we should not give up, impatient at the slowness of reform, and the partiality of any solution.

Thus the argument leads back in the end to questions of political strategy. But it would be facile to conclude that concern with the quality of information is therefore less important. Power rests on consent as much as force, and consent is determined by the way people perceive their society. Reformers and conservatives alike seek to impose their definition of the situation, manipulating the means of communication to command respect for the information they trust. Neither sincerely wishes to advertise fact or argument damaging to their case. But since, in a democratic society, the debate is nominally open to all, the mechanisms of

[47] See *New York Times,* November 18, 1971.

suppression and selective attention are correspondingly subtle. We cannot repudiate these mechanisms, for without selection, the mass of information competing for attention would become unmanageable. But we can acknowledge them and try to understand the way they distort our perception. From this we may be able to change the bias.

The process is circular: without power, you will not be heard; but until you are heard, you cannot influence the basis of consent to the power you seek. Community action set out to change the way problems were perceived, by opening new channels of communication. In this it largely failed, in the short run, because it had no power to alter the priorities of attention. But from its frustrations arose a movement to protest the right of the poor, and all politically disadvantaged minorities to be heard, which over the decade has profoundly influenced our conceptions of democracy. If these rights can be secured and applied, at every level of government, to a more open process of arbitrating the allocation of resources, then the experiment of community action may be vindicated after all.

PRINCIPAL REFERENCES

Individual authors:

BATCHELDER, ALLAN, 'Decline in the Relation of Income of Negro Men', *Quarterly Journal of Economics*, Vol. LXVIII, (August 1964).

BRAGER, GEORGE, 'Influencing Institutional Change Through a Demonstration Project: The Case of the Schools' (Prepared for the Columbia University and Mobilization for Youth Training Institute Programme, April 1964).

BROOKS, MICHAEL P., 'The Community Action Programme as a Setting for Applied Research', *Journal of Social Issues*, Vol. XXI, No. 1, (January 1965).

BURNS, JAMES MACGREGOR, *The Deadlock of Democracy: Four-Party Politics in America* (New Jersey: Prentice Hall, 1963).

CAHN, EDGAR S. and JEAN, 'The War on Poverty: A Civilian Perspective', *Yale Law Journal*, Vol. 73, No. 8, (July 1964).

CLARK, KENNETH B., *Dark Ghetto: Dilemmas of Social Power* (New York: Harper and Row, 1965).

CLOWARD, RICHARD and OHLIN, LLOYD, *Delinquency and Opportunity: A Theory of Delinquent Gangs* (Glencoe, Ill.: The Free Press, 1960).

COTTRELL, LEONARD, 'Social Planning, the Competent Community and Mental Health', *Urban America and the Planning of Mental Health Services*, Vol. V, Symposium No. 10, (November 1964).

CROZIER, MICHEL, *The Bureaucratic Phenomenon* (Chicago: University of Chicago Press, 1964).

DAHL, ROBERT, *Who Governs?* (New Haven: Yale University Press, 1961).

DENTLER, ROBERT, 'Strategies for Innovation in Education: A View From the Top', (Presented at the second workshop of the Public Policy Institute, Columbia University School of Social Work, October 1964, mimeographed).

FREEMAN, HOWARD E. and SHERWOOD, CLARENCE C., 'Research in Large Scale Intervention Programmes', *Journal of Social Issues*, Vol. XXI, No. 1, (January 1961).

GORDON, MARGARET S., 'United States Manpower and Employment Policy: A Review Essay', *Monthly Labor Review*, Vol. 87, No. 11, (November 1964).

HERMAN, MELVIN, 'Problems and Evaluation', *The American Child*, Vol. 47, No. 2, (March 1965).

HIRSCHMAN, ALBERT O., and LINDBLOM, CHARLES E., 'Economic Development, Research and Development, Policy Making: Some Converging Views', *Behavioral Science*, Vol. 7, No. 2, (April 1962).

KAPLAN, MARSHALL, *The Model Cities Program* (Department of Housing and Urban Development, 1970).

KRAVITZ, SANFORD, 'The Implications of Governmental Participation in Health and Welfare Planning—Possibilities and Problems', (Speech to the New York State Association of Community Councils and Chests).

LEVINE, ROBERT A., *The Poor Ye Need not Have with You: Lessons from the War on Poverty* (Cambridge, Mass.: M.I.T. Press, 1970).

LINDBLOM, CHARLES E., *The Intelligence of Democracy: Decision Making through Mutual Adjustment* (New York: Free Press, 1965).

MERTON, ROBERT K., 'Bureaucratic Structure and Personality', in Merton, Gray, Hockey and Selvin (eds), *Reader in Bureaucracy* (Glencoe, Ill.: Free Press, 1952).

MILLER, HERMAN P., 'Is the Income Gap Closed? "No!" ', *New York Times Magazine Section*, (November 11, 1962).

—, 'Poverty and the Negro', (Presented at University of West Virginia Conference on Poverty, May 3, 1965, mimeographed).

MOORE, JOHN E., 'Delinquency: Presidential, Congressional . . . and Juvenile', in *Cases in Urban Legislation* (Washington, D.C.: Brookings Institution, 1967).

MOYNIHAN, DANIEL P., *Maximum Feasible Misunderstanding* (New York: Free Press, 1969).

OHLIN, LLOYD, 'Issues in the Development of Indigenous Social Movements Among Residents of Deprived Urban Areas', (October 1960, mimeographed).

PERLMAN, ROBERT, 'Social Welfare Planning', (Ph.D. dissertation, Brandeis University, 1961).

PERROW, CHARLES, 'Organizational Prestige: Some Functions and Dysfunctions', *American Journal of Sociology*, Vol. LXVI, No. 4, (January 1961).

PIVEN, FRANCES, 'Conceptual Themes in the Evolution of Mobilization for Youth', (Prepared for the Columbia University and Mobilization for Youth Training Institute Programme, April 1964, mimeographed).

—, and CLOWARD, RICHARD A., *Regulating the Poor: The Functions of Public Welfare* (New York: Pantheon, 1971).

SHONFIELD, ANDREW, *Modern Capitalism* (London: Oxford University Press, 1965).

SPARER, EDWARD V., 'The Right to Welfare' in Norman Dorsen (ed.), *The Rights of Americans: What They Are—What They Should Be* (New York: Pantheon, 1971).

SUNDQUIST, JAMES L. and SCHELLING, C. S. (eds), *On Fighting Poverty: Perspectives from Experience* (New York: Basic Books, 1969).

TAYLOR, ALVIN N., 'The Oakland Recreation Department: A Study in Institutional Transition', (University of California Master's Thesis, 1962).

TOCQUEVILLE, ALEXIS DE, *Democracy in America* (New York: Vintage Books, 1945).

VATTER, HAROLD G., *The United States Economy in the 1950's: An Economic History* (New York: W. W. Norton and Co., 1963).

WARREN, ROLAND C., 'The Model Cities Program: Assumptions—Experience—Implications', (Annual Forum Programme, National Conference on Social Welfare, Dallas, May 17, 1971).

—, *Truth, Love and Social Change* (New York: Rand, McNally, 1971).

WEINBERG, JOSEPH L., 'Evaluation Study of Youth Training and Employment Project, East Los Angeles', (U.S. Department of Labour, Office of Manpower, Automation and Training, August 1964).

YLVISAKER, PAUL N., 'Diversity and the Public Interest—Two Cases in Metropolitan Decision Making', (Speech to the 16th Conference on Science, Philosophy and Religion in their Relation to the Democratic Way of Life, August 1960).

—, 'A Relevant Christ—but a Relevant Church?', (Speech delivered at the 'Atlanta Metabagdad' sponsored by the Episcopal Church, February 1964).

—, 'Private Philanthropy in America', (Speech to the National Council on Community Foundations, May 1964).

Community Action Project Reports:

Action for Boston Community Development:
  'The Boston Youth Opportunities Project: a Report and a Proposal', (December 1963).
  A Report on ABCD Activities, September 1963–August 1964.

Community Progress Incorporated:
  'Opening Opportunities: New Haven's Comprehensive Programme for Community Progress', (April 1962).
  Second Annual Programme Review for the Ford Foundation, 1963–64.
  The New Haven Youth Employment Programme: The Six Month Report, May 1964.
  Summary Statistics of CPI Manpower Action, October 1963–April 1965.

Harlem Youth Opportunities Unlimited:
  'Youth in the Ghetto', (1964).

Mobilization for Youth:
  Director's First Annual Report to the Staff, October 1963.
  ' "Employment Shock" At the Top of the Job Ladder', (Manpower Monograph, Department of Labour, OMAT, August 1964).

North Carolina Fund:
'The North Carolina Fund: Programmes and Policies', (November 1963).
Oakland Inter-Agency Project:
Interim Evaluation Reports, 1965.
Philadelphia Council for Community Advancement:
'A Programme for North Philadelphians', Prepared by the Centre for Community Studies, (Temple University, 1961).
'Philadelphia Council for Community Advancement: A Prospectus', (February 1962).
'Analysis of Prospectus of the Philadelphia Council for Community Advancement', (March 22, 1962, mimeographed).
Annual Report to the Ford Foundation, 1963.
United Planning Organization:
'A Proposal for Developing Human Resources for the National Capital Area', (December 1963).

Congressional:
Hearings before the Sub-committee of the Committee of Appropriations, House of Representatives, 86th Congress, 2nd session, 1960.
Executive Order 10940, May 11, 1961.
Public Law 87–274, 'The Juvenile Delinquency and Youth Offences Control Act of 1961'.
'The War on Poverty, The Economic Opportunity Act of 1964.' A compilation of materials relevant to S.2642 prepared for the select sub-committee on poverty, (1964).
Hearings before the Sub-committee on Employment and Manpower of the . . . United States Senate . . . on S.1566 to Extend the Juvenile Delinquency and Youth Offences Control Act of 1961, April 7 and 8, 1965.
Congressional Record, Proceedings and Debates of the 88th Congress, 2nd Session, House of Representatives, June 16, 1964.
Congressional Digest, March 1966 and February 1967.

Ford Foundation:
'Directives and Terms of Reference for the 1960's', (June 1962).

President's Committee:
Policy Guides to the Presentation of Proposals for Funding under Public Law 87–274, September 1963.
'Suggested Guidelines for Federal Support of Neighborhood Organization . . . ' prepared by the Demonstration Technical Review Panel of the Office of Juvenile Delinquency for the Commissioner of Welfare.

Principal References

'The Federal Delinquency Programme. Objectives and Operations under the President's Committee on Juvenile Delinquency and Youth Crime and the Juvenile Delinquency and Youth Offences Control Act of 1961', (November 1962).

Others:

Report of Youth Research Inc., New York State Division for Youth, July 1964.

Newsweek, 'The American Way of Giving', (March 14, 1966).

New York Times for: November 10, 1964; November 5, 1965; James Reston's column, June 24, 1966; and November 18, 1971.

INDEX

Note: All index entries in Roman numerals refer to pages in the British edition of *Dilemmas of Social Reform.*

Index

["